Understanding Evil

Evil is a ubiquitous, persistent problem that causes enormous human suffering. Although human beings have struggled with evil since the dawn of our species, we seem to be no nearer to ending it. In this book, Lionel Corbett describes the complexity of the problem of evil, as well as many of our current approaches to understanding it, in ways that are helpful to the practicing psychotherapist, psychoanalyst, or Jungian analyst.

Psychotherapists often work with people who have been the victims of evil, and, occasionally, the therapist is faced with a perpetrator of evil. To be helpful in these situations, the practitioner must understand the problem from several points of view, since evil is so complex that no single approach is adequate. *Understanding Evil: A Psychotherapist's Guide* describes a range of approaches to evil based on Jungian theory, psychoanalysis, social sciences, philosophy, neurobiology, mythology, and religious studies. The book clarifies the difference between actions that are merely wrong from those that are truly evil, discusses the problem of detecting evil, and describes the effects on the clinician of witnessing evil. The book also discusses what is known about the psychology of terrorism and the question of whether a spiritual approach to evil is necessary, or whether evil can be approached from a purely secular point of view.

In *Understanding Evil*, a combination of psychoanalytic and Jungian theory allows the practitioner a deep understanding of the problem of evil. The book will appeal to analytical psychologists and psychotherapists, psychoanalysts, and academics and students of Jungian and post-Jungian studies. It will also be of great interest to researchers approaching the question of evil from a variety of other fields, including philosophy and religious studies.

Lionel Corbett is a psychiatrist and Jungian analyst in private practice and Professor of Depth Psychology at Pacifica Graduate Institute, USA. His main professional interests are the religious function of the psyche and the interface of Jungian and psychoanalytic psychology. His previous books include *The Religious Function of the Psyche* (Routledge).

Understanding Evil

A Psychotherapist's Guide

Lionel Corbett

Routledge
Taylor & Francis Group

LONDON AND NEW YORK

First published 2018
by Routledge
2 Park Square, Milton Park, Abingdon, Oxon OX14 4RN

and by Routledge
711 Third Avenue, New York, NY 10017

*Routledge is an imprint of the Taylor & Francis Group, an informa
business*

British Library Cataloguing in Publication Data
A catalogue record for this book is available from the British
Library

Library of Congress Cataloging in Publication Data
Names: Corbett, Lionel, author.
Title: Understanding evil : a psychotherapist's guide /
    Lionel Corbett.
Description: New York : Routledge, 2018. | Includes bibliographical
    references.
Identifiers: LCCN 2017045373 (print) | LCCN 2018003255
    (ebook) | ISBN 9781351199674 (Master e-book) | ISBN
    9780815392262 (hardback) | ISBN 9780815392286 (pbk.) |
    ISBN 9781351199674 (ebk)
Subjects: LCSH: Good and evil—Psychological aspects.
Classification: LCC BF789.E94 (ebook) | LCC BF789.E94 C67
    2018 (print) | DDC 170—dc23
LC record available at https://lccn.loc.gov/2017045373

ISBN: 978-0-8153-9226-2 (hbk)
ISBN: 978-0-8153-9228-6 (pbk)
ISBN: 978-1-351-19967-4 (ebk)

Typeset in Times New Roman
by Apex CoVantage, LLC

Contents

Preface

Psychotherapists often work with victims of evil, and occasionally we are faced with an individual who perpetrates evil. However, the subject of evil as such is largely absent from the curricula of our training programs, even though psychotherapists try to help people who have suffered everything from deliberate abuse to subtle forms of hatred, indifference, and inadvertent human failure. I do not believe that the current focus on the specific treatment of particular disorders absolves us from considering the larger problem of evil that is the background to much of this suffering. It is important that we understand how such evil begins within the human psyche. I believe the therapist's attitude toward evil makes a difference to his or her[1] work with both victims and perpetrators of evil, and it helps to deal with evil in others if we acknowledge our own capacity for evil. Furthermore, as difficult as it is to acknowledge this, at times it may be important for the psychotherapist to try to grasp the function and purpose of evil in the life of the individual or society.

We judge an action to be evil when it elicits feelings of horror and incomprehension. However, these feelings do not tell us whether evil is an independent or archetypal force of nature or only the result of human shortcomings. Describing an action as evil does not explain it, and psychotherapists would like to understand what drives such behavior. In this book, I take the position that there are positive forms of evil such as deliberate sadism and cruelty, and negative forms of evil such as neglect, ignorance, or unavoidable deprivation. When these problems occur in childhood, they may have far-reaching consequences, even if their origin is tragic rather than malevolent. Psychoanalytic and Jungian theory are both necessary to clarify the effects of these problems on personality development. These problems produce complexes that allow the incarnation of what Jung refers to as the dark side of the Self, which is then lived out as problematic human behavior.

Some human evil arises out of negligence or stupidity, but a good deal of evil arises out of fear, emotional vulnerability, childhood trauma, and tragic life situations. These developments lead to a personality prone to fragmentation and to places of emptiness at the core of the self. The seeds of evil arise within the resulting emotional pain and helplessness. Evil such as cruelty or destructiveness may arise as a protective mechanism to deal with this kind of vulnerability. A deficit of positive experiences also makes space for the emergence of evil. The psychotherapist's responsibility is to find avenues of healing for such individuals, which requires a sensitive understanding of the dynamics that predispose a person to evil behavior in the context of a committed therapeutic relationship.

Much evil behavior arises from relational failures or disruptions and the failure to repair them. This kind of deprivation in childhood leads to deficits in the structure of the developing self that predispose to hostility or aggression. Evil behavior may be used to prevent fragmentation in the resulting fragile personality. Therefore, the absence of goodness in childhood does not remain an absence; it may lead to later destructiveness. It is as if this absence allows evil to arise that would otherwise never be activated. Once this pattern takes hold, the individual may become caught in an escalating cycle of behavior that is both difficult to control and harmful to the individual and to others. Psychotherapeutic intervention helps to interfere with this vicious cycle.

Psychotherapists may work with individuals who struggle with the urge to behave in an evil manner, and the therapeutic process may tip the balance in favor of not living out this aspect of the personality. In such a situation, I believe that if the psychotherapist understands the situational and psychological factors that predispose toward evil behavior, he or she is in a better position to be helpful. Sometimes these factors are largely the result of intrapsychic dynamics, while at other times the individual's social situation is more important, although these often interact.

This book reviews some of the psychological and social science literature that discusses the problem of evil. I hope the book will allow the reader to gain sufficient perspective on the problem to be able to respond to some of the major questions that arise in clinical practice. I focus on the following questions: Is evil only an emergent property of human psychology, or is there a transpersonal or spiritual component to evil? Can an ordinary person who does not have an evil character carry out an evil act? Is the state of mind or motivation of the perpetrator a critical factor in deciding whether an act is evil, or is the act itself the determining factor? Is there such a thing as primary or pure evil, or is evil behavior always secondary to either psychopathology or irresistible situational pressures that inhibit empathy and evoke a latent capacity for cruelty?

Broadly speaking, social scientists tend to focus on the situational, historical, and other social factors that lead to evil behavior, while psychodynamic approaches look for developmental, intrapsychic, and relational dynamics in the perpetrator. It is important that, although depth psychological theory helps us understand some forms of evil, new phenomena emerge at the larger societal level that are not present within the individual, and these require their own methods of study. Nevertheless, for the depth psychologist, a focus on the societal sources of evil is not sufficient to explain the behavior of people who kill children in schools or who murder people in churches and theaters, without taking into account the perpetrator's psychology. Clinical psychologists, psychotherapists, and psychoanalysts often equate this kind of evil with psychopathology, and this seems preferable to demonizing people. When we can demonstrate major developmental disasters in the childhood of the person who commits evil acts, the resulting psychological difficulties are often seen as mitigating factors, if not total explanations, for evil behavior. However, these psychological factors do not diminish the horror of the evil act itself, and they do not exonerate the perpetrator. We recognize that many people grow up in appalling childhood environments but do not perpetrate evil, a fact that itself needs explanation.

I am concerned with the question of whether evil is some quality of the person, so that there are essentially evil people, or whether evil is only a description of a perpetrator's actions. In other words, can we separate evil actions from the perpetrator's personhood? The clinician's response to this question might radically affect the way in which he or she approaches such a person. A severe personality disorder might lead to evil behavior, and the psychotherapist might wonder if this constitutes true evil or should better be thought of as an emotional disorder, and to what extent these categories might overlap. For many of us, a repeated pattern of evil behavior suggests that we are dealing with a truly evil person. However, if we say a person is evil, we are condemning what he is in his essential nature, not simply what he does. In this view, a person could be intrinsically evil but not have the opportunity to carry out an evil act. This distinction is important because if there is such a thing as an essentially evil person, a "bad seed," the prognosis in psychotherapy is not good. However, the majority of evil seen by psychotherapists is secondary to abuse and maltreatment in the history of the perpetrator.

To understand evil behavior in the psychotherapeutic situation, feelings such as rage, envy, hatred, and indifference toward others have to be understood and explored as much as possible. In the process, the psychotherapist often discovers that the actions of evil people are the result of forces over which they have little or no control. This finding does not absolve them of moral or legal responsibility, but it fosters the therapist's empathy, and this is essential for the therapeutic process.

Many psychotherapists are interested in the spiritual dimensions of the problem of evil – the question of why it exists and whether it might be an irreducible natural principle. I have therefore included a discussion of the metaphysical or archetypal levels of evil and Jung's notion of the dark side of the transpersonal Self. In this context, I believe that even if we understand the human sources of evil, there will still be a dimension of evil that remains a mystery, and this level can only be approached philosophically and spiritually. We must try to understand the problem of evil if we are to understand the human condition, and this understanding is fundamental to the work of psychotherapy. I confess to moments of despair at the levels of depravity to which human beings succumb and to the fact that evil seems to be ineradicable. But we cannot afford to accept that the situation is beyond repair. Our task is to discover mature and realistic hope for the treatment of evil people and for the victims of evil.

Note

1 Throughout this text, I have alternated the use of "he" and "she" or "his or her" to avoid the constant use of "his/her," with the understanding that most of the material applies to both men and women, except where the gender context is clear.

Chapter 1

What is evil?

The problem of evil

The problem of evil is one of humanity's most long-standing and controversial preoccupations, claiming the attention of many disciplines ever since the beginning of human thought. Evil is an inescapable part of our world, to the extent that some people believe that a proclivity towards evil is an intrinsic aspect of human nature. I do not need to rehearse the long list of evils to which we are exposed; suffice it to say that the scale of human evil, and the enormous suffering it causes, demands that we try to understand and confront it. Although evil behavior often seems to make no sense, we cannot afford to dismiss it as ultimately inscrutable, because doing so would make it more difficult to deal with. Perhaps the attempt to make evil more intelligible is a way to manage our fear of it, and certainly we hope that the better we understand it, the better we will be able to deal with it. At the same time, it is unlikely that there can be a single, overarching theory about the nature of evil, given its variety of forms and contexts and the absence of a unifying quality common to all of them. Similarly, if we try to define evil too precisely, we then seem to exclude other types of evil.

Because evil has long preoccupied philosophers, psychologists, and our spiritual traditions, much has already been said about it, mostly from a conscious position. My task is twofold: (1) to see what can be added from the point of view of depth psychology, and (2) to describe the relevance of this problem to the psychotherapist. I think it is crucial for psychotherapists to understand this issue, since so much evil behavior depends on the psychological processes of the perpetrator. Psychotherapists often work with the victims of evil, and there are times when a psychotherapist is able to help perpetrators of evil such as child abusers. With such hurtful people, the gradual development of empathy during psychotherapy may attenuate their destructive behavior.

An important aspect of this problem is the issue of whether all human beings have the capacity for evil, in which case we have to ask why some of us are better at restraining it than others, or whether there is something special about the paradigmatic instances of evil such as Hitler or Pol Pot. My assumption here is that at least some of what we describe as moral evil is motivated by unconscious factors, by complexes in Jung's sense, and by characterological problems such as untrammeled narcissism. These have developmental sources that are fairly well understood.

In the long-standing debate about whether evil is comprehensible or an ultimate mystery, most psychologists (and many philosophers) lean toward the former position. At the same time, we must acknowledge that we may only be able to understand some instances of evil rather than evil as a whole. No single discipline can provide a complete answer to the problem of evil. As Levine (2000, p. 273) says: "Looking for a single cause of evil is like looking for a single meaning of life. It is a sure sign that one is in the grip of a theory and reveals the extent to which theory informs observation."

Psychologists might be able to understand the motivations that drive evil behavior, but understanding the nature of evil itself is a difficult conceptual problem – if indeed there is such an essence, a claim that is often denied. Some writers believe that the word *evil* is inherently demonizing and adds nothing to our understanding, so that it would be better to use specific descriptions such as "unnecessary, gratuitous cruelty to others." But if we do not use the word *evil*, then we risk not conveying or even minimizing the gravity of the phenomena we are describing. We can therefore at least use the term *evil* descriptively, as an adjective rather than a noun, without necessarily implying that evil has an independent ontological reality. However, people who believe that metaphysical evil exists do insist on the objective reality of evil. Some religious writers believe that the divine itself has a dark side, and Jung believed that our image of God must include a dark aspect, since evil cannot be attributed to humanity alone. In contrast, people with a secular worldview want to get rid of the notion of some hidden spiritual force causing evil. Instead, they prefer to understand evil exclusively in terms of psychology and social science, as a disorder, as some kind of aberration, or as the result of historical and political forces. For them, the word *evil* implies too much of a moral absolute, and the notion of evil is seen as an obsolete hangover from simplistic religious thinking. Calder (2013) points out that the word *evil* is ambiguous because although it may be taken to imply a metaphysical agent such as Satan, it is not always clear if this commitment is intended, but it is possible to use the word *evil* without any metaphysical implications. It is also possible to use this word as a way of saying we cannot understand how someone could carry out certain ghastly behavior. Mearns and Thorne (2000) suggest that evil is "a hypothetical construct used to describe someone whom we fear and whom we do not understand. Once our fear diminishes or our understanding increases, the person is no longer evil" (p. 59).

Should we use the term *evil*?

Is evil a metaphysical reality with an essence of its own, or is it entirely explicable in terms of human psychology and social factors? If evil has a supernatural origin, in the last analysis human beings could not fully understand it, and we could not deal with it without supernatural help. In contrast, if evil is purely a matter of social or individual pathology, then we may not need the word *evil* at all. Secular thinkers particularly want to get rid of the notion of the devil or of some hidden spiritual force causing evil. Many of these writers believe we should not use the term *evil* because of its occult references, thereby reducing human responsibility (Masters, 1997). Thus, for Svendsen (2010), theology is irrelevant to our understanding of the problems with which evil presents us; evil is purely a human moral problem. He believes that evil is not primarily a subject for theology, philosophy, or science, but a problem that must be addressed in the political arena. He thinks that the difficulty we have understanding evil makes us reach for mythological explanations of it, such as the devil, but if we attribute evil to the devil, then we make it appear external to us. At the same time, he also realizes that to see evil as only attributable to human beings risks making it seem normal, as if we can thereby justify and accept evil. Svendsen notes that an essential characteristic of evil is that it is "terribly sad" (p. 12).

Knoll (2008), a forensic psychiatrist, argues that evil cannot be defined scientifically because it is an illusory moral concept that does not exist in nature. Levine (2000) argues that psychologists, judges, and journalists should avoid the term *evil* because it has unavoidable historical connotations of sin, disobeying God, redemption, salvation, original sin, and so on. These metaphysical implications are embedded in a particular worldview, and for Levine they are irrelevant to disciplines such as law and psychology. For him, because the word *evil* has roots in a religious attitude, the problem of evil is "extra-scientific" (p. 267). Levine believes we cannot naturalize the word *evil*, meaning use a religious term in a secular context. When we do not use the term in its religious sense, we are referring to seriously immoral acts, or we accuse a person of being heinous or repugnant, but we can refer to a person as a psychopath without using the term *evil*. Levine therefore believes that the idea of evil is anachronistic in terms of contemporary legal and psychological discourse. Thus, some mental illness gives rise to evil, but if we say that evil behavior has its roots in abnormal brain functioning or damaging life experiences, then we can describe it in these terms, and we do not need the category of evil. Religious views have little in common with the views of psychology; religions give qualitatively different accounts of evil than do scientific accounts. Levine therefore believes that to ask "why is there evil?" as distinct from the question of how to relieve suffering or prevent some types of action is not a psychological question. The contrary view is that some acts are so awful that no other word conveys the horror or revulsion they inspire in us. For example, Alford (1997) believes we need a word that takes us beyond terms like *very bad* or *destructive*. He agrees, however, that "evil is not a psychological category but a metaphysical one, about why men and women suffer so much" (p. 20).

Whether or not we should retain the word *evil*, it is clear that this term is sometimes bandied about too readily, without trying to understand the offending individual. The political use of the word *evil* is a good example of the problem of overuse. Comments such as President Reagan's "evil empire,"[1] President Bush's "axis of evil,"[2] and the Iranian description of the USA as the "Great Satan" are all examples of the word being used to express fear, anger, or intense dislike. This usage results from splitting and projection, as if "we" are all good and "they" are entirely demonic. Calling others evil may be a way to imply that we are entitled to attack them. It is typical for adversarial nations to see each other as evil, but Cole (2006) points out that calling those we don't like evil "obstructs our understanding, blocks our way, brings us to a halt" (p. 236). The word *evil* might also be used to imply a questionable notion such as the idea that some people are inherently criminal or inhuman, and so not deserving of humane treatment. The Bush administration was able to mistreat captured terrorists by repeatedly referring to them as evildoers, and this appellation probably contributed to the Abu Ghraib incident (see p. 76, note 6). Thus, as Cole put it, "the attribution of evildoing may lead to further wrongdoing" (p. 178). That is, in the process of trying to deal with what is perceived as evil, more evil may be done, which may be why Jesus spoke against resisting evil (Matthew 5:39).

Many social scientists and postmodern writers see notions of good and evil as entirely socially constructed, and many see good and evil as existing on a continuum. These authors often see deviant behavior purely in terms of the situation that evokes it, without attributing reasons for the behavior to the psychology of the perpetrator. They point out that unacceptable behavior is a function of a given society's values and its historical period, so there is not necessarily anything substantively or essentially identifiable as evil. Other people feel that serious evil cannot be described using neutral language such as "deviant" without trivializing evil behavior. Thus, Delbanico (1996) complains that our society has lost touch with the idea of evil, and affluent Western societies deny the reality of evil, even though it is an inescapable reality. He believes that our postmodern reluctance to name evil puts us in danger of being dominated by it. With this warning in mind, we may note a variety of ways to define evil.

Recognizing and defining evil

Traditionally, evil has been spoken of in two different ways; moral evil refers to acts such as murder, whereas volcanoes and earthquakes are regarded as natural evils. However, the line between these types of evil becomes blurred when natural disasters such as severe storms are the result of human behavior leading to global warming. This distinction raises the question of whether evil is a principle of nature, a natural or archetypal given, or whether evil is a purely human concept, in which case what we call natural evil is simply any process of nature that causes human suffering. Most people feel that evil that is planned and deliberate is the worst kind; if bad things happen by accident, they are tragic but not evil. The magnitude of the act is important; the greater the suffering and loss caused to victims, the more likely the act is considered to be evil.

Part of the difficulty here is that there is a form of moral evil that claims to be good; it follows normative social rules, as we saw in the case of people who sincerely believed in a regime such as the Nazis. Susan Smith, who killed her children by drowning them in a lake, left a handwritten confession in which she said that her children "deserve to have the best," apparently meaning that they would go to heaven, which would be better for them than being on earth. Did she actually believe she was doing something good? Perhaps Hitler thought that what he was doing was good for Germany, but then on what grounds do the rest of us consider this kind of behavior to be evil?

A commonsense approach to the recognition of evil would include whatever produces human sorrow, whatever inflicts undeserved harm onto people, or whatever leads to unnecessary destruction or senseless violence. More broadly, we recognize as evil anything that curtails personal growth and human potential, or whatever is destructive of human relationships. Becker (1975) believes that we identify as evil anything that threatens the perpetuation of our species, just as Pierrakos (1990) thinks of evil as anything that is anti-life. Singer (2004) believes that "evil acts are acts that are horrendously wrong, that cause immense suffering, and are done from an evil motive – the motive to do something horrendously wrong" (p. 193). Magid (1988) thinks of evil as a pattern of behavior that disregards the whole in which we are embedded, for example using pesticides with no thought for their environmental consequences. Katz (1993) defines evil as "behavior ranging from deliberate destruction of human dignity to deliberate destruction of human life" (p. 10). He believes that depriving a person of dignity is a "critical starting point in the genesis of evil" (p. 146). Hering (1996) says that evil is unmitigated destructiveness that is absolute, a state of mind devoid of any care, concern, guilt, scruple, or empathy for the victim. As Benn (1985) points out, however, it is not enough to talk about evil behavior; one could be evil but unable to act. Similarly, Calder (2003) notes that an evil character could be too cowardly or incompetent to succeed in committing an evil act. He also notes that ordinary people without an evil character may cause evil. (This question is discussed further on p. 45).

Some authors see evil on a spectrum of behavior of increasing degrees of gravity. Singer (2004) describes six degrees or gradations of evil. At the extreme, the perpetrator does something knowing it is evil and because it is evil, which Singer refers to as *pure or malignant evil*. Next, the individual does something knowing it is evil but without caring, which Singer refers to as *ruthless evil*. Then, an individual might carry out an evil act that he would judge to be evil if it were to be inflicted on himself or on people he cares about, but not if it is inflicted on others or if he inflicts it; this is *fanatical evil*, exemplified by terrorist groups. One might cause evil for reasons such as convenience, which Singer terms *egoistic evil*. He believes that it is not evil to act harmfully for some greater good or when one mistakenly judges the action to be good. Singer acknowledges the difficulty of discerning or proving which degree of evil is applicable to a given case.

Svendsen (2010) also distinguishes various forms of evil. Instrumental evil occurs in the process of carrying out another purpose, such as the BP oil spill in the Gulf of Mexico, or a person may knowingly and intentionally commit harm in the process of satisfying needs. What he refers to as *stupid evil* is based on human incompetence without an evil motive, such as driver error leading to an injury. Svendsen uses the term *demonic evil* to describe evil carried out for its own sake, in order to deliberately harm others or to watch them suffer.[3] James (1958) believes there are at least two forms of evil; one is the result of a maladjustment to the environment, which is curable either by modifying the self or the environment, while the other is "a wrongness or vice" in the person's essential nature (p. 117). In more modern terms, James might be distinguishing between developmental and situational factors in contrast to an innate aspect of the personality. But if a person is in serious emotional pain resulting from developmental failures in childhood, is he truly evil if his behavior hurts others, or should we think of this situation more in terms of tragedy?

We instinctively feel that it is evil to use another person purely for one's own benefit, or to kill for pleasure, or to use force to humiliate and destroy others. It is evil to rejoice in injustice and to enjoy humiliating others. It is evil to destroy just for the sake of exercising power. We regard it as evil to try to harm others when motivated by hatred, envy, greed, financial gain, revenge, and similar motives. There may even be a form of evil that is entirely unmotivated, that has no explanation; once it begins, it seems to be self-perpetuating.

It is important to note that evil is not only the result of problematic individual traits such as sadism and indifference to the suffering of others; religious traditions also produce evil at times. Medieval Crusaders believed they were waging a holy war against the Muslims while pillaging and murdering on the way to Jerusalem. The medieval Inquisitors sincerely believed they were combating heresy, which justified their violence. The pursuit of religious ideals often leads to evil, as we saw in the case of people such as Osama bin Laden. Kekes (2005) believes that this latter kind of evil arises from distortion and falsification of the relevant facts by the individual's passions, for example when harmless disagreements between religions lead to non-believers being seen as enemies of the truth who must be destroyed, or when political differences are seen as symptoms of immorality. The depth psychologist tries to take into account the unconscious underpinnings of such passions, in order to understand the reasons that people become possessed by affectively toned ideas or complexes to the extent that cognitive distortions occur. When psychologists see toxic behavior, we look for the complex or for other unconscious mental mechanisms driving the behavior, such as self-deception (discussed on p. 61) and perceptual blindness. Conscious intention may be etiologically less important than these unconscious sources of motivation, but even ordinary states of mind such as boredom may lead to evil. Conscious traits such as ambition are healthy up to a point, but overweening ambition may rapidly become evil.

Noddings (1989) approaches evil from a woman's point of view and tries to develop a model of ethics based on caring, relationship, and an appreciation for the importance of feelings instead of a model based on principles and rules. She suggests that evil consists not only of whatever produces pain and helplessness but also of whatever neglects relationship. Moral evil includes the failure to alleviate these problems. Noddings believes that most moral philosophy has been written unconsciously from a male point of view and that the problem of evil has been "suffused with male interests and conditioned by masculine experience" (p. 1). History, politics, and other social structures have obscured the nature of evil because all these systems for dealing with it have been created by men, and men tend to think in terms of power. World religions teach that God is all-powerful and just, but the notion of an omnipotent God allows men to avoid their own responsibility. In contrast to theodicies[4] devised by men, Noddings does not believe that there can be any redemptive explanation for the existence of evil. She believes that women are better than men at dealing with ambiguity, and so they are better able to deal with evil in themselves and better able to work out the problem of evil in relationships.

Noddings believes human beings have a natural disposition to care, and when we fail to be present to others' needs, we easily succumb to the kind of striving that promotes evil. She believes that the incessant desire to have more for oneself in relation to others is a particularly male desire that most women find inexplicable, and this desire contradicts the project of being a mother.

Noddings does not provide many descriptions of evil in women, except to say that they may succumb to the evil of men by agreeing to sacrifice their sons in war, or they may care in the wrong way, for example by being too smothering as mothers. She ignores the fact that women may have their own desire to dominate and destroy. The evidence of history suggests that there are women who can be as motivated as men to be destructive or dominant in an evil manner. Many examples can be cited: women were among those who tortured and murdered the inmates of Nazi concentration camps. Their cruelty was no less intense than the brutality of the male guards.

Attempts at a rigorous definition of evil always lead to more questions. Was Shakespeare (*Hamlet*, act 2, scene 2) correct to say: "For there is nothing either good or bad, but thinking makes it so"? In this view, evil is only a matter of human judgment. Then, evil is nothing more than whatever a particular society or individual defines as evil, based on local and personal values. Related to this view, good and evil can be seen to be on the same spectrum, so that the difference between them is only a matter of degree and opinion. Yet many people insist that there are absolute standards of evil that apply regardless of any particular social consensus. We have no difficulty insisting that events such as genocide are evil, regardless of the culture that inflicted it. If we insist that evil is an ontologically separate category with an essence of its own, we imply that there is an archetypal quality to evil, or even that evil is a transpersonal or spiritual process in which human beings participate. The distinction is important, because if evil is an essence woven into the cosmic order of reality, or if there really are demonic forces as some religions maintain, then we will never be able to fully eradicate it, but to the extent that evil behavior is a purely human reaction to deprivation and abuse, we can be more hopeful. Even if we decide that evil is inevitable, we do not need to invoke its spiritual dimension; evil can be understood as an aspect of the human psyche that arises because of our evolutionary endowment. This would be the case if human beings have evolved to be aggressive, or if envy, hatred, and cruelty are a part of our nature, but evil may not be inevitable if such aggression is secondary to frustration or fear.

Is (moral) evil deeply mysterious, something we are incapable of ultimately understanding, or is evil simply a way of talking about whatever causes unwarranted suffering? In the latter case, evil has no deep properties or essence, and the problem of evil is an empirical one; the problem lies in the way we treat each other. Evil is then the result of fundamental psychological and social dynamics that can at least in principle be understood. However, for many people a purely empirical approach to evil does not do justice to the horror and shock that evil inspires, and lacks explanatory power. There seems to be something more to evil than simply toxic behavior. We wonder if the potential for malignant behavior lies in all of us because it is an aspect of human nature, or whether evil is a primordial force that society must constantly try to suppress. Hence we have definitions such as that of Vetlesen (2005, p. 21), who believes that "to do evil . . . is to intentionally inflict pain and suffering on another human being, against her will, and causing serious and foreseeable harm to her." A broader definition is suggested by Funkhouser (1991), in a cross-cultural study that compared stereotypes of good and evil in several countries. In this work, evil was understood in terms of the misuse of power, as "the motiveless control or influence of other people to their detriment" (p. 861). However, it is not always enough to define evil in terms of harm and suffering caused to others, although that may be part of our definition, because one might be evil without causing suffering; one might enjoy watching the suffering caused by others, or one might simply wish to dominate others without doing much actual damage.

There are some people who deliberately choose evil *because* it is evil, like Milton's Satan, who, having lost hope of any goodness, said: "Evil be thou my good." But these are probably the exceptions. I noted earlier that people who commit what most of us consider to be evil acts may actually believe they are doing good. Another example is given by Ruth Stein (2002), who analyzes a letter to the 9/11 hijackers by Mohammed Atta, one of the ringleaders of the attack, in an attempt to understand their motivation. She notes that the letter has a "solemn, serene, even joyful tone that is infused with love of God and a strong desire to please him" (p. 393). The letter tries to reassure and calm the hijackers, calling for restraint and control; it does not stress hatred, but rather stresses God's satisfaction with the act they are about to perform. She believes that the terrorists were in a trance-like state of mind as a result of incessant incantation of prayers while focused on God, so they were able to function while in a euphoric state. They saw what they were doing as God's will. For Stein, the letter is reminiscent of the voice of a wise father instructing his sons about a mission of great importance. Stein stresses the joy and self-surrender found among these devotees. (This letter is discussed further on p. 173). Perhaps the fact that one might do evil while convinced one is doing good is the reason Camus (1991) says that "the evil that is in the world always comes of ignorance, and good intentions may do as much harm as malevolence if they lack understanding . . . the most incorrigible vice being that of an ignorance that fancies it knows everything and therefore claims for itself the right to kill" (p. 131).

Here it may be useful to distinguish intention from motivation; one's intentions are what one consciously wants to do, but one may have an unconscious motivation that is driving one's behavior. Intention alone is not a sufficient criterion for describing an act as evil, since we sometimes commit evil unwittingly, with no intention to do so, because of circumstances beyond our control. Evil intention and motivation may not lead to an evil action if circumstances do not allow the act to be carried out. Calder (2013) thinks that a certain type of motivation is necessary for an act to be considered to be evil; the evildoer must desire to cause significant harm, or he must lack the desire that others not be significantly harmed. Calder thinks that for a person to be described as evil, he must have a consistent propensity for these desires, so a person who is not consistently evil may occasionally commit evil acts without himself being evil. However, if we allow intention as part of our definition of evil, then an attempted murder that is unsuccessful would be an evil even if no harm ensues. Furthermore, good intentions may produce an evil outcome, so that intention alone is not necessarily sufficient to describe an act as evil. Motives such as ideology or religion may not be evil in themselves, even if they lead to evil outcomes for victims. Evil that causes harm could be due to negligence or recklessness rather than a wicked motive, and an act that is motivated by diabolical intentions may only inflict small amounts of harm, so it may not have evil results. Authors who believe that an evil motivation is critical in deciding that an action is evil argue that even if serious harm results from an action, we should not refer to the action as evil if no harm was intended or if the harm could not be foreseen by the agent (Singer, 2004).

Haybron (1999, 2002) points out that definitions of evil based on the amount of harm caused do not take into account motive and affect (whether one enjoys the evil one does). One might be evil but never cause any harm; a quadriplegic who lives silently while spitefully wishing nothing but suffering for others may enjoy watching others suffer. Harm-based theories also do not support a bad/evil distinction; how much harm qualifies as evil rather than bad? Motivation may then be very important. Haybron (2002) believes that "most evil actions are not the product of evil people. . . . the connection between evil-doing and evil character is much lower than most writers suppose" (p. 279). Haybron says that to be evil is to be consistently vicious in the sense that one is "not aligned with the good to a morally significant extent" (2002, p. 270). Truly evil people have no good side, and they show no real compassion or conscience, even if they never perform evil acts or do any harm at all – although that is unlikely. Evil people may also do their duty as long as this is not grounded in respect or concern for others. An evil person might be positively opposed to the good, and misalignment from the good is vicious; it requires complete or near-complete lack of concern for the welfare of others. He believes that evil people are motivated in ways that are radically different from ordinary wrongdoers.

Formosa (2008) argues that there are four different ways to conceive of evil acts: (1) the consequences for the victims, especially the amount of harm they suffer; (2) the motive or intention of the perpetrator; and (3) the inability of evaluators to understand why the act was done combined with (4) our feeling of utter horror or disgust at the act. A combination of these approaches may be used to distinguish an act that is evil rather than just wrong. Formosa points out that to defend a theory of evil, authors typically give examples of acts considered to be evil and use them to show that the author's theory matches our moral intuitions better than other theories. However, he believes that although our moral intuitions are important, this process is not definitive for various reasons; for example, the intuitions that are relied on are often too vague to make the sort of distinctions that are required. There is also the question of how much weight can be given to our intuitions when deciding on a moral theory and the question of whose intuitions are correct, since people from other cultural groups may have different intuitions. Formosa suggests that a useful theory of evil should provide a set of conceptual tools that help us identify evil when it occurs, help to minimize or prevent future evils from occurring, and help us respond to evil in appropriate ways. Practically speaking, these conditions do not differentiate among competing theories of evil that are all useful but that also face intuitive difficulties. A combination of approaches may be used to distinguish an act that is evil rather than just wrong. An act that is motivated by diabolical intentions or that includes silencing the agent's empathy may only inflict small amounts of harm, so it may not have evil results.

Formosa (2008) defines an evil act in this way:

> [A]n evil act is an act of wrongdoing in which the perpetrator of the act is at least partly responsible for other individuals suffering what would at least normally be a life-wrecking or ending harm, and where in so acting we judge the perpetrator, in the light of all the relevant details, to be deserving of our very strongest moral condemnation.
>
> (p. 230)

Life-wrecking harm means "harm that violates the minimum conditions of human well-being in such a way that it interferes with a person's ability to function as a fully-fledged agent" (p. 229). Life-wrecking harm interferes with a person's ability to live a full life. It is harm that causes intense suffering, inhibits the performance of ordinary activities, produces severe trauma, undermines one's moral character, hinders the ability to maintain, nurture, develop, and begin new relationships with people, and undermines the person's ability to be autonomous and cultivate dignity and self-worth. However, it seems entirely possible that an act might be evil without causing life-wrecking harm.

Formosa points out that perpetrator accounts alone are inadequate approaches to evil. He believes we need a combination approach with three components: (1) a perpetrator component that identifies what makes the act deserving of condemnation; (2) a component that identifies what makes the act unjustifiable; and (3) a victim component that identifies the harm done to victims. An evil act is an act of wrongdoing that meets several criteria. The perpetrator of the act is morally responsible for causing suffering that produces very significant harm, including harm that ends life or that significantly impairs a person's autonomy. Taking into account all of the relevant factors (including deliberativeness, reprehensibility of the motive, and the degree, type, and gratuitousness of the inflicted harm), the perpetrator has acted very badly. But Formosa believes that we can only condemn the perpetrator if he is morally responsible, and so this would not apply if he were insane. Then, a horrible act would be akin to a natural disaster rather than evil, because no one is morally responsible. Deliberativeness means that the perpetrator acted knowingly, with foresight, prior deliberation, and planning, rather than mere recklessness or negligence. Reprehensibility means that the perpetrator's motive was something akin to racism or sadism rather than anger. Formosa suggests that harm is gratuitous if the harm is itself the goal of the act, as in sadism, or when the degree of harm inflicted is excessive, given the perpetrator's own goals. Formosa (2008, p. 233) defines an evil person as "an unreformed person who repeatedly perpetuates, or at least intends to perpetuate, evil acts." In this view, a person who commits an evil act in a moment of weakness or frenzy is not an evil person, or he does not have an evil constitution or character, whereas an evil person repeatedly acts in an evil way. Some evil deeds are out of character and not typical of the person's usual behavior, so the words *repeatedly* or *habitual* are important.

Victim approaches to evil are those such as described by Card (2002): "An evil is a reasonably foreseeable harm (that need not be highly probable) that falls within a certain range of magnitude and importance and is brought about, seriously risked, sustained, aggravated, or tolerated by culpable wrongdoing" (p. 3). She believes that evil is any kind of intolerable or atrocious behavior. Card believes there are two major components of evil: the harm that is caused by it and the wrongdoing itself. She does not believe we should define *evil* in terms of the motives of those responsible, because we can recognize evil without knowing the perpetrator's motives. These motives do not need to be evil in order for the act to be evil; the motives may even be good under other circumstances. She believes that wrongdoing alone is not sufficient to make something evil; wrongdoing is only evil when it causes intolerable harm to others. An evil act is one that produces harm that is reasonably foreseeable, culpably inflicted, and deprives or risks depriving others of the basics needed to make a life possible, tolerant, and decent. The necessary basics include decent food, water, air, sleep, freedom from prolonged pain and debilitating fear, the ability to form and maintain affective ties, the ability to make choices, and a sense of one's own worth as a person. A tolerable life is a life that is at least minimally worth living for its own sake, not just as instrumental to the ends of others. An institution can be evil, not only if its purpose is inhumane but if it can be foreseen that its normal operations will produce intolerable harm. Card thereby removes the focus from the motivation and the psychology of the perpetrators to the suffering of their victims. She believes that the perpetrator is culpable when the perpetrator intends to do intolerable harm, is willing to do so in the course of pursuing an otherwise acceptable aim or principle, or fails to attend to risks to others. Card subsequently extended her ideas to non-sentient life (Card, 2002), and Davion (2009) has applied Card's theory to the problem that global warming has produced for Alaskan villagers that have been forced to relocate.

Baumeister and Campbell (1999) point out that acts that seem evil to victims may be experienced differently by the perpetrators; evil is therefore best defined from the victim's perspective, since the victim's suffering constitutes the evil consequences of the act. There is often a gap or discrepancy between the victim's and the perpetrator's view of the nature of an act. The perpetrator may not see the act as important and may regard the victim's suffering as trivial and irrelevant to the perpetrator's goals and satisfactions. Victim accounts of evil involve a longer time span than perpetrator accounts (as the example of slavery shows), and victim accounts see clear moral issues whereas perpetrator accounts see more gray areas. Perpetrators may see extenuating circumstances or justification for their action, but victims judge perpetrators more harshly and unambiguously. Perpetrators may acknowledge wrongdoing but also see provocation by the victims that victims may deny. Victims may see the actions of perpetrators as purely gratuitous even though the perpetrators have explanations. Perpetrators rarely see themselves as simply sadistic, although the evil deed may be attractive to the perpetrator. In this context, Vetlesen (2005) believes that there can be no impartiality or objectivity by an external observer or neutral third party in judging moral evil; the victim is the privileged source.

To be labeled evil, Darley (1992) suggests, an action "has to have a quality of egregious excess, such as a murder committed in the course of a crime" (p. 201), triggering moral outrage because of complete disregard for the humanity of the victim. Or, he believes, evil consists of depraved excess, such as pleasure gained from the torture of the innocent, especially if the perpetrator carefully plans his actions ahead of time, for example by planning to kidnap someone in order to torture him. In this vein, Garrard (1998) suggests that the nastiness of an act rather than the amount of harm it causes could be sufficient to judge the act to be evil. She believes that an evil action "is one in which the agent is entirely impervious – blind and deaf – to the presence of significant reasons against his acting" (2002, p. 330). The perpetrator has silenced any consideration for the suffering of the victim and cannot see that these considerations are reasons for acting or not acting. Thus, the torturer does not see the screams of his victims as reasons to desist. Garrard believes this is due to a cognitive defect, a distorted capacity for practical reasoning, but it also sounds like a serious defect of empathy. Her account does not explain why the evil person was so blind or indifferent to his victim's suffering.

Staub (2003) points out that doing nothing or ignoring the suffering of others may be evil; the bystander who passes by someone suffering on the street, family members who know a child is being abused but do nothing, the nation that ignores genocide or that sells arms to countries that murder its own people, are all behaving in an evil way. Staub gives the example of psychoanalysts in Berlin during the Nazi era who ignored the persecution of their Jewish colleagues. Some of these analysts participated in the Holocaust and the Nazi euthanasia of mentally ill and handicapped people. In his analysis of genocide, Staub (1989) considers evil to be not only the deliberate killing of others but also "the creation of conditions that materially or psychologically destroy or diminish people's dignity, happiness, and capacity to fulfill basic material needs" (p. 25).

Because some people who commit evil acts do not regard their actions as evil, Baumeister (2012) believes that we have to define evil as an experience in the eye of the beholder, not through the lens of the myth of pure evil. Terrorists are evil from the point of view of their victims, but they regard themselves as freedom fighters or religious devotees. For Baumeister, we have to understand them on their own terms or we "abandon the project of scientific understanding in favor of moral condemnation" (p. 369). He believes we cannot condemn their actions at the same time as we try to understand them scientifically. "Refusing to recognize the humanity of the perpetrator is probably an insuperable obstacle to fully understanding the genesis of his or her violent acts" (p. 369). After we have understood them, we may condemn them morally.

According to Verhoef (2014): "Very broadly, evil can be understood as everything that hinders the realization of a good life (which includes natural catastrophes). In a narrow sense, evil is those premeditated human actions that are intended to cause harm to others." Or, for Waller (2007, p. 19), evil is simply the destructive intention to do harm or cause suffering. Waller says that a purely evil person is "just as much an artificial construct as a person who is purely good. Perpetrators of extraordinary evil are extraordinary only by what they have done, not by who they are" (p. 19). They are not beyond understanding. Therefore, the root of evil is the action itself, not the person who commits it. To determine moral culpability, we must take into account human will, genetics, the situation, and the psychology of the individual.

Schmid (2013) defines evil as "everything that opposes personal being. If the meaning of being consists of being-for-each-other, then evil is opposition to love" (p. 50). Here *love* is used in the sense of agape or Rogers' unconditional positive regard; evil arises from a deprivation of love, either for oneself or for others. Berkowitz (1999) suggests specific criteria for deciding if an act is evil: (1) the victim is helpless; (2) the perpetrator is responsible for his actions; and (3) there is an imbalance between the amount of injury done to the victims and the magnitude of the objective gains achieved by the perpetrator. He notes the debate about whether President Truman's 1945 decision to drop the atomic bomb was truly evil. For many people, the devastation of Hiroshima and Nagasaki was balanced by the lives of the U.S. soldiers that were not lost in the invasion of Japan that would otherwise have been necessary. However, this was one of many occasions on which it is debatable whether an act is evil or not, because at the time of the bombing of Hiroshima, according to some historians, the Allies were aware that the Japanese had asked the Soviets to act as an intermediary for negotiating a Japanese surrender. The fire-bombing of Dresden in 1945 is widely regarded as unnecessary, because the bombing, which killed about 25,000 civilians, did not affect the outcome of the war.

Thomas (1993) believes that an evil act is not just a wrongdoing; it is "a wrong-doing that evinces a profound deadening of moral sensibilities" (p. 75). For him, evil does not arise from understandable conditions, such as a crime of passion, but from moral deadening; the evildoer realizes he will cause harm but this does not stop him. Thomas believes that such moral deadening is the definitive distinction that differentiates evil from an understandable condition such as a crime of passion.

Horne (2008) believes that the term *evil* should be restricted to evil acts rather than evil characters; for him, "evil" is an adjective rather than a noun. Evil acts can only be examined in their specific contexts. He would therefore eschew "foundational" explanations of evil based on secure, basic beliefs, such as the notion of evil as a kind of force. Horne suggests that to derive knowledge of what is evil from *a priori* postulates without reference to historical or contemporary contexts is to give that knowledge "the cloak of universality and permanence" (p. 670). In contrast, he wants to conceptualize evil hermeneutically and phenomenologically, such that understanding evil emerges by means of interpretation within its cultural and historical contexts. For him, such understanding is always provisional and context-dependent. He points out that Freud, Jung, and Melanie Klein all write as if evil is a noun and there is an evil tendency in human nature, but later psychoanalytic theorists such as Winnicott and Fairbairn only use a hermeneutic, phenomenological approach.

Levi (1989) warns against the danger of oversimplifying when discussing good and evil; he describes a "gray zone" in his discussion of the complexities involved in dichotomizing good and evil in the concentration camps. He points out that the Nazis degraded their victims to the point that the victims' behavior sometimes resembled that of the Nazis, for example when certain prisoners were singled out to perform special tasks for which they received extra food. These prisoners, known as *Kapos*, acted as administrators who supervised forced labor, and they could be cruel and ruthless, but this was the result of the harsh conditions of the camps that made survival very precarious. The *SonderKommandos* were prisoners who were forced to run the gas chambers and crematoria. After a few months, they too were murdered, to ensure there were no witnesses. Levi also discusses Chaim Rumkowski, the Jewish head of the Lodz ghetto in Poland, who was power-driven and grandiose and suppressed resistance in the ghetto. He made lists of those to be sent to concentration camps. These cases reveal how the victims of persecution can themselves become corrupt, but Levi makes the point that we cannot judge them, because none of us know how we might behave if we were driven by necessity or the seduction of power. It is more difficult to place the Nazis into the gray zone, according to Levi, but he believes that most of them were average people who were not monsters. In his words, "they had our faces" (p. 169).

Is *evil* qualitatively different than *very wrong*?

There is no agreement about the difference between acts that are merely wrong, such as behavior based on selfishness and deceit, and actions that are truly evil. Intuitively, however, we feel there is a difference; it would not be possible for instance to think of a Nazi concentration camp as merely wrong. If we are justified in making this distinction, what makes the difference? Does evil have a special quality of its own? For most authors, to describe an act as evil rather than wrong, the act must have either a hateful or malicious motivation, or it must produce particularly harmful effects that we judge to be much more serious than the effects of ordinary wrongdoing. There is no agreement however on the *amount* of harm or suffering that has to be inflicted in order for an act to be considered evil. Harm can be understood to include physical and emotional damage of all kinds. However, *harm* is a very broad term, since it may refer to any form of pain or suffering or restriction of human potential, so the harm must be considerable for the action to be considered to be evil. Therefore, some authors define *evil* only in terms of an event that causes great harm, whether or not an evil outcome was intended; others insist on the importance of intention when deciding whether an act was evil. If we allow intention as part of our definition of evil, then an attempted murder that is unsuccessful would also be evil even if no harm ensues. On the other side of this coin, good intentions may produce evil outcomes if they result in serious harm. Even if serious harm occurs unintentionally, an action might still be considered evil.

Shafranske (1990b) is among those who believe that we can distinguish true evil from human failings. He suggests that, because true evil lies outside the boundaries of humanity, it involves a conscious disavowal of the possibility of the good, of one's "teleological call to be in relation with the other and to oneself as a member of humanity" (p. 6). For him, fallibility does not sever one's relationship with others, but in his view, true evil does so.

According to Perrett (2002), evil is more profoundly wicked than just wrongdoing. He says that Evil, as distinct from ordinary moral and natural evil, is intentional wrongdoing that flows from a particular kind of depraved character. The act must be motivated in a particular way; it is done *because* it is wrong. The perpetrator takes pleasure in the wrongness of the action and shows no morally appropriate guilt, shame, or regret. A moral monster who can truly be described as Evil is therefore a rarity. If we just pursue our own interests and desires at the expense of others, we are not necessarily choosing to do evil for its own sake. Perrett points out that if we understood all of the circumstances and motivations behind such behavior, we will see complexities that prevent us from judging the individual as Evil.

Darley (1992) is among those writers who believe that although we think we can intuitively recognize evil when we see it, it is not possible to unequivocally define the difference between an act that is evil as distinct from merely bad; it is more difficult to define evil than wrongdoing. He points out that it is difficult for us to justify our moral preferences, and we have no easy way to designate some actions as morally wrong. He therefore suggests that we base our definition of wrongdoing on principles such as utilitarianism,[5] since we can all agree that the essence of wrongdoing is intentionally, knowingly, recklessly, and unjustifiably causing harm or pain to others.

Morton (2005) suggests that a "weak" reading of the term *evil* refers to wrong-doing such as willingness to follow immoral orders, moral incompetence, lack of imagination, and overreaction, whereas a strong reading of evil implies an atrocity that arouses horror or moral revulsion. Morton does not believe there can be a common psychological profile to those who commit atrocious acts, although the conceptual commonality shared by evil people is that they do not experience the usual human "barrier to inflicting pain, death, or humiliation on another" (p. 257). Evil people have a barrier against the awareness that they are doing wrong. Self-deception is obviously important here; if we convince ourselves that evil means are justified by a certain end, then we can justify evil acts by pointing to our good intentions. (Self-deception is discussed further on p. 61.)

Calder (2013) agrees that for evil to be qualitatively different from ordinary wrongdoing, the evil act must have a particular quality that merely wrongful acts do not have to any degree. He suggests that evil acts have at least two essential components: they cause significant harm, and they inexcusably intend to bring about, allow, or witness significant harm for an unworthy goal – harm that a normal, rational person would take considerable pains to avoid. Calder says that ordinary wrongdoing does not have these essential properties. In contrast, Russell (2007) believes that evil is only *quantitatively* not qualitatively distinct from ordinary wrongdoing. He denies there is anything substantially different between evil and wrongdoing, even though in everyday usage we distinguish between them. In this context, when we use the term "the lesser of two evils," we imply that the degree of evil can be calibrated in some way.

Given this controversy, can we insist that evil has a special quality of its own? Darley believes it is impossible to "definitely and unequivocally categorize certain acts as evil and others as merely bad" (p. 201). However, many people believe that we can make this distinction on the basis of our emotional reaction to the act.

Acts we describe as evil have a particular quality; their nature seems ghastly and appalling, often impossible to understand, filling us with a kind of revulsion and disgust. (Although an act could be disgusting but not necessarily evil if it does not cause harm.) Morton (2004) notes that evil acts produce a "visceral revulsion" (p. 13), and Garrard (1998, 2002) agrees that evil acts are more than just very wrong because they possess some "especially horrific quality" (p. 321). Read (2014) also argues that for something to be called evil, it must produce intense emotional distress and have the power to shock or disturb. Horne (2008) suggests that we use the word *evil* as a metaphor to refer to the kind of subjective arousal that results from our witnessing destructive acts. Evil therefore seems to produce a kind of moral pollution that is not found in ordinary wrongdoing. Singer (2004) suggests that the test of evil, as distinct from an act that is simply wrong or bad, is that "no normal decent reasonable human being can conceive of himself (or herself) acting in such a way" (p. 195).

Levine (2000) points out that to call someone evil is to condemn the person in a special way; this description denies that the person is best understood as simply immoral or ill. He suggests that true evil produces a combination of a sense of horror combined with moral condemnation. Overall, at least subjectively, the word *evil* therefore goes deeper than the word *immoral*, implying a qualitative distinction. It seems that evil is a distinct moral concept, qualitatively distinct from wrongdoing.

Does evil always involve aggression and violence?

Many people describe evil in terms of destructive aggression, especially violence against the innocent. For Read (2014), there is an inextricable link between violence and evil; it is violence that moves us to categorize the case beyond wrong and into the realm of evil, because of the physicality of violence and "the unquestioned malevolent connotations accompanying it" (p. 51). She believes that we are less sensitive to crimes such as fraud that do not incorporate violence. Read points out the difference between a crime of passion compared to the creativity of "imaginative serial killers or other repeat offenders" (p. 54). We are more understanding of a man who kills as he stumbles upon his wife *in fragrante delicto* than we are of a cold, calculating murderer who constructs an elaborate plan to harm his victim. The former seems to "snap" in the heat of passion, whereas the latter has a passion for harm. This suggests, she points out, that creativity may be required for the definition of a crime as evil. Yet evil cannot be entirely equated with aggression or violence, because some evil actions are more complicated or subtle, and some forms of violence are emotional rather than physical. We see emotional violence between intimate partners when one member of the couple is subject to offensive or degrading behavior by the other, in a way that arouses shame or fear. Or, one partner is overly dominant and abuses his or her power. This kind of cruelty is psychologically very damaging (Yoon & Lawrence, 2013) and may escalate into physical violence.

For most people, interpersonal violence is aversive, producing psychological distress, so that the average person avoids deliberately hurting others, sometimes at considerable personal cost (Grossman, 1996). This innate human disposition contributes to the intuitive notion that it is evil to deliberately, consciously, inflict unjustifiable violence on others. Consequently, the military has to train recruits to overcome their in-built aversion to killing. However, once people have engaged in violence they become increasingly likely to be violent in the future (Bushman, 2002), apparently because they become desensitized.

Baumeister (1997) has a general concept of evil as "intentional interpersonal harm" or unjustified aggression, and he uses the word to encompass not only "great crimes and horrendous acts" but also "petty cruelties and minor transgressions of everyday life" (p. 8). Baumeister believes that restricting the term *evil* to horrendous acts is to succumb to the "myth of pure evil" (p. 18), meaning a stereotyped conception of evil that is essentially different from less extreme but unjustified aggression. His definition would not necessarily distinguish between mere badness or real evil, as we see in the case of the psychopathic personality.

The Machiavellian character and the psychopath

The term *Machiavellian* is based on Machiavelli's 1532 text *The Prince*, which describes the ruthless ways in which a ruler must be willing to behave in order to maintain power, even as he appears on the surface to be benevolent. This behavior includes strategies of cheating, manipulation, deception, stealing, and lying. Machiavelli believed that evil in politics is inevitable, and the ruler should work with it rather than trying to resist it. Machiavelli's view of human nature was cynical; he saw people as greedy, self-serving, stupid, and easily deceived. He believed that moral standards cannot provide any realistic guidelines for politics, so the ruler must learn how not to be good. The ruler must utilize fear and punishment to control the population and prevent rebellion; for Machiavelli, threats are more likely to motivate people than are promises of good things to come. If the ruler is seen as kind, he may be seen as weak; he must therefore be cold-blooded. When a situation requires firm control, Machiavelli recommends hiring agents or proxies to commit the necessary unpleasant acts, then turning against these agents and punishing them for committing these acts, thus defusing people's anger by finding a suitable target for it. All of this is done in the service of political stability, which for Machiavelli is a cardinal virtue.

Christie (1970) pointed out that Machiavellian individuals see others as objects to be manipulated, rather than individuals with whom one can empathize. Such characters have no concern with conventional morality; any form of lying and cheating is acceptable to them. They are not necessarily motivated by ideology; rather, they simply wish to achieve particular ends. These individuals surface in many areas of life, including science, academia, politics, and business. Christie believes that people fall on a spectrum, at one end of which are those who are very successful at manipulating others, whom he called "high Machs," whereas people who are sometimes willing to be helpful are "low Machs." Highly Machiavellian people are exploitative, prioritize competition and winning at all costs, and place low value on community and family. This trait is negatively associated with agreeableness and conscientiousness and positively correlated with a strong sense of personal control. These individuals use persuasion, self-disclosure, and ingratiation to get their way, and may be willing to betray others when the others cannot retaliate. They have low ethical standards and tell more falsehoods than most people. Many Machiavellian characters are found in important social positions where they are able to take advantage of kindhearted people, and they are quite difficult to detect. Some literature in this area suggests that Machiavellian intelligence may have evolved as a social strategy for personal advancement (Jonason et al., 2012).

McHoskey et al. (1998) argued that such people are no different than psychopaths, and some of them are similar to borderline personality disorders. The true psychopath does not develop any moral values. He has little or no capacity to love and he is unable to generate feelings of compassion or emotional (as distinct from purely cognitive) empathy for others, so he is incapable of sustaining normal relationships. He is capable of dehumanizing and exploiting others with no compunction or conscience. He has a very limited ability to identify with his victim, so he is able to treat people as if they were things. He may therefore not be sadistic in the usual sense of the word, since his destruction of a person means no more to him than destruction of a material object. Some clinicians see malignant narcissism as the common quality that underlies these features, since this personality trait is associated with arrogance, preoccupation with oneself, and indifference to the feelings of other people (see p. 87).

Psychopathy seems to have a substantial genetic component, based on twin studies. Character traits such as indifference to hurting others and lack of emotion can be seen in young children. Viding (2005) believes that this genetic vulnerability makes such children resistant to psychotherapeutic intervention, and they are at high risk for becoming adult psychopaths. It is suggested that psychopathic traits in children occur because of brain anomalies that reduce their ability to have empathy for others and impair moral reasoning (Frick & Marsee, 2005; Meloy, 2000). Such children are less able than normal to recognize expressions of distress on others' faces. Using functional magnetic resonance imaging (fMRI), criminal psychopaths have been shown to have significantly less affect-related activity in the limbic system (Kiehl et al., 2001). Some researchers believe that abnormal functioning of the amygdala (normally associated with fear conditioning) may be central to the psychopathology of the psychopath (Blair, 2003). Other research has shown abnormalities of the corpus callosum, the prefrontal and temporal cortices, and other parts of the brain (Raine et al., 2003; Raine & Yang, 2006). As well as genetic abnormalities, factors such as maternal alcohol abuse may play a part in the etiology of this disorder.

It is possible that environmental rather than genetic influences have molded the brains of vulnerable children towards becoming psychopaths. Because most psychopaths were severely abused in childhood by predatory parents, their brains were exposed to a constant barrage of stress hormones, so they become relatively inured to stress and its associated emotions. Consequently, the autonomic nervous system does not respond normally to stress, for example with an increased heart rate. A child who is chronically severely abused may end up unable to experience his own feelings or the feelings of others. Vulnerable minds of this kind are susceptible to propaganda and hate literature.

For psychopathic people who are indifferent to others, evil behavior is sometimes a way to deal with boredom. There is a correlation between proneness to boredom and psychopathic, sensation-seeking behavior. Even psychopaths who are socially successful are often chronically bored, partly because they have a very sparse inner life. Kekes (2005) points out the connection between boredom and evil. He regards boredom as an unpleasant state of mind that consists of a combination of apathy, discontent, and restlessness, in which everything seems to be pointless, nothing is interesting, and nothing matters. Instead of leading an empty life, evil is an exciting outlet for the bored psychopath because it allows him to be active and energetic while planning to outwit law enforcement. Success allows him a feeling of pride and accomplishment, and proves his self-sufficiency and independence. His evil actions are an authentic, free expression of his nature rather than the result of external influences. Keke's description correlates well with the traditional understanding of boredom as a state of low arousal in situations in which there is insufficient stimulation. Psychopaths are intolerant of boredom and routine because of chronic cortical under-arousal, as a result of which they are pathologically stimulation-seeking (Zuckerman, 2014).

It is startling to discover that, according to Stout's estimate (2005), 4% of the U.S. population has some degree of anti-social personality, while about 1.5% are full-blown psychopaths. She points out therefore that there are more psychopaths than there are anorexics or schizophrenics, so this character type poses a very real social problem, and it is likely that psychotherapists have had some experience of them whether or not we recognized what we were dealing with. Many psychopaths are successful in business, politics, law enforcement, or other professions that involve control of other people, partly because they have no conscience and no capacity for remorse, so they can treat others only as a means to an end, with no reservations about how these ends are to be achieved. The only thing that matters to them is winning at all costs, which is a major defense against dysphoric affect and allows a sense of safety in a world that they perceive as dangerous. Psychopaths may be superficially charming and able to simulate real relationships, but only for the purposes of manipulation. Although they do not actually experience real love, empathy, or devotion, they may be able to mimic these feelings. Such personalities are difficult to spot partly because they are experts at creating a good first impression. They are confident in their abilities and can make others see them as effective. They lie without concern for the consequences, and if confronted with the truth, they seem surprised that the lie matters to others. If challenged about their lying, they may be prone to rage.

The relevance of the problem of evil to psychotherapists

Psychotherapists typically receive little or no training on the subject of evil, although they commonly find themselves working with someone who has been the victim of evil, and they may be faced with an ordinary person behaving in an uncharacteristically reprehensible manner. Psychotherapists may meet a character they believe to be evil or one who admits to being a frequent perpetrator of evil. Occasionally the therapist meets someone who is accused of being evil but who denies this appellation. Not uncommonly, psychotherapists work with a person who is unrealistically convinced that he is evil, or who feels that something in him is destructive or evil. This is a common feeling among severely depressed people or among those who have internalized the sense of a shameful defect in the self as a result of harsh parenting or early religious indoctrination about their sinful nature. Such a belief may be initially unconscious and emerge during the course of psychotherapy. An individual in psychotherapy who has committed real evil may eventually experience regret as a result of the therapy, and he may attempt restitution or penance. This process may be fostered by psychotherapeutic work.

One characteristic of the psychotherapist's experience of evil in the consulting room is a reaction of fear, or sometimes of bewilderment or rage at the patient's behavior. Rarely, with some individuals, the therapist experiences a sense of absolute dread that convinces her that she is in the presence of evil (Grand, 2000). Another common countertransference response is one of revulsion and the wish to escape, which Peck (1983) believes is so specific that it is a diagnostic pointer towards the presence of evil. In these situations, it may seem that ordinary therapeutic responses are not sufficient, and psychotherapists are forced to rely on personal experience and beliefs about evil, combined with the assumptions of their culture. These situations bring to the fore the question of whether evil can be objectively defined, or whether it is a purely subjective judgment. If the latter is true, then the issue of projection and the therapist's personal biases become very important determinants of the countertransference.

Working therapeutically with an individual who believes he or she has experienced true evil, the therapist has various choices. If the notion of evil does not fit with the therapist's personal belief system, as Goldberg (1996) suggests one might listen to this description as metaphorical, focusing on the meaning it has for the patient. Usually, the psychotherapist will work from within the patient's frame of reference, but the psychotherapist may have a different worldview and radically different moral standards than those of the patient. A patient might speak of evil while the therapist believes that what is really being described is better thought of as cruelty or abuse. The patient may rather coolly describe his behavior in a way that fills the therapist with horror, leading to a subjective assessment of the presence of evil. When the therapist feels such an intuitive sense of evil in the room, the treatment may not proceed in the usual way, and the therapist might feel alone and disorganized because of a combination of confusion and fear. The therapist might feel helpless or unsure what to do in the felt presence of evil, or she may find it difficult to establish a therapeutic relationship. Sometimes the therapist feels a coldness in the room, or an ominous sense of a dark presence, as if the patient is possessed by something that wants to destroy him. In this context, von Franz (1972) makes the important point that even if the therapist believes the patient to be evil, this kind of possession is not deliberately chosen. In her words: "It is a tragic fate which should be respected in silence" (p. 179). Different psychotherapists have different tolerance for specific types of evil behavior based on their own psychology, their countertransference response to the perpetrator of evil, and their theoretical approach. It may help to acknowledge that the emergence of evil, either in an individual or in a society, at least gives us a chance to confront it.

Most psychotherapists are trained to see themselves as morally neutral, although in practice psychotherapists cannot free themselves from the issue of values. In principle a severely narcissistic character who makes life miserable for those around him, who lacks empathy and commits acts of cruelty and indifference, can be looked at as psychologically disturbed without being thought of as evil. Needless to say, this strictly psychotherapeutic approach gives rise to the concern that psychology somehow lets evil behavior off the hook. However, the psychotherapist's primary task is to look at behavior psychologically rather than as a moral judge. But since psychotherapists are human, judgment often springs to mind and has to be taken into account as part of the countertransference.

It is often argued that psychotherapy is not about morality, yet questions about traditional values and morality do occur in the psychotherapeutic setting. Sometimes, conflict with collective values causes great suffering. Tensions often arise between conscience and personal desire. The patient's ideas about good and evil may or may not coincide with collective morality or with the therapist's personal standards, and when these are in conflict, the psychotherapist is faced with something of a dilemma in terms of which attitude to support.

Psychotherapeutic witnessing of evil

The experience of actually witnessing evil can be very traumatic, making the world seem less safe, calling into question the reliability of good internal objects, and threatening our sense of how the world operates and our sense of a moral order. The psychotherapist is of course not immune to such reactions. Gozlan (2016) describes the case of Dr. John Bradford, a forensic psychiatrist who broke down emotionally and became suicidal after watching a video of rape and murder made by the perpetrator. Bradford could not tolerate the helplessness of the victim, although he had previously seen many such images without experiencing much affect. It seems that on this occasion he identified with the suffering of the victim, as if he was the helpless woman on the video who was about to be killed. Gozlan suggests that Bradford's personal crisis represents a larger crisis in the field of psychiatry, which uses diagnosis as a defense against affect, as if the clinician is outside of the experience. In order to be "objective," the clinician has to become psychologically numb as a defense against being "response-able" (p. 174). Bradford's defenses broke down, and he experienced a "primal dread" for which his professional frame was no protection. Gozlan wonders if Bradford's breakdown was a response to the trauma he witnessed or to the return of his own repressed material. Gozlan believes that the mental health profession's tendency to treat people with techniques that have no emotional influence on the clinician is a defense against affect and helplessness, which generate dissociative responses in the clinician, especially when the painful material is (perhaps unconsciously) relevant to the clinician's own life. Trauma destroys meaning, meaninglessness fosters detachment, and diagnosis defends against the inchoate experience. Diagnosis "may be used as an armor, transforming the position of expert into a tool with which to repel the chaotic otherness of trauma" (p. 181). Gozlan believes that psychiatry has an illusion of knowledge; it tells itself a story of mastery that tries to "mask the messy encounter between the patient's and the therapist's unconscious . . . through a one-dimensional, exhaustive story" (p. 182). In Bradford's case, Gozlan believes that the sheer meaninglessness of the evil he witnessed contributed to his inability to process the violence he was witnessing.

Gozlan asks the important question of how one can create meaning and sustain affect in the face of horror, watching events that have no reason to them, without losing one's mind. He points out that we face the dilemma of being simultaneously fascinated and repelled by un-representable evil, which leads to a breakdown, but breakdown is also the point of transformation or breakthrough that forces us to encounter our own subjectivity. Bradford was forced to watch his own trauma. "In facing evil we face an irreducible otherness, but in facing this troubling excess, we encounter ourselves" (p. 183). Bradford's professionalism could not protect him. Gozlan points out that

> elaborate attempts at classification, objectification, and normalization transform what should be a practice of care into a perverse search for mastery. The preference for explanation rather than interpretation as well as the promise of objectivity, predictability, and emotional distance translates into totalitarian thinking and omnipotence in the clinician's thinking.
>
> (p. 184)

Covington (2016) addresses the question of why a group of bystanders may watch evil without intervening, for example during episodes of genocidal violence such as the Nazi era, in which people are massacred while onlookers do nothing. She suggests that persecuting others gets rid of one's own group's feelings of helplessness and vulnerability and makes another group feel these unbearable feelings. Not only might this be a form of identification with the aggressor, but she suggests that witnessing extreme violence perpetrated on others might function as a kind of ritualized cleansing that tries to restore purity within the group. The group can identify with the killers "who serve as a conduit for their own sadism, omnipotence and fantasies of revenge"; the group is then able to "keep its own hands clean and maintain the paranoid splitting necessary to keep what is bad outside and 'other' as a defense against past trauma" (p. 197). The group's approval of mass killings transforms an evil act into something moral, part of the common good.

Covington also points out that witnessing evil is traumatic because it destroys our beliefs that allow us to go on being in the world safely, and also threatens our relationship with internal objects who created these beliefs – these internal objects can no longer guide us. Our old belief system and expectations about the world are shattered, and we struggle to accommodate a new reality. One might not intervene in trauma that we witness, according to Covington, because one has to maintain some distance from the event in order to sustain one's own belief system. The bystander is not passive simply because of repressed sadism or unconscious complicity. In her words: "The bystander is in a twilight zone, neither actively engaged in the event nor entirely passive, simultaneously identifying with both abuser and victim" (p. 202), although identification with the abuser might be unconscious. To take action means that "one enters the world of abuser and victim with the attendant risk of becoming one or the other."

Wicked or evil?

Singer (2004) suggests that it is not sufficient to call Hitler merely wicked, since that term does not do justice to him; for Singer, *evil* is the term of ultimate opprobrium. Is there in fact a distinction between evil and wickedness? These terms are sometimes used interchangeably, but their exact meaning can be ambiguous. The term *wicked* is not often used today, perhaps because it used to have religious connotations, as if it were synonymous with *blasphemous* or something similar. However, the political and social philosopher Stanley Benn (1985) believes that wickedness is not synonymous with evil, and wickedness may be more serious than evil. He suggests that wicked people not only have a wicked attitude, but they knowingly do evil with evil intent. In contrast, an evil deed may be done by someone who is weak or misguided but not necessarily wicked, and one may do wrong with good intentions. In this view, someone who is evil through and through – full of hatred and malicious fantasies – may be paralyzed and unable to actually do wrong. Benn believes that a wicked attitude is based on an evil maxim or rule for living, such as "only my personal welfare is important." This kind of maxim may simply be mistaken, and there are culpable and non-culpable mistakes, but a truly wicked person knows he is acting according to an evil maxim. Benn acknowledges that there are weak-willed and morally indolent people who cannot control themselves but who are not wicked.

Benn (1985) has a typology of wickedness. The least problematic form of wicked person is the selfish individual, or one who devotes himself exclusively to the promotion of his own family or business or nation, with ruthless lack of concern for the maxims of others. He acts for the sake of his own well-being and self-interest, which excludes everything except self-centered goodness. He is therefore governed by some notion of goodness, if only his own good. For such a person, self-love takes precedence over moral law, which seems to be what the psychologist would regard as a narcissistic issue. Benn regards psychopathy as a form of moral imbecility, but because the psychopath does not see what he does as evil, in Benn's sense he is not wicked. The psychopath lacks the capacity to decenter, to look at the world from someone else's standpoint. Whereas the selfish person does understand that his action may affect the well-being of another person, but disregards this reason for acting, the psychopath is unable to see the other's well-being as a reason for him not to carry out an action. Benn likens this to the psychopath being asked to take into account the color of someone's hair when stealing his wallet – this reason would be irrelevant to the psychopath. The psychopath knows what others regard as good or bad, and knows what he would or would not enjoy, but only in a self-centered way, never taking into account the interests of others. He does not act on an evil maxim knowing it to be evil, so from Benn's point of view he may be evil but not wicked. The psychopath is morally defective in the sense of an amoral, dangerous animal, but because he is a person we have to apply moral constraints when dealing with him that do not apply to man-eating tigers.

For Benn, malignant wickedness is evil done in the full knowledge that it is evil, even done *because* it is evil. Benn also describes the conscientiously wicked person as one who believes that the maxims underlying his actions are universally valid and necessary. All other considerations are secondary to the maxim guiding his actions. Thus, the conscientiously wicked nationalist believes in the universal validity of his nation's supremacy, as if this were so good for humanity that any rational person would recognize his nation's overriding excellence. This kind of wickedness may arise even when the ideal is good but it is pursued with ruthlessness and insensitivity that excludes other goodness or ignores other horrors that ought to be taken into account.

Benn believes that doing evil so that good may come of it, or so that a greater evil may be avoided, is not necessarily wicked. He suggests that the wicked person is one who is callous enough to do the evil that needs to be done, for example in politics, where political action may involve violence. In the case of both selfish wickedness and conscientious wickedness, the individual refuses to acknowledge the moral significance of behavior that he could reasonably be expected to know as evil.

Citing the case of Eichmann and the Nazis who claimed they were merely following orders, Benn describes heteronomous wickedness, the condition of being dominated by an outside authority, as actions that are not entirely due to the will of the individual even if he appears to be free to choose whether to follow the orders of a superior. An individual such as Eichmann is acting on principles that he has assimilated from his social environment; he had handed over his conscience to the Nazi party and did not challenge this system. He therefore willfully made himself an instrument of wickedness. Benn believes that one should not submit to the guidance of an external authority such as a church or party while surrendering one's own judgment about its principles, or we may obey wicked orders. Benn acknowledges that such submission might be based on a disposition to act in accord with an evil maxim, and many people are only saved from wickedness by circumstances; had they been a guard in a concentration camp, they too might have acted wickedly.

Benn points out Kant's disbelief that human beings would adopt as a maxim for their behavior something like "do evil for evil's sake." That would make the person devilish, and Kant did not believe that human beings could be satanic. However, Benn believes that a malignant person would use the suffering of others as a reason for his action, not because the evil he recognizes is good for himself but just to take delight in the suffering of others. Unalloyed wickedness hates the good because it is good, and seeks its destruction on that account. Benn raises the issue of whether we have properly understood such evil and whether we perceive something as unalloyed wickedness because we have not fully understood it.

Benn takes on the claim made by Socrates that no one who knows the good would choose evil. This is plausible if we suppose that all voluntary action is directed at something that is considered to be good. So, for Socrates, whoever commits evil is ignorant because he misperceives something as good that is actually not so. On Socrates' account, therefore, self-destructive behavior prompted by self-hatred is perplexing – how can someone find good in hating himself? Furthermore, contra Socrates, the malignant person desires things precisely *because* they are not appropriate. Benn uses the example of Claggart, a character in Melville's novel *Billy Budd*, who hates Billy, a young sailor, and falsely charges him with sedition in order to destroy him – based purely on envy and hatred. Envy wants to destroy the good because it is good; Billy's goodness is a reproach to Claggart, so he must try to destroy it. Benn also quotes Schopenhauer's belief that, for the wicked, the suffering of others is an end in itself, not simply a means for the attainment of the individual's own ends. Schopenhauer believed this is due to an "intensity of will" that nothing can assuage; such an individual seeks to mitigate his own suffering by seeing the suffering of others, in which he delights, and hence cruelty results. In other words, some people behave in evil ways just because they are evil, not because of a perceived good.

Milo (1984) also has a typology of wickedness. He distinguishes between people who consciously recognize that their behavior is morally wrong and those who are guilty of unconscious wrongdoing. Unconscious wickedness is of three types: perverse wickedness, moral negligence, and amorality. An individual who believes that his wrongdoing is actually right is guilty of perverse wickedness; the morally negligent individual recognizes that certain types of behavior are wrong but does not recognize that his particular action is wrong. The amoral individual is also guilty of unconscious wrongdoing but has no moral principles and believes that what he does is neither right nor wrong. Milo also defines three different types of conscious wickedness, or morally depraved people who know that their actions are wrong. Preferential wickedness means behavior that results from a desire to do something wrong that is stronger than a desire to do something right, in contrast to evil people, who have no desire at all to do something right. Moral indifference and the Christian concept of wickedness involve conscious wrongdoing without any morally redeeming emotions such as shame or remorse.

Milo believes that true wickedness, or wickedness in its worst form, consists in deliberately doing what is morally wrong. He and Singer use the term "Satanic wickedness," following Milton's Satan, who infamously proclaims: "Evil be thou my good."[6] That is, a truly evil person, rather than a merely bad person, does evil knowingly, for the sake of evil, or wants to do evil or acts "with evil intent" (Benn, 1985, p. 796) or "under the aspect of evil" (ibid., p. 805). But it can be argued that a person can do evil without doing it for the sake of doing evil – this would probably not characterize Hitler or Stalin, for example, who were evil for other reasons.

Is evil banal? Hannah Arendt

Arendt's (1973) *The Origins of Totalitarianism* discusses the components of totalitarianism that allow the existence of what she calls radical evil. She points out that the Western moral and political traditions were unable to provide the resources necessary to deal with the overpowering evil of the Nazi regime. She believes that, rather than seeing evil as originating in wicked desire and behavior, the atrocities committed by totalitarian states are committed because large numbers of citizens follow the laws of the state without challenging social conventions. Horrible acts are committed or permitted by ordinary citizens, not only by a few demonic individuals. A totalitarian state controls every aspect of its subjects' lives – their culture, bodies, education, technology, media, and industry. It is therefore hostile to human freedom; such a state destroys the human capacity to be genuinely human.

Arendt defines radical evil as the attempt to make human beings superfluous or less than human; people are then dehumanized, deprived of rights, and treated as if they do not matter. Human individuality and spontaneity are destroyed, and difference is eliminated. The extermination of whole populations through total terror, for no intelligible reason, constitutes radical evil. The perpetrators of evil within the regime become mere vehicles that inflict the regime's ideology on its victims. These regimes condition people as if they were Pavlov's dogs. Therefore, rather than seeing evil as a metaphysical problem, Arendt understands it as the result of inadequate moral, legal, and political structures. She points out that history shows the dehumanizing effect of state policies that begin by seeing people as radically other, followed by colonization, discrimination, and eventually extermination. This process helps us to understand a source of genocidal behavior. People who become stateless may also become irrelevant; they are denied recognition of their humanity and legal status, and they become disposable. When people are superfluous, radical evil can emerge. The problem of statelessness continues, as we see in the case of the world's current refugee crisis.

Totalitarian systems allow the individual to identify with the larger group and its leader, so that the individual feels the regressive pull of being part of a powerful whole. This allows one's conscience, or the superego, to be ignored or submerged by the goals of the group, so that the superego now works for the ego ideals or the ideology of the leader. Murder may then be justified in the name of the ideal. Many observers of the Holocaust initially believed that the perpetrators made no moral judgments of their own and did what their superiors told them to do. Later it was realized that many of the perpetrators were not unaware of what they were doing, but they thought what they were doing was right.

Arendt appeared to change her views about evil while she covered the 1961 trial of Adolph Eichmann[7] for *The New Yorker*. In her 1965 *Eichmann in Jerusalem*, she developed the notion of the banality of evil. This suggested that Eichmann was "terrifyingly normal," and he was not driven by hatred or sadism but by his sense of duty to the Nazi regime, combined with his wish to rise in the Nazi hierarchy. Arendt believed that Eichmann lacked the imagination to realize empathically what he was doing to others. He had been certified as normal by several psychiatrists, and he was said to have had an exemplary family life. According to Arendt, he was incapable of looking at his behavior from the other person's point of view; he never realized what he was doing; he was not motivated by ideology as much as by the wish to please his superiors and advance his career by demonstrating his efficiency. He had no other motive. Adding weight to the notion that ordinary people in the right circumstances can commit evil, Arendt believes that Eichmann was an ordinary bureaucrat, a thoughtless, dutiful operative who was following his conscience, believing that what he was doing was a good thing. This kind of thoughtlessness can wreak havoc. Supporting the distinction between evil deeds and an evil personality, Arendt thought that although Eichmann's deeds were monstrous, he was personally neither monstrous nor demonic. She did, however, believe that he was guilty and deserved to be executed.

Arendt's approach dismisses the idea that evil acts presuppose evil intentions and motivation. She thought that most people could have behaved similarly under the kind of circumstances in which Eichmann found himself, implying that evil is an innate human potential. For her, Eichmann is not so different from the rest of us. Arendt believed that the frightening aspect of Eichmann was the very fact that he was so utterly normal, bland, and simple. She believes that such a person in a totalitarian regime surrenders his mind and his capacity for self-reflection and shame to the regime. Blinded by an illusory and wicked ideology, Eichmann became part of a movement that allowed him to be capable of terrible acts. Such an individual has become a kind of nobody, with no personal identity. Arendt distinguishes this banal form of evil from evil perpetrated with the deliberate intention of making other people superfluous. However, she seems to think that remaining this kind of personality is a matter of conscious choice; she thereby ignores the unconscious sources of our behavior. But her point that personal moral awareness can be distorted by social factors is very important. We are reminded of Himmler's Posen speeches,[8] in which he says that although the work of exterminating Jews was difficult, the murderers had to become tough but remained decent, while they remained true to a "higher purpose." In other words, the usual meaning of words such as "right," "higher," and "wrong" were turned upside down in that society. If Arendt is correct, intention and motivation are not as important as the result of an action in deciding whether it is evil.

Another question arises here: if Eichmann was banal, if he was so thoughtless and clouded by propaganda and ideology that he did not realize the significance of what he was doing, he was not acting autonomously or fully consciously; was he then responsible for his actions? Arendt believed that Eichmann was fully responsible, and it was correct for him to be held accountable. It is also possible that he was so involved in a psychological merger or *participation mystique*[9] with the Nazis that he did not differentiate himself from his surroundings, and hence exerted no personal judgment.

The origins of Arendt's idea of the banality of evil are found in her correspondence with the philosopher Karl Jaspers. She suggested to Jaspers that evil can be defined as "making human beings as human beings superfluous" (Arendt & Jaspers, 1992, p. 166). Evil means to dehumanize people, strip them of dignity, and treat them as expendable. In a 1946 letter to Arendt, Jaspers says that we should see the Nazis not as "demonic" but as "total banality, in their prosaic triviality. . . . Bacteria can cause epidemics that wipe out nations, but they remain merely bacteria" (ibid., p. 62). In her response to Jaspers, Arendt says that we should resist the impulse to "mythologize the horrible" (p. 69).

Arendt's notion of the banality of evil has been discussed by Covington (2012) from a psychoanalytic point of view. Covington says that Eichmann's commitment was the result of his identification with an ego ideal, the Nazi ideology. She points out that although Eichmann was not able to think about his prisoners, he did show concern for the lives and welfare of his own family, so he wasn't a "nobody" in every respect, only in certain respects. Covington also points out that Arendt "confuses the apparent lack of hate with a lack of motivation" (p. 1220). In fact, Eichmann had other motives, such as his commitment to the Nazi ideals with which he was identified, so-called role narcissism. His lack of empathy, which Arendt refers to as a lack of imagination about the effects of his actions on others, for Covington "is the danger zone in which evil is born" (p. 1221). Covington believes that Arendt's point about Eichmann's lack of thought and self-reflection is important because otherwise we may relegate evil exclusively to psychopaths or tyrants. In this way, we might absolve ourselves of responsibility for our own destructiveness, which must not be split off and projected onto people who are either bad or sick, so that evil only seems to be committed by others who are not one of us. Covington also suggests that what Arendt calls Eichmann's thoughtlessness, or his ability to commit evil with no feeling, results from the lack of an observing ego. He had no ability to have an internal dialog with himself, which would have allowed some self-reflection. Such an internal dialog, she suggests, is an expression of innate morality, and it can be perverted through self-deception or when it is ignored. Also: "When there is no internal dialog, there can be no awareness of an internal world or unconscious and no space for thought or memory . . . no feelings have meaning because they are dissociated and obliterated" (p. 1224). This lack may be why the "nobody" is susceptible to unquestioningly following the orders of an authority. He becomes an automaton; because there is no thought, there is no remorse or guilt. The orders he obeys "serve to suppress feelings that cannot be thought" (ibid.). There is no observing ego because the ego exists in the shadow of the collective superego. Covington points out that the nobody who retreats into mindlessly following orders also derives unconscious pleasure from killing the subjectivity – the inner life – of others. This is an externalization or enactment of an internal envy attack (Bion's–K)[10] that tries to destroy creativity and imagination.

In Arendt's *Eichmann in Jerusalem*, she appeared to be denying the existence of radical evil, which she had described in her earlier work. This apparent change in her thinking produced great controversy, since it seemed to exonerate Eichmann. She now claimed (Arendt, 2007) that evil is never radical because it has no depth; it can spread like a fungus but it has no deep roots (the source of the word *radical*) and no demonic dimension.[11] She did, however, continue to use the phrase "extreme evil" to describe the dehumanizing of people in a way that makes them superfluous. Thoughtlessness allows ordinary people to participate in social policies that produce extreme evil. She questioned the traditional idea that people who commit evil must have evil intentions and must be wicked, pathological people, since Eichmann was none of these things. The point she made is that while evil itself is not banal, those who commit evil may be ordinary people. She did not want to mythologize evil by calling it satanic. However, an important problem with her idea is that calling evil "banal" risks making evil seem too ordinary, or even somehow normal.

Some commentators dispute Arendt's view of Eichmann, pointing out for example that he was a participant in the infamous 1942 Wannsee conference that planned the final solution. Lipstadt (2011) notes that Eichmann's memoir was full of support for Nazi ideology; he agreed with the Nazi doctrine of racial purity; and he was very committed to killing Jews as fast as possible. She points out that Arendt does not pay enough attention to the anti-Semitism without which the Nazis would not have been able to mobilize the population to participate in the murder of European Jewry; this ideology played an essential role in the Holocaust. Some historians believe that Arendt was fooled by the deceptive way Eichmann represented himself, even though her concept of the banality of evil was true of other perpetrators if not of Eichmann himself. From this point of view, Arendt simply did not understand Eichmann's ruthlessness, his psychological makeup, and his adherence to Nazi ideology. She seemed to believe his assertion that he had not harbored ill will towards his victims, which to many people seems unbe-lievable. She was only able to infer what he was like from court documents and his appearance at the trial, without the benefit of an interview with him.

Arendt believes that the Western tradition has not fully faced the human capacity for evil. She rejects both the Christian notion of evil as a *privatio boni* (see p. 130), and also the idea that evil actions always result from demonic motives. She sees evil not as something supernatural but as the result of purely human actions and the power relations within society, acknowledging that the Holocaust can no longer be explained by the "malice, insanity, or character defects of a few monstrous individuals" (1973, p. 591). Her notion of the banality of evil contrasts traditional views of evil as the result of a wicked individual. She points out that atrocities may be normalized within powerful political regimes, which consist of the activity of individuals such as Eichmann whose motives are mundane rather than demonic. This means that we cannot use the psychopathology of a few individuals as a full explanation of evil, which is an historical and political phenomenon. She thinks that evil originates in human desolation and loneliness, which used to be covered up by authority, tradition, and religion, but these structures have splintered, and evil occurs because we refuse to endure this ordeal. We disavow our own nothingness and desolation and the impossibility of being. One of Arendt's (1994) important warnings is that evil may occur in new and unexpected ways.

Various contemporary writers believe that Arendt's writing on evil is still relevant, given the continuing prevalence of totalitarianism, the plight of refugees, widespread poverty, deprivation, and other factors that dehumanize people and make them expendable or superfluous. Hayden (2010) suggests that Arendt's work is still useful "because her conception of the banality of evil draws attention to the central role played by organizational structures, institutions, and policies" (p. 462). These structural conditions that destroy the status of human beings enable individuals to participate in dehumanizing policies; we cannot blame evil on a few deviant and pathological individuals. Bernstein (2008) echoes Arendt's belief that the appeal to absolutes such as good and evil or other simplistic dichotomies and moral certainties should not be introduced into the political realm, which they corrupt. As an example, he cites the "War on Terror," in which "nuance, subtlety, and fallibility are (mis)taken to be signs of weakness and indecision" (p. 66). For Bernstein, the discourse on good and evil is a cynical political weapon used to stifle critical thinking and obscure complex issues. Phrases such as the "axis of evil" play on people's fears and anxieties but corrupt politics.

Calder (2003) agrees it is conceptually possible for ordinary people without evil characters to cause evil, but he contests Arendt's claim that Eichmann falls under this category. He believes that Eichmann was a moral idiot rather than a moral monster, but he had an evil character. Wolfe (2011) also questions the notion of the banality of evil, saying that political evil recruits people who are not ordinary; they are people who are attracted to brutality. They feel like victims, and they want to make right what they consider to be long-standing wrongs; therefore, they are not merely conforming to authority. Wolfe writes that Arendt seemed determined to normalize the evil of the Holocaust in the way that St. Augustine tried to normalize evil in general (see p. 130).

Arendt's book about the Eichmann trial was also attacked because it seemed to some of her critics that she was trying to exonerate Eichmann because he lacked evil intentions. In fact, she was simply pointing out that ordinary people in the right circumstances can perpetuate evil; we do not have to be a monster to do so. Hollander (2014) believes that the notion of banality is only appealing because it is an original idea that demonstrates the difference between appearance and reality, or between conventional wisdom and iconoclastic thinking.

An important implication of Arendt's work is that not all evildoers are psychologically unusual. Several psychological studies of the Nazis found no specific psychological abnormalities among them, although others dispute this (Browning, 1998; Zillmer et al., 1995). Although a few Nazis were psychopaths, most were apparently psychologically unremarkable, which is a frightening discovery because it makes one wonder if evil is a latent capacity within all human beings. The problem can be stated succinctly by asking whether only cruel and sadistic people become Nazis or whether Nazi ideology made people cruel and allowed the release of malignant aspects of the German culture of the time. Irrespective of which of these is true, writers such as Kekes (1998) insist that people who perform such actions should be held to be morally responsible for them.

Is there a background moral order?

Materialists and atheists believe that "natural evil," events such as earthquakes or tidal waves, are only the result of chance or natural forces, with no ultimate meaning or purpose, simply part of the tragic side of life. For them, the universe is morally neutral, and it operates according to the laws of physics, with no special regard for human beings. From this point of view we should not project human concerns onto nature, which is impersonal. Human beings have to develop their own moral principles, either based on reason, our emotional sense of right and wrong, and on practical experience or as mutually agreed conventions, because good and evil are entirely human judgments. For atheists, the very idea of divinely given morality is nothing more than a myth, and so cannot be used to explain anything; there is no overarching moral principle governing the universe. Or we can take the view of the world's religions that there is an underlying intelligence or moral order behind the visible universe, some kind of spiritual reality that affects us and with which we can have contact. This intelligence has expressed its moral preferences in revelations such as the Bible. One of the debates among religionists lies in the question of whether or not evil is attributable to the divine itself, or whether evil is a purely human affair. In the Abrahamic traditions, evil means deviation from divine will, and evil is a power that can be defeated with divine assistance. People who feel a spiritual reality behind appearances have to contend with the question of the relationship of that reality to the experience of evil and suffering. For many such individuals, this is one of the central questions of human existence. For religiously oriented people, the divine created natural evils such as earthquakes as part of the cosmic order, whereas human evil is a matter of free will.

Are there objective moral truths?

The very fact that we use the term *evil* implies a moral judgment and a human moral sense, although opinions vary about the ways in which we derive our moral scale. There has been a long-standing debate about whether morality is purely relative or whether there are objective, divinely revealed moral standards and truths, as our religious traditions would insist. In contrast, writers such as Freud believe that morality emerges as we learn to manage our impulses and become socialized by our family and society. Feelings such as shame and guilt make us conform to group expectations and an idealized view of behavior. Psychoanalysts such as Melanie Klein see morality develop in the depressive position with the development of empathy, concern for others, and the recognition of our own destructive potential.

Moral objectivists like Kant or Plato believe that there are absolute ethical standards or principles,[12] but moral relativists point out that different cultures have very different moral codes and practices. In today's atmosphere of multiculturalism and diversity, it is unfashionable to judge other cultures as if moral standards were independent of culture. In this view, we can only judge our own culture. Moral relativists believe that moral principles can only be based on the beliefs and values of particular societies. What is considered good or evil, or even normal and abnormal, is a function of a social system; practices that to us are evil, such as infanticide, cannibalism, or the killing of elderly people, have been practiced by many societies. The cultural relativist does not believe that moral standards apply to all cultures. Despite this, and impossible to reconcile with a position of complete relativism, we instinctively recoil at certain practices such as slavery, which we regard as barbaric and inhuman, whilst we automatically judge some behavior as good, such as helping those in need. Although cultural anthropologists have not found moral standards that are invariably found in all societies, we do see many different cultures with similar moral codes (Wilson, 1979). Murder and incest, for instance, are prohibited in many societies. Even cultural relativists feel subjective horror at certain cultural practices such as female circumcision. Moral relativists nevertheless insist that moral judgments are only true or false in relation to a particular cultural standpoint. There are many critiques of this view, which implies that there are no absolute standards of good and evil, so that a practice such as slavery might not be considered evil within a particular society. The moral objectivist position might insist that practices such as capital punishment or abortion are always wrong under all circumstances, while the relativist might suggest exceptions. Relativists tend to see all morality as purely conventional.

We cannot divorce ourselves from our cultural training, at the same time as it is important to recognize that our cultural standards change, as we see in cases such as slavery and attitudes toward same-sex marriage.

Some writers believe that morality is not only a function of the society in which we live, but also depends on subjective or individual factors, as if it were a matter of taste. The obvious problem with this attitude is that no judgment would be really meaningful if taste is merely a matter of opinion or aesthetic preferences. Serial killers or ruthless dictators would be entitled to their subjective moral standards. However, we are not isolated individuals, and we obviously need social agreements about behavior even if we cannot agree about whether there are absolute standards of morality.

Traditional monotheistic religionists tend to assume that there are objective and absolute moral truths that are divinely given. However, the view that there are objective moral values has some problems, including human fallibility and the question of whose intuitions about morality we should trust, not to mention the difficulty of proving whose view is correct. Well-intentioned people throughout history have insisted that their moral standards are absolutely true (think of the Inquisition), and many of these people have been willing to persecute those who disagreed with them. Accordingly, Hollander (2014) writes that: "Balancing moral certainty and moral relativism may seem impossible, but trying to do so might enable us to acknowledge the reality of evil without being consumed or demoralized by our awareness of it" (p. 56).

Theoretically, the cultural or moral relativist would even be tolerant of intolerant societies, but in practice it is emotionally impossible not to feel critical of groups such as ISIS. Given the way they behave, most of us simply cannot believe their cultural standards could be valid. In this kind of situation, judgments about good and evil are necessary, even if tempered with understanding the ignorance of the perpetrators. Furthermore, a relativism that has no independent basis for morality, which insists that cultures make their own standards, would then find it hard to justify reformation, such as the attempt to abolish slavery. Jesus and Buddha would look too subversive, and there would be no basis for civil disobedience.

From within our monotheistic religious traditions, evil means a transgression or rebellion against a received moral code of conduct, one that is divinely given or inspired. Religious traditions appeal to revelations such as the Ten Commandments or the Qur'an to justify their standards of behavior. Eastern traditions tend to think of evil in terms of ignorance or unconsciousness. Atheistic ethical humanists point out that it is possible to list rules of conduct that are universally valid, maxims such as "it is wrong to kill innocent people for no reason," or "concern for others is a good thing." These principles do not need to be based on religious edicts, since they might be products of human thought, although it is arguable that religions have influenced their widespread adoption. These kinds of principles seem to be based on moral emotions such as shame and empathy. They may simply be emergent properties of social systems that would have evolved without religion, or they may be archetypal realities in their own right, but this distinction is not important for practical purposes. They are simply commonsense rules that allow society to function well. All human beings have common needs and fears, and our moral codes and rules of social behavior can ultimately be based on these.

Notes

1 In a speech delivered to the National Association of Evangelicals on March 8, 1983, President Reagan used the phrase "evil empire" to refer to the Soviet Union. Needless to say, this phrase was felt to be demeaning and was resented by Soviet leaders.
2 President George W. Bush used the phrase "axis of evil" in his State of the Union address on January 29, 2002, and he repeated this phrase on several subsequent occasions in reference to governments he believed to be fostering terrorism.
3 Svendsen believes that demonic evil is carried out for the sake of something that the agent considers to be good because it satisfies a desire, even in cases such as rape and murder that are evil in themselves. The logic of this position seems dubious.
4 Theodicies are attempts to justify God in the presence of evil and suffering.
5 Utilitarianism is the doctrine that an action is right if it increases the welfare and happiness of the greatest number of people.
6 But Satan's behavior is very complex. He is remorseful and sad at times, as well as being envious. He recognizes that it was his pride and ambition that made him rebel. If he acts out of envy and pride, he is not acting purely for the sake of doing evil.
7 Adolph Eichmann was responsible for administering the transportation of European Jews to the Nazi death camps.
8 Himmler realized that his behavior violated moral norms. In 1943, in the Polish town of Posen, he admonished a group of SS officers not to speak openly about the death camps and required them to swear an oath of silence. Apparently, the Nazi leadership believed that what they were doing was necessary but realized it would horrify ordinary people.
9 The phrase *participation mystique* originated in anthropological descriptions of tribal cultures; it denotes a kind of feeling of identity or non-differentiation between subject and object. This is one aspect of crowd psychology, where there is little differentiation of the individual in favor of a group consciousness.
10 Bion's–K refers to un-metabolized, un-mentalized, beta elements, which are unmanageable affects or raw, incomprehensible experiences that attack thought.
11 Mariano (2009) believes that Arendt did not really change her view, even though she thought she had done so, because her *Origins* already spoke explicitly of banality.
12 For the technically minded, I should note the distinction sometimes made between the validity of a moral principle and its truth. A principle may be a valid and practical guide to behavior, but to say it is true implies that the principle has a special ontological status.

Chapter 2

Can we understand evil?

Introduction, with a caveat

Although there is a school of thought that would like to get rid of the concept of evil, for many of us the word *evil* is an important way of talking about some of the unspeakable things that happen in the world. This chapter deals with a variety of attempts to explain or at least understand evil, either in terms of psychology or social science or with some combination of these approaches. While acknowledging the power of the notion that evil is ultimately beyond reason and explanation, I prefer to take the position that we must try to understand evil from as many points of view as possible, or we will not find adequate ways to cope with it. I should, however, acknowledge the views of philosophers such as Richard Bernstein (2002), who believes that no matter how much we use social and psychological explanations for evil, there will always remain a gap in our accounts. It is certainly true that even if we find a psychological disorder in an evil person, we can never be quite sure that the disorder is responsible for his evil actions.

Is there a danger that by explaining evil in some way, we implicitly condone it? One approach to evil behavior is to say that it is a kind of emotional disorder, but do we then somehow lessen its reality? If we say that someone is evil because he is sick, do we diminish his responsibility? These fears are overstated: Staub (1989) points out that to understand evil is not necessarily to forgive it, and many authors (e.g., Kekes, 2005) believe that people must be held responsible for their intentional actions. Even if evil is a disease, understanding a disease does not make it less real. At the same time, Baumeister (1997) notes that "there is ample reason to fear that understanding can promote forgiving. Seeing things from the perpetrator's point of view does change things in many ways" (p. 386). Baumeister makes the point that while we should not allow our moral condemnation to interfere with our attempts to understand evil, it is a bigger mistake to allow our understanding to interfere with our moral condemnation. However, there is some experimental evidence that explanation does tend to have an exonerating effect (Miller et al., 1999). Thus, we might be less willing to call an act evil if it occurs when the agent is under extreme duress or in the grip of overwhelming emotion, suggesting that there are situations that make evil more understandable. As well, a person may only engage in evil actions under particular circumstances or in relation to particular people. Fortunately, the truly monstrous individual, who perpetrates evil for its own sake rather than in response to social or psychological pressures, seems to be a rarity. In fact, it is partly our difficulty in understanding such behavior that makes us want to call such a person evil. Some moral philosophers reject the notion of pure or absolute evil, or malice for its own sake that wants to make others suffer for no reason at all. These writers insist that this behavior is always motivated by some kind of gain or goal (McGinn, 1997).

No single discipline can provide a complete answer to the problem of evil. As Levine (2000, p. 273) says: "Looking for a single cause of evil is like looking for a single meaning of life. It is a sure sign that one is in the grip of a theory and reveals the extent to which theory informs observation." Yet theories about the source of evil abound.

An overview of the causes of evil

Many questions arise when we discuss the sources of human evil. The problem is to discern the factors that allow the capacity or the will to deliberately inflict needless suffering on another person, either by deliberate acts of malice or through callous indifference. We must also try to understand what makes an apparently ordinary person behave monstrously. Is the breeding ground of evil something that happens as a result of developmental factors in childhood, which lead to an intrapsychic predisposition to evil, or is the ground of evil largely situational and social, or some combination of these factors? It sometimes seems that when we do understand the situational and psychological factors that lead to evil behavior, this understanding makes the behavior seem less heinous, and possibly even less culpable. There is also a risk that if we refer to someone as evil, we distance ourselves from that person as if we are entirely guiltless. We may even regard the evil person as less than human. These are defensive maneuvers that fail to acknowledge that traces of the same feelings that afflict the perpetrator of evil afflict all of us, but most people can contain these feelings without acting them out. As we will see, perpetrators of evil are often evacuating their unbearable emotional states onto others.

There are many predispositions to evil behavior; the obvious factors are those such as envy, hatred, greed, revenge, spite, bitterness, excessive ambition, and prejudice. Adherence to a malignant ideology is a further factor. All of these can be subjected to psychological scrutiny, and several have developmental sources, or they are part of complexes or the shadow. Because some people do evil in the belief that what they are doing is good, the issue of self-deception becomes particularly important (see p. 61).

Some individuals feel a need for more wealth, power, and status because they cannot be comfortable with how they are; they feel incomplete or deficient in some way, or they cannot accept or contain their own flaws and frustrations. As a result, tragically, various types of evil behavior seem to be ways in which the individual is trying to make himself either more comfortable or happier, but he is doing so in a perverse manner. That is, in some individuals the search for happiness, which may result in problems such as greed or violence, may cause evil, or at least be responsible for the suffering of other people. Sometimes, therefore, self-interest and the conditions of the person's life make evil actions seem reasonable to the perpetrator.

Kekes (1993) argues that wickedness is caused by unknowing participation in the essential conditions of life. He points out that we are vulnerable to contingent forces we cannot control that undermine our attempts to live good lives. Reinforcing this problem, he believes we have insufficiently developed capacities for moral conduct – either we have a cognitive lack such as thoughtlessness, an emotional lack such as insensitivity, or a volitional lack such as weakness of the will. Nature is indifferent to us, and we are vulnerable to indifference through exercising the vice of expediency; we pursue goods "without regard for the evil that may result from their pursuit" (p. 75). Expedient people just work to achieve their goals; their energy is directed towards success, ignoring the ways in which their preoccupations affect others.

Kekes also believes we are prone to vices, which are enduring character traits that manifest themselves as unjustifiably injurious actions. Thus, we are vulnerable to destructiveness, which we express through the vice of malevolence, the "disposition to act contrary to what is good. Its emotional source is ill will, a desire for things not to go well" (p. 79). Malevolence is an active vice; unlike expediency, "it carries with it no prospect of gain" (p. 80). Kekes says that malevolence arises when people feel treated by society with contempt; they feel like losers or they belong to an ethnic or religious group that is offensive to those in power, or they do not have the physique, education, opportunity, or ability to improve their situation. Their lives are "informed by futility, indignity, and meaninglessness" (ibid.).

Kekes's (2005) reflections on evil are based on his analysis of six historical episodes of evil behavior.[1] He believes that explanations of evil based on religious, political, or scientific approaches try to explain away evil, as if evil is a kind of interference with the good. He does not like the religious approach to evil because it rests on the idea that there is a morally good order underlying the world, and at the same time he believes the Enlightenment approach inflates rationality too much as a tool for ridding us of evil. He finds no single cause of evil; motivation for evil varies from time to time and in different places and historical situations. He believes we need a mixed, multidimensional, or multifactorial model that includes internal factors such as envy, external factors such as an abusive childhood, combined with social, psychological, and unintentional factors, as well as the active and passive roles of individuals and society.

Kekes is among those writers who believe that evil people are not very different from ordinary people. He traces evil to factors such as fanaticism rooted in faith or false reason, ambition, envy, a depraved sense of honor, and boredom. He stresses the need for self-restraint of our darker impulses, but he does not discuss integration of the shadow. He points out the potential dangers of ideologies that produce passionate beliefs that make people prone to wishful thinking and self-deception; such passions may overwhelm reason and morality. He believes that in order to deal with evil, we need to cultivate moral imagination, a greater appreciation for different ways of life, increased self-understanding, and more awareness of alternatives to evil actions. In his words (2005): "Weakness of will, ignorance of the good, defective reasoning, human destructiveness, bad political arrangements, excessive self-love, immoderate pleasure-seeking, revenge, greed, boredom, enjoyment, perversity, provocation, stupidity, fear, callousness, indoctrination, self-deception, negligence, and so forth may all explain some cases of evil. None, however, explains all or even most cases." Kekes believes that a root cause of wickedness is the desire to have more for oneself relative to others, especially when this desire goes unchecked by critical self-reflection, sympathy, and self-control. This desire becomes problematic when we want more so badly that we are willing to diminish the goodness of whatever stands in our way. A lack of self-control and self-knowledge are also crucial factors.

Kekes points out that much evil is due to vices that we do not choose. His examples include dogmatism that results from uncritically holding mistaken opinions; such a dogmatist might feel justified in owning slaves, and similar evils, because the dogmatist and his peers adhere to a pernicious set of principles. Other vices describe people who are cowardly, lazy, or intemperate, who do not have the capacity to do what they know they should do. Their actions reflect their character, which they are unable to control.

Kekes believes that there is no transpersonal moral order in the universe, only impersonal, purposeless natural processes. For him, good and evil are human values and human ways of judging events according to the ways in which they affect us. His is a tragic view of human nature, and he admits that he has a "deep and profoundly depressing view of human life" (p. 5), because in his view human character is fundamentally flawed; we are tainted by our vices. Nature is indifferent to us, and the many contingencies we face in the world adds to the tragic sense that we are not in control of our lives even if we aspire to live good lives.

Social scientists tend to focus on evil as the result of unjustified violence. Thus, Staub (1989) defines evil as the deliberate killing of others and also "the creation of conditions that materially or psychologically destroy or diminish people's dignity, happiness, and capacity to fulfill basic material needs" (p. 25). Baumeister (1997, 2012) believes that violence is an evolutionary hangover; for our early ancestors, aggression conferred status and enabled the strongest to survive and reproduce. However, because of our legal and cultural development, aggression is now obsolete because we have better ways of resolving conflicts. Yet we are still social animals, and if culture fails us, we fall back on aggression to get what we want. He thinks threatened egotism is a root cause of evil; perpetrators of violence typically have favorable views of themselves, and narcissists are more aggressive than others. He thinks that violence occurs when their favorable self-image is threatened or attacked; they lash out when criticized, as a way of avoiding loss of self-esteem. He also believes that idealism may motivate people to believe that what they believe to be noble goals justifies violent means – witness the slaughters carried out by totalitarian governments or those carried out in the name of religion. He suggests that our best way to contain evil is to strengthen our internal restraint against aggressive impulses, since they cannot be eliminated – self-regulation is critical. Baumeister also suggests that some evil acts are simply a means to an end – a way of getting what the evil person wants, such as money, power, or sex, when such a person cannot get what he wants legitimately. These factors lead to the breakdown of internal restraints against committing evil.

Midgley (2001) focuses on envy and pride as motivations for evil – she thinks that at the heart of these states of mind is the desire to enhance oneself at the expense of others, or the desire to have more for oneself relative to others, which when combined with hostility turns into a demand for their submission and destruction and the "violent hatred and rejection of all that seems to be superior to oneself" (p. 138). This is essentially an explanation of evil behavior in the context of malignant narcissism. Midgley claims that wicked people are deliberately blind to relevant facts, ideals, and principles; evil is therefore not something positive as much as it is a lack, "a denial and rejection of positive capacities" (p. 16). This approach implicitly involves self-deception.

Ross (1988) suggests that vicious characters produce vicious actions, and these arise from three types of desires: (1) the desire to do wrong; (2) the desire to produce a bad state of affairs; and (3) the desire to inflict pain on another. This philosophical account does not tell us the psychological sources of these desires, but it is true that some people have a character structure that predisposes them to commit evil. An evil disposition allows situational or social factors to release evil behavior, but it is also clear that, under certain circumstances, apparently ordinary people can do evil things. Sometimes this happens because they are under the influence of evil authorities or mass psychology, and sometimes because they believe that what they are doing is right.

Horne (2008) believes that evil begins when an individual or a group asserts that only their actions are natural or human, and this group claims foundational knowledge or absolute truth about what is normal. This group's naturalness is compared to the "unnaturalness" of others, who then become non-persons or impure, leading to a fear of contamination. Horne describes this as the "heart of darkness" at the core of individuals and groups, which he believes reflects the residues of early infantile trauma. This refers to material that is repressed, or to internal persecutory objects, or to Jung's shadow. Horne believes that we all contain a pocket of such material, and he suggests that evil acts are an expression of this nidus, which is the point of origin of our own "unnaturalness." Because of the fear of contamination by the "unnatural" group, these individuals seem dangerous and may be shunned or even killed. Evil may start when we make decontextualized assertions about others, whom we measure according to standards that we insist are the only natural ones. Horne points out that we tend to name phenomena around death, gender, the body, and the processes of nature as potentially unnatural. These may create a sense of otherness that makes people anxious, which is why they are termed evil, instead of thinking of them as frightening or puzzling or needing further understanding. It is possible for those who consider themselves to be natural to change their opinion about the other group, as we saw when homosexuals gradually became naturalized.

Becker (1975) believed that human destructiveness towards other people is the result of our unwillingness to accept the reality of death, combined with our yearning for immortality. For him, the root of human evil is our urge to deny our mortality and achieve a heroic self-image. Because of our denial of death, we identify ourselves with our favorite ideologies, which give our life significance. We are willing to die for this ideology, as if participation in a system of belief will confer individual immortality. This feeling is so strong that we would rather die in defense of our ideologies than live without the solace they provide. Ideologies are therefore a way of denying death, and anyone who threatens our ideology is seen as evil. Becker also believes that much evil is not the result of human aggression but follows from our submissiveness to authority. We perpetuate evil in the name of waging war against it, with good intentions but also deriving emotional satisfaction from killing others. He believed that a promising way for us to deal with our propensity to evil is to develop independent critical judgment so that we do not succumb to "herd enthusiasms and herd fears" (p. 161).

Becker believes that in war we buy our own life by killing others, or we kill others to affirm our own life. Our lust for power is dangerous: "We feel we are masters over life and death when we hold the fate of others in our hands" (p. 114). He points out that in war the enemy has a ritual role to play, "by means of which evil is redeemed" (p. 115). We are also dedicated to war because wars reveal our fate; wars test divine favor, and they seem to be a means of purging evil from the world. Surviving war means we are specially favored by the gods. We show that we are on the side of purity by cleansing the world around us of evil, and this striving for perfection reflects our attempt to be eligible for immortality. He thinks that our fear of extinction is linked to our dread of insignificance, and human sacrifice is a form of ritual triumph in the contest with evil. To ceremonially kill captives affirms our power over life and death. He believes that "men spill blood because it makes their hearts glad and fills out their organisms with a sense of vital power" (p. 102). We kill out of the notion that we are doing the good and righteous thing, so we may kill out of joy and lust as well as out of fear. This heroic attempt to make the world pure and good is ultimately self-defeating; the attempt to vanquish evil results in more evil. Becker also believes that war is a kind of social safety valve because it focuses the energy of the masses towards an external enemy or scapegoat. We can then project our hatreds onto the enemy; "somebody has to pay for the way things are" (p. 122). Becker does not believe that we only kill out of frustration and fear, but also out of "joy, plenitude and love of life. *Men kill lavishly out of the sublime joy of heroic triumph over evil. Voilà tout.* What are clinical classifications and niceties going to do with that?" (p. 141; emphasis in original). Becker believes that we cause evil by trying to heroically triumph over it, because we will not admit that we are vulnerable, no matter how much of others' blood we spill trying to deny our vulnerability.

Camus also connected evil with anxiety about death; he believed that our horror of death might allow us to do anything to fight it. Camus was an atheist, and he could not reconcile the Christian notion of a loving God with the presence of evil, so in his novel *The Fall* he insisted that evil is found only in the human heart. In this book, Camus depicted a narcissistic character named Clamence, whose intense fear of death allowed him to be contemptuous of others, vain, hypocritical, greedy, and hateful, with an intense will to power. Clamence believed that people are only kind to others in order to make themselves happy. He behaved well on the surface, in order to be admired and feel self-satisfied, but actually he despised people and felt superior to everyone else – in fact, he saw himself as "something of a superman" (p. 23). He only loved himself: "I looked merely for objects of pleasure and conquest" (p. 44). The sources of such narcissism cannot be reduced to the fear of death, but it is true that the narcissist may see the prospect of death as an intolerable narcissistic injury.

Graham and Haidt (2012) suggest that a major cause of evil is to make a moral principle or a symbol sacred or too idealized. They define *sacredness* as the tendency to invest people, places, or ideas with importance far beyond their utility. They point out the danger of believing there is a single correct truth, an attitude that is at the root of extremism. Moral convictions may have a dark side – they produce idealistic evil, exemplified by people such as Timothy McVeigh,[2] whose values included white pride, racial purity, and the like. Apparently moral ends can be used to justify violent means, because strongly held values lead to the making sacred of specific people, places, or ideas, acting as a foundation for deciding what is evil.

Koestler had various suggestions about the causes of human evil. He suggested that: "We ought to give serious consideration to the possibility that somewhere along the line something has gone seriously wrong with the evolution of the nervous system of *Homo sapiens*" (1968, p. 239), as if there is a flaw or an engineering error in human neurological circuits. He believed that our emotional constitution is dominant over our rational capacity (p. 272). Our intellectual faculties have advanced, but our moral faculties remain primitive. Koestler also believed that our species has an "integrative tendency" that leads to our desire to submit to authority, identify with a social group, and give uncritical acceptance to closed systems of belief (1978, p. 79). In these ways we abrogate personal responsibility, and this allows ordinary people to become torturers, devoted to a cause that is elevated into a delusional transcendent reality by the human "pathology of devotion" (1968, p. 233–235). Human beings don't listen to reason because our mutually exclusive belief systems are walled off from each other, so that we are a "mentally sick race, and as such deaf to persuasion" (1968, p. 339). We engage in "self-transcendence" (1968, p. 260), which allows us to participate in the group's projected delusions, so that we feel part of something greater than ourselves that we believe will endure after death – a transcendent reality manufactured to fit our prejudices. We identify with clan, tribe, nation, church, or party, and uncritically accept these "emotionally saturated system of beliefs" (1978, p. 93). Examples are the Nazi Nuremberg rallies, lynchings, and so on, which lead to a surrender of our independent personalities and synchronize our behavior, so that we identify with the group at the price of our personal identity. The collective mind allows people to be aggressive and becomes the psychological basis for war. Loyalty binds the herd together; without loyalty to the tribe or flag, Koestler believes there would be no war.

Koestler also points out that our language and symbols incite aggression; we are as susceptible to being hypnotized by slogans as we are to infectious diseases. The hypnotic effects of words play a dominant role in ideologies, which are inflated belief systems to which we have an emotional commitment. Ideologies that are closed systems of thought are paranoid, according to Koestler. These systems are delusions that purport to express universal truths that provide answers to all human needs and explain everything; they cannot be refuted by evidence because their adherents only think in terms of the system to which they are committed. The surrender of personal identity to such delusions anesthetizes our critical faculties. All this leads to evil, especially when combined with low intelligence, primitive moral development, and a propensity to kill others. He thought that the answer to the rift between the phylogenetically old and new levels of the brain, or between instinct and intelligence or emotion and reason, might be a pharmacological intervention, some kind of mental stabilizer, as distasteful as that sounds (1968, p. 336).

Human need theory

Human need theory posits that certain fundamental human needs motivate human behavior, and these needs must be satisfied if we are to prevent or resolve destructive conflicts (Burton, 1997). The list of basic human needs varies among different theorists, but there is general agreement that if our needs cannot be met constructively, they may be expressed destructively. Typically, needs that motivate us are thought to be those such as the maintenance of self-esteem, dignity, relatedness, identity, independence, responsiveness, stimulation, security, recognition, justice, meaning, freedom, and feeling effective. Needless to say, the boundaries between true needs and simple wants are not always clear, and some needs may be relatively more or less important.

Theorists such as Maslow (1943) made the satisfaction of a hierarchy of needs central to their approach to psychotherapy. Maslow's list lay on a spectrum, beginning with physiological necessities and physical safety, moving to the higher-order needs of love and belonging, self-esteem, self-actualization, and self-transcendence. His list of needs was criticized for not acknowledging its ethnocentric, Western bourgeois values, because the needs of people raised in societies that value individualism and self-actualization are different from the needs of people raised in more collective societies that value acceptance and community.

Staub (2003) also makes a case for finding the source of evil in the frustration of universal psychological needs. He believes that this frustration gives rise to psychological and social processes that make aggression more likely. For example, during difficult times the need to identify with one's group enhances one's sense of security, strengthens a sense of identity, and "may give people at least the illusion of effectiveness and control" (p. 55). However, the need for security means that aggression is a likely response to attack or the fear of attack. The need to enhance relationships with people in one's own group may lead to scapegoating of another group, at the same time as it diminishes one's own group's responsibility for its problems. Scapegoating others gives one an explanation for one's difficulties and suggests a way to deal with problems by acting against the scapegoat. Ideologies such as extreme nationalism also serve such functions, but they have the drawback of identifying another group as an enemy who must be destroyed. This situation may progress to mass killings.

In most people, empathy for others inhibits or moderates our expression of aggression. The lack of empathy found among psychopathic or severely narcissistic people is therefore very important. Baron-Cohen (2012) would replace the concept of evil with the notion of a lack of empathy resulting from brain changes beyond our control. He therefore sees evil as a medical condition. As well as brain changes, there are also important developmental origins of a deficit in empathy; it is difficult to develop empathy if one never experienced nurturing, empathic responsiveness in childhood. Infants need empathically responsive selfobjects in order to cope with overwhelming affects and to develop affect regulation. The experience of an empathic parent fosters the development of empathy for oneself and for others. Narcissistic defenses such as grandiosity seem to prevent empathy, and the psychopath or malignant narcissist has none. For the average person, reactions of horror and disgust are increased when we see evil because we empathically sense the evil motivation underpinning an evil action. However, empathy is sometimes suppressed, because to imagine what a suffering person feels may be to awaken our own suffering and the suffering of those close to us.

In this context, defenses are important; splitting, dissociation, and psychic numbing make ordinary people more able to commit evil by reducing our empathic awareness of what we are doing to others (Lifton & Markusen, 1992). Self-absorption also makes us less open to the suffering of others and to the evil that causes it. Indifference to evil may result from what Kekes (2005) refers to as deficient moral imagination, which is the "attempt to appreciate other ways of life by coming to understand them from the inside" (p. 236) – empathy described in a different key. He points out that the lack of this faculty allows gross misunderstanding and misperception by the evildoer of his victims.

Garrard (1998, 2002) similarly suggests that the evildoer is unable to hear the significance of the victim's screams; the perpetrator silences considerations against committing evil and ignores any consideration for the suffering of the victim. Thus, the torturer does not see the screams of his victims as a reason to desist. Garrard believes this is due to a cognitive defect, a distorted capacity for practical reasoning, but it also sounds like a serious defect of empathy. Her account does not explain why an evil individual can be so blind to his victim's suffering.

Can ordinary people commit evil?

It does not make sense to place a sudden act of impulsive violence by an otherwise average person in the same category as the behavior of a professional torturer acting in a premeditated, cold-blooded manner. However, there is no doubt that ordinary people may commit or tolerate evil, given the right social situation. For example, Browning (1998) does not think it is sufficient to attribute the causes of the Holocaust to the specific social and historical conditions in Hitler's Germany. He believes that the same kind of behavior could happen in contemporary society, perpetrated by ordinary people. Browning describes how ordinary, middle-aged men from Hamburg who were members of Reserve Police Battalion 101 became savage murderers of the Jewish population of Poland. They killed about 38,000 Jews and deported about 45,000 to the Treblinka concentration camp in 1942–1943. Browning points out that only 12 out of 500 of these men accepted the offer to be relieved of the duty of executing Jews, even though there were no serious consequences when people refused an order to kill unarmed civilians. Browning argues that these men willingly committed massacres out of a combination of obedience to authority, conformity to group norms, peer pressure, and because of state authorization of their behavior, not because of hatred. They did not think they were doing anything evil; they believed they were doing their duty as ordered by a legitimate authority. They were therefore willing executioners but not primarily genocidal. Browning (1998) believes that there was no special type of person who took part in these massacres. In this view, the Nazi core was distinct from the general population.

Only 12.5% of the *Einsatzgruppen*, the mobile SS killing units in Poland and Russia, were Nazi officials; a few of the leaders were well-educated academics and professionals, but most of them were "ordinary" people (Bauer, 1982). Perhaps the "ordinariness" of these men explains why, according to eyewitness accounts, killing innocent people took a serious emotional toll on some of them (Noakes et al., 1988). It is true that a small number of these murderers enjoyed their task and adopted a predatory identity (Prince, 2016), and a small number refused to kill, but most of them did what they were asked to do, even if they had to be routinely given large amounts of alcohol to enable them to function. Others broke down psychologically. Even the SS general in Russia who directed these murders was hospitalized for a psychological breakdown in 1941.

In his review of Browning's work, Goldhagen (1992) agrees that many of these men had the option not to kill, but he disagrees that they were ordinary, because he believes they were members of a barbaric culture that was murderously anti-Semitic. In his controversial[3] *Hitler's Willing Executioners*, Goldhagen (1997) argued that age-old, deeply rooted German anti-Semitism led to the willing participation of the majority of Germans in the Holocaust. He believes that the Holocaust could not have happened without the tacit or explicit consent of the German population, who wanted to kill Jews because they were hated, so in his view the Holocaust cannot be exclusively attributed to a psychopathic, sadistic minority. He points out that the men of Battalion 101 willingly murdered and tortured Polish Jews in particularly brutal ways. They expressed enthusiasm for their behavior, so that the situation alone does not account for their behavior. However, other authors argue that most Germans were only casual supporters of the Nazis, or they were only passively complicit, or they were bystanders who were overwhelmed by the situation rather than determined racists.

Most observers of the Nazis note that only a few of the SS were sadists or true psychopaths (Hohne, 1989). At the same time, it is unlikely that the population was coerced into submission to the Nazi regime; as Zukier (1994) points out, the newsreels of the time do not suggest that people were acting under duress. As well, Hitler backed down when the churches protested the regime's euthanasia program to get rid of people the Nazis considered "unworthy of life," such as the mentally retarded, the severely disabled, or those with hereditary disorders. This suggests that widespread opposition to the persecution of the Jews, if it had existed, might have made a difference. However, many Germans cooperated with the Nazis by denouncing their Jewish neighbors even when they were not coerced into doing so. Furthermore, the historical evidence is that Nazi propaganda was not the deciding factor in changing attitudes – the population was receptive to this propaganda because it coincided with their prior attitudes (Kershaw, 1991). Zukier (1994) also makes the point that the Nazi electoral success occurred during a period of improving economic stability and prosperity; this success largely came from support by the middle class and social elite. In this view, the Nazis did not use a process of psychological selection to choose their agents; they were able to "transform ordinary personalities into murderous temperaments. Almost any individual . . . could be in due time, remolded into a mass murderer" (p. 439).

Although one might imagine that only people who are strangers to those they kill can commit mass murders, another example of the effects of embedded racism occurred at the Jedwabne pogrom in 1941, which occurred in German-occupied Poland. In this small town, many of the Poles who had lived with their Jewish neighbors since the eighteenth century joined in the slaughter (Gross, 2001). It resulted in the deaths of 340 people, many of whom were locked in a barn that was set on fire. The Jewish population, long subjected to prejudice, became scapegoats for the violations that the Poles had experienced during the Russian invasion. Feelings of helplessness and victimhood were evacuated onto the Jews, who were seen as destructive and somehow alien.

The Hutus and the Tutsis in Rwanda had long been ruled by the Belgians, who had deliberately inflamed hostilities between these ethnic groups for strategic purposes. This tension erupted in genocide.[4] Although the Tutsis were a vilified group, the fact that many Hutu perpetrators had Tutsi relatives makes it less likely that purely ethnic hatred was responsible. The perpetrators were willing participants in the mass murder of their rivals in order to establish political dominance and gain materially, even though many of the Hutu killers in Rwanda were the neighbors of the Tutsis they dehumanized and killed. They were not forced to kill, but only a few tried to prevent the killing. Evidently, fundamental social and psychological processes may make such crimes possible among ordinary people. This phenomenon urgently needs explanation and is discussed in more detail in Chapter 3.

There is clearly a powerful tendency for people to conform to the behavior of the group in which they belong. But in situations such as genocide, it is important to note that there is no way to predict who will succumb to the social pressures to commit evil and who will resist such pressures. It may be very difficult to oppose the dominant social attitudes, especially when these are backed up by armed soldiers and an atmosphere of fear. The individual in this situation feels helpless, often leading to rationalization about doing nothing. The person who tries to think for herself in such a situation feels extremely isolated. One's own safety or the safety of one's family may be at stake, and the loss of one's occupation is another risk. This was the situation faced by decent Germans and others during the Nazi regime, many of whom had to split off normal human feelings about the victimization going on around them, although a brave minority was able to shelter Jews despite the danger to themselves.

The more fearful and powerless one feels, the more one is susceptible to the seduction of demagoguery, and the more one is open to racist and ethnocentric propaganda. This social dynamic is visible today. Below the surface of the dominant ideals of a culture lie a variety of negative or shadow traits that emerge when social conditions permit. Group pressures then allow apparently ordinary people to become agents of evil, either actively or passively. This is sometimes called the "sleeper" problem. Behavior that was once considered wrong may be justified by the state or by a demagogic leader.

Zukier (1994) asks the important question of how millions of ordinary people in Germany could have been transformed into evildoers. Like most social scientists, he does not believe that evil is an "inner force" that emanates from a wicked individual. Instead, he believes that evil arises as a result of natural psychological processes, so that the Holocaust is an example of the "self-seduction of a nation" (p. 442) and not the "discharge of natural wickedness." For him, therefore, evil is not something that waits in the heart for an opportunity to act; it is a carefully nurtured quality of the mind. In Nazi Germany, ordinary people were induced to participate in evil by means of ordinary psychological processes of learning, human interaction, and social forces. Zukier believes the Nazis became murderers by inches, taking gradual, small steps towards greater and greater atrocities. The individual so affected does not realize he has crossed a moral Rubicon until it is too late, whereupon he has to silence his conscience and struggle with his natural aversion to committing atrocities. To maintain his psychological equilibrium, such a person then focuses away from his actual behavior towards his duty to the authorities and the details of his work. Zukier believes that the Nazis did experience moral conflict about their behavior, but they regarded it as a heroic task to overcome the conflict between their behavior and their feelings and personal preferences for the sake of their cause. This author believes that genocide is an injury to the human spirit, and that "genocide is foremost a psychological crime . . . the monstrous aftermath of the soul murder of perpetrators, victims, and bystanders" (p. 441). The perpetrators were guilty of the deadly sin of killing love in the human soul.

There is no doubt that "ordinary" people also carried out evil acts during the Bosnian and Rwandan atrocities (Lu, 2004; Vetlesen, 2005). Most of them were not known to be hateful or sadistic. But are people who commit evil really ordinary? Staub (1989) believes that perpetrators of evil manifest lack of self-awareness, decreased empathy, and a cognitive orientation to aggression. He points out that some of the Nazis enjoyed violence before they joined the party. Many authors protest that to attribute such evil exclusively to psychopathology is really a way of emotionally distancing ourselves from the perpetrators, which we feel a need to do. However, we are not necessarily so different from them. Even though social forces are important contributors to evil behavior, so that personality only plays a partial role, there are important psychological factors to consider.

Psychological approaches to evil behavior

As a discipline, psychology can only comment on human behavior that is considered to be evil, but not on the possible ontological status of evil itself, which is a metaphysical problem.

Different psychological schools approach evil behavior in their own ways: behaviorists in terms of learning, psychodynamic theorists in terms of unconscious destructive impulses or problems such as hatred and envy, Jungians in terms of complexes and the shadow, and so on. Whatever theory they use, psychotherapists of all schools take into account personality structure and the meaning and motivation of behavior as well as the social context of the behavior.

For many years, psychologists paid little attention to the problem of evil because it seemed to belong to the domain of theology or philosophy. Today, however, people with a secular orientation often believe that psychology can tackle the problem of evil in a way that is more convincing than the traditional theological approaches. In general, psychological approaches speak in terms of specific personality traits such as cruelty, selfishness, or sadism, without recourse to metaphysical notions of evil such as the devil, which are not part of the purview of psychology. Many psychotherapists view evil behavior as the result of relational disasters and abuse experienced in childhood. Evil is then seen to represent an intrapsychic potential that is promoted, released, or permitted by situational factors.

It is possible that we are defining people as evil who are really psychologically disturbed. Perhaps it would be more humane to see evil as sickness. However, some theorists dislike any such psychological approach to the problem of evil, because they believe that psychological explanations are "based on disreputable thinking." For Kekes (1993, p. 232), speculation about psychological motives for evil is intellectually shoddy. The problem with psychological thinking, according to Kekes, is that such explanations are too general. There are an incalculable number of influences that affect a person's motives, the explanations given by psychologists cannot be tested, there are no control groups, no effort to consider people in similar circumstances who behaved differently, and no way to decide upon the merits of incompatible psychological explanations. However, in a later (2005) text, Kekes acknowledges the importance of familiar psychological propensities of the kind used by novelists and historians – propensities such as the desire for a meaningful life, the need to be loved, self-deception, resentment at injustice, and fear of the unknown. To such a list of conscious factors, the depth psychologist would add that complicated, often unconscious, psychological mechanisms must also be involved in the commission of evil. The unconscious plays an important part in driving behavior, and the fact that depth psychological theories are often incomplete and contradictory is a function of the complexity of the psyche. We cannot wait for the field to become unified before we try to understand evil.

There is a legitimate concern that psychological explanations will be used to excuse evil; the term *excusiology* is sometimes used to describe this phenomenon. However, understanding what motivates evil behavior from a psychological viewpoint does not necessarily imply pardon or forgiveness; accountability and punishment may still occur. Nevertheless, various authors point out that by speaking of evil exclusively as psychopathology, we avoid the moral and existential issues involved. Thus it is that part of the traditional bias against psychological explanations for evil results from a concern that to understand evil psychologically will remove moral responsibility from the perpetrator, or we risk making evil somehow more acceptable or we strip it of its true horror. Some writers are concerned that if we regard evil behavior purely as a type of sickness, we thereby free the perpetrator from guilt and responsibility. We might thereby indirectly remove the label of evil from such a person, no matter how terrible is his behavior. Hitler is an example of this problem; he was severely abused as a child, but even if this were to help us understand his actions, we do not want to make him less culpable. However, it is surely possible to both understand such a person psychologically, historically, and socially while we condemn his behavior at the same time. Kekes is clear that holding evildoers responsible for their actions is indispensable, and most psychologists would agree, with the proviso that significant mental illness may mitigate responsibility. Child murder is often due to a mother's delusional depression, in which the sufferer believes that the world is so terrible that her children must be saved from it.

Given that the human will can be compromised by intense emotions such as rage or severe depression, it is not always clear when we should hold accountable the perpetrator of an evil action. In the case of a truly psychotic person who commits evil in response to delusions or hallucinations, it is clear that responsibility is diminished, but the question of responsibility is much less obvious in the case of personality disorders.

Morton (2005) points out that there is probably no common psychological pro-file among those who carry out different forms of evil, but there is a conceptual commonality in that to carry out an action that arouses horror in us, a person has to overcome a psychological barrier to inflicting pain, death, or humiliation on another person. There is a barrier against the awareness that one is doing wrong. If we convince ourselves that evil means are justified by a certain end, we can justify evil acts by pointing to our good intentions.

Peck (1983) stresses the importance of self-deception that produces a barrier against knowing that what we are doing is wrong. He believes that because psy-chopaths have no conscience, they do not need self-deception, but evil narcissists use self-deception to keep the consequences of their crimes out of awareness. However, Morton points out a problem with Peck's stress on self-deception; this process does not explain *why* atrocities are carried out by those who commit them; it only describes a feature shared by people who commit atrocities. An evildoer may deceive himself about his terrible act, but he does not commit the act because of self-deception. (Self-deception is discussed further on p. 61.)

The real evildoer does not care about the effects of his evil on others, and this indifference needs an explanation. Lack of empathy for the victim is an obvious candidate, as discussed previously. Another possibility is that some perpetrators are attracted to evil acts *because* they are evil and hence exciting to perform. Such a person might have to silence internal self-criticism even as he unconsciously rebels against any form of moral authority. Typically, however, when the possibil-ity of doing evil crosses their mind, most people do not follow up on the possi-bility, partly out of moral self-respect. Morton (2005) points out that evildoers deceive themselves about the moral character of their actions, but that does not mean that everyone who is systematically mistaken about the rightness or wrong-ness of their actions is evil. We might feel a pull in two opposite directions, as in the abortion debate, and we use denial, for example when we ignore our aware-ness that money we spend on luxuries could be contributing to famine relief. Morton (2005, p. 259) warns against construing

> malignant self-deception as an archetypal psychological complex in which the person is enabled to satisfy some impulse to atrocity solely by the capac-ity to close their eyes to the suffering of others or their own role in causing it. That complex would be so far from the psychology of any actual human per-son that it could serve only to reinforce the pernicious cultural stereotype of the evildoer as a diabolical force utterly different from the rest of us. To think that way is itself to enter into a kind of self-deception. It is to blind ourselves to the amount of horror in the world that results from the actions of normal, well-intentioned, kindly people, struggling to evaluate the actions they are agents of or accomplices in.

Spinelli (2000) is typical of those authors who are concerned that if we talk about evil purely in terms of psychopathology, personality disorder, or emotional immaturity, we avoid the moral and existential dimensions of evil. He is also concerned that the intrapsychic approach to evil actually mimics the attitude of evil people because, just as the evil person makes his victim less than human, so the psychological view makes us see evil people as different and separate from the rest of us. He suggests that we are interested in accounts of evil in the media not because the perpetrators are so different from us, but rather because "they provoke a sense of queasy kinship" (p. 564). Spinelli prefers an interpersonal approach to evil. However, the intrapsychic and the interpersonal are not really separable. Although the average person may share some traits in common with the truly evil person, there is usually a qualitative or quantitative difference in the intensity with which these traits express themselves.

Goldberg (1995) believes it is a mistake to reduce the cause of evil to a problematic character structure or a psychiatric disorder. In his mind, such a diagnosis does not explain the mystery of evil, which he believes to be a moral affliction and not an illness. Akin to Peck's emphasis on self-deception, Goldberg believes that the crucial dynamics that lead to evil are rationalization and denial, which lead to contempt for and manipulation of others. He proposes a five-stage process in the development of evil behavior. The first stage begins with the shame and humiliation of a vulnerable child, leading to the development of a sense of self afflicted with a sense of badness combined with a critical inner voice, both of which leave the individual vulnerable to further abuse. To avoid painful shame, lying and deceit begin the second stage, which makes self-examination impossible and leads to a sense of self that is full of self-contempt. This feeling can be warded off by attempts to regain self-esteem by means of bravado and risky behavior, which reduce shame. Goldberg believes that in the early stages the perpetrator finds it difficult to commit acts of violence, but over time this becomes easier and more justifiable. Magical thinking may supervene in which the individual is convinced of his ability to triumph over limitations and weakness, and he is increasingly able to ignore any doubts about the meaninglessness of his life. An illusion of invincibility is expressed by aggression and contempt for the world – magical thinking vanquishes shame. When the individual attacks and overpowers others, he feels important, and at least in his own mind he thereby overcomes weakness.

The authoritarian personality and evil

Authoritarian personalities (Stone & Lederer, 1993) are particularly prone to develop irrational, destructive social attitudes, ethnocentrism, and prejudices such as anti-Semitism. This personality type provides an interesting example of the interaction of personality and culture. It is characterized by rigid adherence to conventional values, submission to an idealized moral authority, aggression, projection of the individual's personal difficulties onto an out-group, concern with strength, and the devaluation of introspection. This development is usually attributed to rigid, unloving child-rearing practices with harsh or traumatic discipline that emphasizes obedience and fear. This combination arouses hostility against parental authority, which must be repressed and is then projected onto out-groups. Such an individual feels he must submit to authority but feels impotent and angry about doing so, and often needs to find a scapegoat for his difficulties. To overcome any sense of personal weakness, he has to appear to be strong and shows intolerance of weakness in others.

Staub (1989) notes that overly strong respect for authority and a tendency to obey authority without question is a cultural characteristic that leads people to turn to authority in difficult times. These societies, such as Germany at the time of the Nazis, accept the authority's view of problems and solutions and do not resist authority when it acts harmfully towards others. German families and schools at that time were authoritarian, with punitive child-rearing practices. Staub also notes that group violence such as that of the Nazis is more likely in a monolithic culture with a limited flow of ideas, in contrast to a pluralistic society.

Resistance to hurting others

Deliberately harming others may lead to the perpetrator feeling physical and emotional distress. Thus, some soldiers who participated in the 1968 massacre at My Lai were crying, and some shot themselves as a way of getting out of the work of killing (Kelman & Hamilton, 1989). A high proportion of veterans suffer from problems caused by their own violent acts, especially when civilians are killed, and veterans sometimes develop psychiatric and physical problems as a result. This kind of evidence suggests it is extremely unpleasant for the average person to kill someone, and many people are unable to do so. Professional torturers sometimes report psychological problems, such as nightmares and depression, associated with their work. Nevertheless, there are people who enjoy inflicting suffering on others; torturing and humiliating others enhances the sadist's sense of self-importance, and such people slowly develop a habit of inflicting harm. This has been compared to an addictive process. Sexual sadism is similar; it emerges incrementally. Baumeister and Campbell (1999, p. 213) therefore suggest that

> we can outline the following requirements for an adequate psychological account of sadism. First, the initial reaction to hurting others (at least among adults) appears to be quite aversive, and the distress seems to be at a visceral level rather than a moral or abstract one. Second, the distress one experiences over inflicting harm appears to subside over time. Third, the pleasure in harming others also seems to emerge gradually over time and is described by some as comparable to an addiction. Fourth, the majority of perpetrators do not seem to develop sadistic pleasure or a feeling of addiction.

That is, there is typically an initially aversive response to hurting others, but this reaction diminishes over time, so it becomes easier to kill after many repetitions. Guilt usually occurs when we harm others, so that guilt is a deterrent to sadism; such guilt is partly based on empathy, which makes the perpetrator feel discomfort. Only a small number of people do not feel guilt or empathy when deliberately hurting others.

Humanistic approaches to evil

During the 1980s, Carl Rogers and Rollo May exchanged a series of letters that centered around the question of whether evil is inherent in human nature (Spinelli, 2000). Rogers believed that cultural influences form the basis of evil behavior by human beings, who, for Rogers, remain "essentially constructive in their fundamental nature, but damaged by their experience" (quoted in Kirschenbaum & Henderson, 1989, p. 238). He did not believe that evil is inherent in human nature. May, however, takes issue with this position; he attacks what he sees as its naiveté and one-sidedness because he believed that human beings have the potential for both constructive and destructive behavior. May points out that people constitute culture, and culture reflects human tendencies, so culture alone cannot be blamed. He argues that evil is best understood as the expression of a non-integrated daimonic urge. Here the word *daimonic*[5] implies something innate in people, part of our system of motivations. The daimonic is any natural function such as sex or rage that has the power to take over the whole person. The daimonic is not an entity but is "an archetypal function of human experience – an existential reality" (May, 1969, p. 123). (Jung [1965, p. 337] notes that the daimon is a synonym for the unconscious.) The daimonic is an urge for self-affirmation and self-assertion that can be expressed either constructively or destructively, depending on whether it is integrated into the rest of the personality. When this power goes awry, so that one element takes control over the total personality, we have a situation of possession by the daimon. From Jung's point of view, this would represent possession by a complex.

Like Jung, May is concerned that psychologists not think of evil as simply a lack. The daimonic becomes evil when it usurps the total self, when it appears as excessive aggression, a craving for power, or cruelty. But these are the other side of the same assertiveness that empowers our creativity. All life is a flux between these two aspects of the daimonic. This idea echoes Jung's notion that the archetype is ambivalent, with both positive and negative poles. May's (1969) critique of Jung in this context was that May thought that Jung's concept of the autonomy of the unconscious could lead to an attempt to evade responsibility for one's shadow, whereas May thought that there is always a degree of freedom of choice, no matter how driven we are by the daimonic. (Jung would probably reply that this may not take into account the power of the unconscious in some individuals, and that choice can only arise when the shadow has become conscious.) For May, the self always participates in and interacts with the daimonic. It does not seem that this distinction is very sharp; Jung also invoked the importance of the ego in ethical decision-making and pointed out that the autonomy of the unconscious is relative and not absolute.

For May (who was a minister before he became a psychologist), evil is an onto-logical, not just a moral problem; it is a vital force of nature. The daimon is the basis on which a person actualizes his or her unique potentialities; it is the funda-mental force of psychic energy that is the source of both good and evil potentials in the self. The daimon comprises both extremes and potentials, which are both conflicting and complementary. The daimonic urge has to be integrated into the personality in psychotherapy and harnessed to life-affirming values, which means the therapist is a guide in the confrontation with evil. May believed that the use of the anachronistic term "devil" is a way of avoiding personal responsibility for our own participation in evil; the devil is a scapegoat term.

In his debate with May, Rogers denied that there is such an innate human ten-dency toward destructiveness or evil. He believed that people are essentially con-structive by nature, given the right social and interpersonal conditions, and people are only destructive when they have been injured or damaged. He believed there is a "formative tendency" in the universe that tends toward greater order, related-ness, and unity; the human actualizing tendency would make us grow construc-tively if our environment is sufficiently facilitating. Rogers disliked the idea of the person as a beast that has to be tamed. He therefore inclines towards the *privatio boni* idea (see p. 130). He had been a theology student and was influenced by Christianity. He does, however, acknowledge that every person has the capacity for evil behavior: "I, and others, have had murderous and cruel impulses, desires to hurt, feelings of anger and rage, desires to impose our will on others" (quoted in Kirschenbaum et al., 1989, p. 254), but he sees this problem as the result of nega-tive life experiences. He realized the destructiveness that these could produce:

> I am quite aware that out of defensiveness and inner fear individuals can and do behave in ways which are incredibly cruel, horribly destructive, immature, regressive, anti-social, hurtful. Yet one of the most refreshing and invigorat-ing parts of my experience is to work with such individuals and to discover the strongly positive directional tendencies which exist in them, as in all of us, at the deepest levels.
>
> (Rogers, 1961, p. 27)

Rogers believed in an inherent urge to self-actualization and fulfillment. For him, people have the potential to be good, whether or not they actually are good. Self-actualization may take an antisocial direction, but the actualizing tendency develops in positive ways if the necessary elements and a facilitating relation-ship are present. Given such a relationship, he believed we tend to move towards pro-social behavior. In contrast, because May believed that innate human poten-tials are the source of both our constructive and destructive impulses, he felt that Rogerian therapists are too blind to the shadow side of human nature, resulting in a naive failure to acknowledge and confront the dark side of their own and their clients' behavior and personalities. For example, May believes that Rogerian therapists do not provide the kind of environment in which their clients can experience anger (May, 1982).

It is worth noting that Rogers may have misunderstood May as saying the daimonic is inherently evil; May believes it is simply a force of nature, which can manifest itself either creatively or destructively depending on how it is integrated into the personality.

Evil as a result of an evil ideology

Truly evil behavior is typically associated with personality disorder, but it might also be the result of ideology, as we saw in the case of Anders Breivik in Norway,[6] who, from what one can glean from his published statements, seems to be a psychopathic, malignant narcissist. But there is a relationship between ideology and personality; certain types of people are attracted to certain ideologies, and ideology can allow the personality to express itself and give it meaning (Virtanen, 2013). Staub (1989) points out that ideology was central to the genocides in Nazi Germany, Armenia, Cambodia, and Argentina. The French Revolution of 1789 cruelly murdered and tortured many thousands of people in the name of a fanatical ideology, and there are many similar examples. Needless to say, sincere belief in an evil ideology does not exempt the individual from responsibility for his evil actions. As Kekes (2005) points out, even if an individual believes his actions are not evil, and he is acting in good faith, we must still hold him responsible for evil actions, or else we would have to exempt from responsibility concentration camp guards, terrorists, and the like.

Depth psychologists are interested in the extent to which adherence to a malignant ideology is a function of the extent to which the ideology fits with the individual's character structure. For example, sadistic, cruel, or unempathic personalities are attracted to inhumane political ideologies. Whether or not the ideologue is able to act on his beliefs depends on the political and social situation in which he finds himself, but in general, extreme narcissism predisposes to evil behavior. Timothy McVeigh believed he could inspire a revolt against the government by bombing the Federal building in Oklahoma City in 1995, or at least he could retaliate for the killing of civilians at Waco. Since character structure itself is dependent on unconscious factors, the ideology to which one is attracted cannot be attributed exclusively to the effects of propaganda, indoctrination, and other social pressures.

Psychoanalytic self-psychology suggests that a cohesive sense of self might form around a fundamentally evil ideology that is used to stabilize and energize the self. The living out of evil ambitions or evil ideals based on this ideology may reinforce the cohesion of the self but be harmful to the lives of others. In this vein, Magid (1988) points out that evil may exist within a cohesive, conflict-free self in the form of socially malignant values, perhaps based on a destructive political system, which function as compensatory structures in Kohut's sense.[7] These are

psychological structures that shore up structural defects in the self; they func-
tionally rehabilitate the self by making up for a weakness in one pole of the self
by strengthening the other pole. A child may idealize one parent when the other
parent fails to adequately mirror the child, or the child turns to a particular parent
for the emotional support that is unavailable from the other parent. For example,
a potential weakness in the area of self-cohesion can be compensated for by the
pursuit of ideals that shore up self-esteem (Kohut, 1977).

The adoption of strongly held ideals and values may build or buttress intrapsychic structure, and a system of meaning that is important to the person, such as a
religious or political system, may closely correlate with the individual's mental
makeup. The choice of content is not important for this process to succeed. The
intense, fanatical belief found among political and religious ideologues may be
used for defensive self-stimulation or self-cohesion, and it is like an addiction
used to ward off deadness in the absence of a secure sense of self. The content of
the belief system is no guide to its psychodynamic function; an evil content may
help to build intrapsychic structures. Similarly, some people may engage in evil
actions in an attempt to re-vitalize an enfeebled or fragmenting sense of self.

Based on Fromm's account of Hitler, Magid suggests that Hitler's ideology took on the force of an addiction that sustained his (and his followers')
narcissistic equilibrium, further sustained by increasing doses of violence and
hatred. Hitler's absolute certainty about his ideology allowed him a degree of
self-cohesion – it acted as a selfobject. Magid uses Henry Kissinger as an example of a self whose structural integrity is based on ambitions and ideals that
maintain his cohesiveness, even as they cause damage to others. Kissinger was
powerless and bullied as a child, and his father also suffered because of anti-
Semitism. Kissinger denied that this persecution had much effect on him, but
Magid believes that out of this early powerlessness "emerged a man devoted to
maintaining the balance of order between nations – at whatever the cost" (p. 107).
For Kissinger, according to Magid, "order takes priority over justice" (p. 107).
Magid believes that Kissinger displayed a degree of narcissistic vulnerability,
quoting his biographer David Landau, who described him as "a combination of
arrogance and insecurity . . . compounded with internal self-doubt," and also that
he has "an unusual impulse to power and authority" springing from "a strong
sense of personal mission" (p. 107). Kissinger was also extremely accomplished
with undeniable strengths. Magid believes that in order to deal with an underlying defect in his sense of self, Kissinger developed compensatory structures
in the form of ambitions and ideals, which allowed him to function well without overt symptomatology. Magid quotes William Shawcross, another Kissinger
biographer, who believes that under international law Kissinger could be found
guilty of war crimes for planning the indiscriminate killing of civilians in Cambodia. In other words, Magid suggests that the evil self may not be a "demagogic
madman," but "an eminently respectable, highly principled individual" without
the histrionic qualities seen in Hitler.

The conviction of personal evil

Psychotherapists sometimes work with people who feel that there is something about them that is innately bad, evil, or destructive. This kind of deeply rooted belief is often spoken of during an episode of depression, or it may be initially unconscious and emerge during the course of psychotherapy in the form of an organizing principle or a complex. Sometimes, such a person blames himself for the difficulties his family experienced during his childhood, as if it were his birth that caused these problems. Miller (1996) describes this kind of situation as the result of the child's becoming a prisoner of his parent's narcissistic needs, so that the child must mold himself to meet the needs of his wounded parents' unbearable pain. This may be accompanied by a deep sense of shame about having come into being. Miller borrows from Winnicott (1960), who points out that the infant's developing sense of self is largely formed by what he absorbs from the type of "holding environment" provided by his caretakers. It is as if the infant imagines that everything in the environment is created by him, so anything bad in the environment is absorbed into his own sense of self. Miller points out that if the child is in an evil situation, he will not be able to separate out his own sense of self from the environment, which is the only one available, and the toxicity seems normal. As Eigen (1984) points out, when the organizing capacities of the ego are disrupted and deformed by faulty mirroring early on, the sense of self feels tainted: "The self gives in and sides with demonic promptings as a way out" (p. 92). Coen (1986) points out that a parent may project his own defective sense of self into the child, and the child must identify with this projection in order to maintain a relationship with the parent. The other parent encourages the child to comply and not question what is wrong with this arrangement. This is partly what Jung meant when he said that the unlived life of a child's parents has a major effect on the child's development.

Free will

The question of free will has long occupied philosophers.[8] For the psychotherapist, the issue is the extent to which developmental factors such as childhood trauma, psychosis, or severe personality disorders limit our capacity to behave freely. If we describe an individual or his actions as evil, do we imply that he had the ability to choose his action freely? Abuse in childhood predisposes to evil behavior, but it is not clear whether such abuse fully determines this behavior. Some serial killers are alleged to have no control over their impulse to kill, but our legal system assumes that killers who are not overtly mentally ill must have a degree of control over their impulses. In practice, we morally condemn evil behavior and at the same time hold the perpetrator responsible, even if we assume the behavior was not under the agent's control, although we tend to be less punitive in the latter case.

At first glance, it seems that unless the evildoer has free will, he cannot be subject to moral disapproval, and he may not even be fully culpable. Not only may powerful intrapsychic (often unconscious) forces affect behavior, but the individual may also be radically affected by an extreme situation, often beyond his or her ability to resist. Severe regression, of the kind seen in combat or mob violence, may prevent us from behaving as we normally would. Regression impairs critical thinking and empathy, and makes the person susceptible to ideological propaganda and demonization of groups seen as hostile. If the individual is caught up in a war or a mass movement and is subject to overwhelming social pressures to conform to group behavior, is he still morally autonomous and responsible? Examples are legion; during the Cultural Revolution in China, millions of people were subject to serious abuse if they did not conform to Maoist directives. During the Nazi era, opposition to the government led to death or imprisonment. Nevertheless, we have many examples of exceptional people who resisted negative social and environmental forces, people such as Jesus, Socrates, Abraham Lincoln, Gandhi, Martin Luther King Jr., and Nelson Mandela. It would be important to understand what such individuals have in common that allowed them to resist external pressures.

It may be that the degree of freedom one has to choose one's behavior lies on a spectrum, depending on the intensity of intrapsychic and social pressures. Some people are clearly capable of being good but fail to be good by choice or because of indifference. In fact, Haybron (2002) defines the corrupt character as one who has the basic ability to be moral and good but does not use this ability.

The work of M. Scott Peck

In his early work, Peck (1978) defines evil as the use of power to impose one's will on others by overt or covert coercion, in order to protect a sick, unloving self. Later, Peck (1983) thinks of evil as anti-love, a negative force that "seeks to kill life or liveliness" (p. 43), and as "militant ignorance," refusing consciousness of one's own evil by a process of self-deception. For Peck, evil is a malignant form of self-righteousness in which one cannot tolerate personal imperfection and the guilt it would produce; thus, evil has to be projected onto innocent victims who are scapegoated. Evil arises because we do not put ourselves on trial. By projecting our own evil onto others, the evil person can maintain a persona of righteousness; self-deceit and self-deception avoid self-reproach. Evil people project and scapegoat instead of asking for forgiveness. They attack others instead of facing their own failures because they want to maintain an image of perfection. Because of this pretense, Peck calls them "people of the lie"; the lie is at the heart of the evil character. They lie because they cannot tolerate self-reproach, and they are continuously afraid that their pretense will become obvious to others and they will be exposed. In Jungian parlance, they refuse to examine their shadow and insist on hiding it behind the persona. Presumably, this avoidance is necessary because the shadow aspect of the personality is too painful or shameful to acknowledge.

Evil people may deny hateful or vengeful feelings. Especially when they are narcissistically vulnerable, they become very concerned with a public image of respectability and goodness, and they are often excessively intolerant of criticism.

For Peck, evil is a kind of mental illness, a malignant subtype of narcissistic personality disorder. Evil is a matter of human character; evil deeds themselves do not make us evil. Peck suggests that the problem of evil has to be addressed by educating children in the dangers of laziness and narcissism. We must pay attention to the danger posed by members of a group who surrender their personal capacity for ethical judgments to a leader.

Most of the reviews of Peck's work are in journals of religion rather than psychology.[9] Although Peck's views deserve to be taken into account, psychologists have largely avoided Peck's *People of the Lie* because in it he confesses his Christian commitment, talks about sin, God, and the devil, and takes an interest in demon possession and exorcism. However, he makes it clear that he thinks that genuine possession is very rare, and this topic is not connected to the majority of the book, which is about the psychology of evil. Theologians attacked Peck partly for taking the notion of demons seriously and partly for discussing evil in naturalistic terms, without connecting it to sin, as if overcoming evil were merely a matter of self-improvement. Klose (1995), for example, believes that Peck was not sufficiently explicit in separating his psychological account from his personal religious beliefs. In fact, Peck draws a clear distinction between evil and sin (1983, p. 70–71). He thinks that evil is the absolute refusal to acknowledge and tolerate one's sense of one's own sinfulness (1983, p. 71) because of a character problem. This refusal results from an unwillingness to "suffer the discomfort of significant self-examination" (p. 72). Peck thinks that evil people have an unacknowledged awareness of their own evil character, which is intolerable and which they constantly try to escape because it is too terrifying to face. They deny or hide evidence of their evil from their consciousness.

Peck (1983) thinks that an evil person is characterized by (a) consistently destructive behavior, often subtle; (b) excessive, usually covert, intolerance of criticism or other form of narcissistic injury; (c) marked concern with a respectable image, which leads to pretentiousness and denial of hateful and vengeful feelings and motives; and (d) intellectual deviousness. He thinks this personality disorder serves a defensive function that is learned in childhood as a way of coping with the onslaughts of evil parents. Or, this character type develops incrementally as a result of a series of evil choices. For Peck, malignant narcissists are people who will not submit to something higher than themselves; their behavior is motivated by the need to maintain a grandiose self-image at all costs, often desperately avoiding any awareness of their evil nature. Any evidence that contradicts an image of self-importance or goodness is suppressed.

Reminiscent of Kohut's view of the origin of narcissistic disorder, Peck thinks that in such individuals normal infantile narcissism is preserved as a way of protecting the child against an intolerable life with damaging parents. Peck thinks that evil people act according to maxims such as "protect your self-image at all costs," even if it means hurting others to do so. Such a maxim is an uncon-scious organizing principle, but because it is unconscious the person has to lie to himself about it. Because this principle is unacknowledged, their behavior seems inexplicable. Unlike the psychopath, who has no moral sense, the evil person splits off evidence of his evil from awareness. Evil therefore comes in the effort to escape guilt, to deny conscience, and thereby to hide from oneself. Because the psychopath has no conscience, Peck does not regard psychopaths as truly evil.

Peck seems to be saying that a defense against the awareness of the nature of one's actions may be necessary to prevent shame or fragmentation anxiety. Peck does not discuss what Kohut would describe as a vertical split within the personal-ity, in which incompatible conscious attitudes and different values can exist side by side, allowing evil behavior on one side of the split that may be disavowed by more mature behavior on the other. Peck describes this phenomenon in terms of self-deception, which allows one to erect a barrier to knowing that the act is wrong. This idea may be true for some people who commit terrible acts, but it does not explain the action itself.

Peck accounts for group evil, such as the My Lai massacre, in terms of regres-sion (the stress of combat and hardships in Vietnam), the diffusion of responsibil-ity, and the abdication of personal autonomy. As a defense against stress, these soldiers were psychically numb, which made them insensitive to the suffering of others. Peck accounts for the attempted cover-up of the My Lai incident by sug-gesting that it was motivated by fear of punishment combined with fear of ostra-cism or retribution from others. It is difficult to assert one's own moral feelings if doing so means that we have to struggle with the force of group cohesion acting in the opposite direction.

The major advantage of Peck's (1983) approach is that he believes that des-ignating evil as a disease obligates us to treat evil people with compassion; they need help. A disadvantage is that to restrict the definition of evil to one type of person, the malignant narcissist, ignores the potential for evil in the rest of the population. Ellenbogen (2013) points out an inconsistency with Peck's approach; although Peck claims that evil is a sickness and should be considered a psychi-atric diagnosis, he also insists that evil people are blameworthy and accountable. Ellenbogen points out that to call someone evil is to imply that he acts freely, but if evil is a sickness that makes people behave in an evil way, then the sickness is determining the behavior, so that the person is not blameworthy. Furthermore, Ellenbogen believes that the injunction to judge others as evil "flies in the face of the intuition most of us have that there is a moral imperative to be charitable" (p. 1142), and to the degree we fail to understand people it becomes much more difficult to be empathic with them. She does not believe that we should judge people who commit evil acts as evil people; we should adopt a methodology of compassion and only judge their actions. Many ethicists believe that it is possible to hold people responsible for their actions even if they have a personality disor-der, without blaming them for being the way they are.

Peck claims that evil people are unwilling to submit their will to their conscience. They resist self-scrutiny and cannot tolerate guilt, which they hide using rationalization and self-deception, and by lying to themselves. Ellenbogen points out that this presupposes that the narcissistic individual has free will to choose and is therefore accountable for his behavior, but we may not be able to choose the use of defenses such as resistance to self-scrutiny and self-criticism. This may feel too dangerous for a very insecure person with low self-esteem. If this problem has developmental origins, she believes the person is not necessarily blameworthy. She argues that even people with evil intentions may not conceive of these intentions as evil; they may have misguided beliefs that their intended acts are justified and morally right. Thus, the narcissistic individual who has been wronged may feel that revenge is justified, and the contemptuous person feels that others are inferior, which in the extreme leads to enslavement and genocide. Such an individual's lack of empathy may not be within his control. To help such people, Ellenbogen believes the psychotherapist must refrain from thinking of them as evil and not make moral judgments about their character. "Acceptance is a necessary condition for helping a habitual wrong-doer to change" (p. 1146). She also makes the point that to judge others as evil hinders us from understanding them and makes us think of them as alien. In her view, we need to assume that their behavior makes sense and that they share the same basic human nature as we do. Respect for others is a duty and is incompatible with the judgment that someone has an inherently evil character. The term *evil*, in her mind, should be reserved only for evil behavior.

To cope with evil, Peck recommends a methodology of love, defined not as a feeling but as an act of will, the willingness to extend oneself "for the purposes of nurturing one's own or another's spiritual growth" (1978, p. 119). The psychotherapist must "allow his or her own soul to become the battleground. He or she must sacrificially absorb the evil" (1983, p. 269). This is a special calling of the therapist, requiring committed engagement with the evil individual.

Self-deception

Much of Peck's analysis depends on the presence of self-deception in the evil person. Kubarych (2005) points out that self-deception is "one of the most difficult and controversial problems in philosophical psychology" (p. 248). Self-deception means that one desires not to know some truth about oneself that one wishes were false. Kubarych uses a model of self-deception that suggests that the individual irrationally rejects what the available evidence suggests is probably true. This process is different from weakness of the will, in which the subject's intention is in conflict with his values, but these two mechanisms often coexist and reinforce each other and allow us to act against our better judgment. Kubarych (p. 249) points out that this means that one "must hold two contradictory beliefs simultaneously, be unaware of holding one of the beliefs, and that the act of keeping one of the beliefs out of conscious awareness must be motivated." (This sounds like the ego defense of compartmentalization.) Self-deception also applies at the group level; Kubarych uses the example of Nazi Germany to illustrate the fact that the German people knew that something very wrong was occurring, but they "accepted the legitimacy of forbidden knowledge" (p. 253) because it was too dangerous to know, so they deceived themselves. Similarly, based on Solzhenitsyn's account in *The Gulag Archipelago*, in Soviet Russia people protected themselves from knowing that their ideology was flawed and the Soviet system was failing, in order to maintain loyalty to the regime. Self-deception is often understood to be a way in which we protect ourselves from a wound to our self-esteem by ignoring aspects of ourselves that we wish were not true. Some authors, such as Fingarette (1969), believe that the capacity for self-deception is inherent in the human personality. (See p. 120 for a discussion of the neurobiology of self-deception, which is also discussed further on p. 61.)

Goldberg (2000) believes that the problem of self-deception, the human need to keep us from acknowledging painful truths about ourselves, led Freud to his discovery of the unconscious. Goldberg believes that self-deception is a form of crippling fantasy in which the individual feels that if only people would treat him as he wished they would, with no effort on his part, then he would no longer be insignificant. Goldberg goes so far as to suggest that this fantasy lies at the heart of all forms of psychopathology and relational conflict. He believes that constructive inner speech – an internal conversation with oneself about oneself – facilitates self-awareness and discourages self-deception. However, if the individual has a sense of personal badness as a result of ill treatment in childhood, the individual has to lie and pretend, and self-examination becomes more difficult.

Notes

1   The six episodes are the bloody, thirteenth-century Catholic crusade against the Cathars of France; Robespierre's year-long reign of revolutionary terror; the operation of the Treblinka death camp; the Tate-LaBianca murders by Charles Manson's "family" in 1969; Argentina's state-run terror campaign – the Dirty War – in the late 1970s; and the deeds of John Allen, a psychopath who published an autobiography detailing his criminal life in 1977.
2   McVeigh was responsible for the Oklahoma City bombings.
3   There were many accusations that *Hitler's Willing Executioners* was overstated, not based on good historiography, and lacking in factual evidence. Some critics believe that Goldhagen underestimated the power of situational explanations for the Holocaust and overestimated the importance of the prior disposition of the German population. It is debatable whether there was something specific about German anti-Semitism that made it so lethal, compared to the endemic anti-Semitism of the rest of Europe. Given the many genocides that occurred before and after the Holocaust, it may be a mistake to assume that the Holocaust could only have occurred in Germany, rather than seeing this kind of evil as a potential within all human beings. Fortunately, mature democracies with well-developed civic institutions are less likely to engage in genocide than those that are socially fragile.
4   The Hutus killed approximately 500,000 Tutsis, and millions were displaced or became refugees.

5 The *daimon*, a Greek term for a divine power, was used by Socrates to mean a warning, inner voice, or a kind of ethical intuition.
6 Breivik bombed a government building in Oslo, killing eight people, then murdered 69 people at a summer camp. He electronically distributed a text of his far-right ideology, which describes his opposition to feminism, to Islam, and to multiculturalism.
7 The term "structures" refers to enduring psychological patterns of beliefs, organizing principles, or complexes in the Jungian sense.
8 In brief, determinists believe that all of our actions are determined by prior events, causes, and conditions. In the extreme, this leads to a kind of moral nihilism that suggests we have no moral responsibility for our actions. The doctrine of compatibilism asserts that even if our actions are caused by prior events, people can act freely if they are not being coerced or constrained, and they are responsible for their actions.
9 This is partly because there was a misleading review in the *New York Times* in 1984, which erroneously reported that Peck said that evil people are possessed by the devil.

Chapter 3

The approach of social science to evil

Introduction

To understand evil, we need a combination of situational, social, and psychological (characterological and psychodynamic) factors. In this chapter, I will consider some of the social conditions that can either foster or discourage evil behavior, both in predisposed personalities and sometimes in ordinary people. Social psychologists focus on the conditions that allow evil to be perpetrated and the ways in which people are socialized into becoming perpetrators of evil (Staub, 1989, 2003; Miller et al., 1999). Social systems can be a source of evil when they are oppressive, using power, propaganda, and violence to maintain control by special interests. Social policy is based on a combination of ideological, economic, historical, psychological, and religious influences, so the social sources of evil are very complex.

Social constructivists and other postmodern writers see notions of good and evil as largely or entirely socially constructed, and many see good and evil as lying on a continuum. These authors often see deviant behavior in terms of the situation that evokes it, not because of the psychology of the perpetrator. They point out that an individual's behavior is a function of a given society's values and its historical period. Social psychologists typically think of evil in terms of the importance of the individual's immediate social situation, and less so in terms of personality and disposition; they focus on the environmental pressures that force or allow people to do evil. These are pressures such as the need for group acceptance and group pressures, obedience to authority, or simply social conformity. It may be frightening and difficult to resist the pressures of the group to which one belongs, and in some situations it may be dangerous to act independently.

Social scientists tend not to value the notion of evil as "springing from the depraved minds of evil persons" (Darley, 1992, p. 202), because they point out that evil may well be done by ordinary individuals who behave in an evil manner because they are caught up in complex social forces. Human beings are often thoughtless and sometimes easily influenced, factors that may lead to evil by default. We are not good at resisting situational pressures. In recent years, therefore, many investigators have turned away from a purely intrapsychic focus towards studies of the social conditions that predispose people to evil, in an attempt to sort out the interaction between the relevant intrapsychic and societal factors. However, as Kekes (2005) points out, only some people who live in adverse social conditions turn to evil, and the same evil acts are carried out under different social conditions. It is therefore not sufficient to attribute evil to conditions such as poverty or injustice; these social conditions exist because of the evil of those who created and maintained them, so that psychological factors are crucial.

Nevertheless, Grand (2015) believes that the shift from the study of individuals to the systemic and social levels is more fruitful than a purely individual approach, based on the assumption that "all intrapsychic, interpersonal, and group operations are culturally embedded, including sadism and historical and inter-generational interpersonal trauma" (p. 254). (The implication of this approach is that at the level of the social system, new factors emerge that are not operating at the purely personal level.) Grand acknowledges that "by displacing the focus from the individual perpetrator, the systemic approach risks reducing individual responsibility" (p. 255), implying that all of us could commit atrocities given the right conditions because evil is nested within a social nexus. She notes that there are always individuals who refuse to participate in mass violence, instead acting with integrity even at risk to themselves. Grand also points out that none of us knows how we would behave in extreme situations, and she stresses the problem of "othering" the perpetrator of evil or of describing him as inhuman, making it hard for him to find redemption.

Social conditions that contribute to evil

Extreme poverty dehumanizes people and fosters evil. Poverty is responsible for the illness and deaths of millions of people. Extreme poverty may render people superfluous in the eyes of the state, a condition Arendt (1973, p. 612) refers to as "the experience of not belonging to the world at all." Pogge (2002, 2005) believes that global poverty and radical inequality constitute the largest crime against humanity ever committed – and these conditions are avoidable. He shows how extreme poverty is not due simply to factors such as natural disasters but also to human-made institutional structures and policy decisions.

Staub (1989, 2003) provides a list of factors that predispose us to societal evil. He believes that evil such as genocide begins when a society or a particularly powerful group within a society experiences difficult life conditions such as economic hardship, large-scale unemployment, loss of control of the political situation, and perceived threats to the group's power and way of life. Such events produce feelings of insecurity and threats to national prestige and well-being, or to the society's identity and worldview. This situation may lead to positive changes but could also produce hostility towards those who seem to be responsible for the problem. This group, usually a minority within the dominant culture, is typically scapegoated, which diminishes individual responsibility among the dominant group and allows its members to feel connected in a common cause. History has shown that when a population has been made to feel vulnerable, committing geno-cide on another group may be a way of reversing the population's trauma. This is a form of identification with the aggressor that evacuates feelings of helplessness by making others feel helpless. People may then commit evil under pressure from their own group.

In the face of difficult life conditions, a subgroup that has been historically devalued within a particular society is quite likely to be further devalued and scapegoated. Staub points out that devaluing another group enhances one's own group's sense of identity, offers an explanation for social problems, and offers a sense of control by taking action against the scapegoat. By devaluing the targeted subgroup, any low self-esteem of the majority is improved. Nationalistic ideolo-gies offer hope, fostered by identifying another group who seem to stand in the way of an idealized future. Members of this group are eventually excluded from the moral realm. Thus, the Nazis offered the German people a sense of their own racial superiority; the Jews were ready-to-hand internal scapegoats for Germany's social difficulties because of generations of anti-Semitism, and the Soviet Union was identified as the external enemy.

A further factor that may lead a society to turn against others is a belief in cultural superiority, especially when the society is struggling with an underlying sense of vulnerability. The Germans of the Nazi era believed they were culturally superior to other countries in many ways, but they also felt weakened and humili-ated following their defeat in World War I and by the imposition of the Treaty of Versailles. A society that has experienced a history of victimization and suffers from unhealed wounds produces a sense of vulnerability that makes other groups seem dangerous, which may lead to aggression against them. Many governments have used and still do use fear as a political weapon, which often leads to irra-tional, thoughtless violence. A cultural history of aggression as a way of dealing with conflict also contributes to a predisposition to violence.

A group's ideology provides a worldview and a vision of a better society for its members. Being part of a powerful group enhances the individual's sense of iden-tity. As well, it is easier to act cruelly to others if one is part of a large group, since this allows individual identity to be disguised and removes fear of retaliation or punishment. The process proceeds incrementally, with initial criticism of the target group followed by increasing derogation, brutality, and dehumanization leading to systematic killing or genocide. In the case of Nazi Germany, for instance, we see the influence of a pernicious ideology combined with intense propaganda and the long history of anti-Judaism fostered by some strands of Christian theology. In Staub's words (2003, p. 295), anti-Semitism was a "deep structure of German culture [that] provided a cultural blueprint, a constant potential, for renewed antagonism" towards Jews. Similarly, in Turkey, "deep seated cultural devalu-ation of and discrimination against Armenians had existed for centuries," lead-ing to the Armenian genocide. When an ideology such as Nazism excludes or devalues certain groups, it is particularly difficult for individuals to resist social pressures to conform to the group's beliefs. The group ideology may become the source of an entirely new belief system and is incorporated into the individual's conscience and moral beliefs, so that people feel they must obey the social and behavioral standards demanded by the authorities.

Staub (1989) notes that the perception by group members that they are facing difficult life conditions may increase the likelihood of collective violence as a solution to social problems. Among a group or nation that feels threatened, afraid, oppressed, or traumatized, primitive mental states such as paranoid thinking, splitting, and regression may be evoked in predisposed people, leading to an increased likelihood of aggression. Staub stresses that human beings tend to differentiate between "us" and "them," or people who belong to their own group and those outside that group. "The group may be defined by ethnicity, religion, nationality, race, family, political affinity, or in other ways" (p. 14), and this differentiation may affect whether we treat someone well or badly. To see others as "them" contributes to violence against others, and seeing people as "us" contributes to empathy and caring. Staub suggests that the sources of this problem lie in human stranger anxiety[1] and attachment needs.

Being part of a group fosters a sense of security, an identity, and connection to others. The group's worldview may become incorporated into, or even take over, the individual's view of reality. Tribalism, or in-group and out-group psychology, makes members of other tribes seem less important than members of our own tribe, so that an us-and-them psychology allows projection and scapegoating. Projection of shadow material allows us to expiate guilt or blame by attributing problems to others. Mass violence results when the entire group regresses and becomes paranoid, deploying splitting and projective defenses in a way that undermines the individual's ability to make clear moral choices. During the regression produced by being part of a large group or part of a nation faced with a crisis, the individual's values, or his personal ego ideal, can be replaced by the values of a charismatic or demagogic leader. The individual may radically identify with or idealize such a leader, so that the individual is no longer making personal choices about his behavior. The individual who is swept away by group values becomes relatively anonymous. When the group's values are evil, destructiveness that at one time would have been unimaginable gradually becomes acceptable or even praiseworthy. By excluding another group from the moral restraints that apply to one's own group, the opposing group can be persecuted (Bandura, 1999). Here it is worth noting Morton's point (2004, p. 54) that "far more evils are performed by perfectly normal people out of confusion or desperation or obsession than by violent individuals or sociopaths." He stresses a "barrier" theory of evil that suggests that evil motivation fails to block actions that should not even have been considered. Most people filter out actions that would be harmful to others when considering a course of action.

The psychoanalyst Eric Erickson used the term *pseudospeciation* to refer to the depiction of one's own ethnic group as fully human while other groups are seen as less than human. Presumably, this is partly the result of our evolutionary heritage, when small tribal groups competed for resources and mistrusted strangers.

This has led to an unfortunate human tendency towards tribalism, which leads to seeing other groups as less valuable than one's own. The resulting ethnic conflicts have caused immense evil and suffering throughout the course of human history.

Theories that deal with the psychology of individuals, and notions about the sources of evil in personal development, are not necessarily helpful when dealing with evil committed by a large mass of people, because new phenomena emerge in large group situations. Responsibility becomes diffused, and the individual feels relatively anonymous, so individual guilt is lessened and the individual is not conflicted about his behavior. The appeal to conscience is also not helpful; during the Nazi era, abuse of devalued groups became a positive moral value, so that to obey one's conscience meant to join in the abuse or ignore it without cognitive dissonance. Here the bystander effect is also important; in the presence of a group, individuals are less likely to intervene to help a suffering individual, because everyone assumes that someone else will take the necessary action to help. As we saw in cases such as Nazi Germany, bystanders may ignore gross cruelty to others when it is assumed that the state authorities condone or instigate this behavior, especially when fear of reprisal is added to the situation. Few individuals can resist such large group pressures and maintain their own standards of behavior. Staub (2003) describes the importance of bystanders who do not protest harm done to minorities; lack of protest is often taken as tacit approval by both perpetrators and victims, allowing the perpetrators to continue with their destructiveness – for example, witness events such as Kristallnacht,[2] which was not protested by the majority of Germans.

Typically, during religious and political conflicts, the parties describe each other as evil to justify the killing or the persecution of the other group. When we persecute others, we feel uneasy or guilty, but if this guilt is repressed, we just feel uncomfortable in the presence of those we persecute, so we attack them even more.

Deindividuation and dehumanization

Social psychologists describe the processes of deindividuation and dehumanization as a way of explaining anti-social behavior such as lynch mobs. Deindividuation means that victims are not seen as having any personal identity, as if they were anonymous, not individuals, and even less than human (Zimbardo, 2007). This attitude is usually accompanied by contempt and disgust. In Nazi concentration camps, the inmates were not only dehumanized, but they were given numbers and stripped of any identity, which made the brutality of their captives more possible. Evil may be easily perpetrated on a person who is seen as less than human, so the effects of dehumanization are very serious. This process may occur unconsciously. Although consciously one might only feel fear or anger towards a particular group, if we unconsciously dehumanize people, we may behave without our customary restraint towards them. We then do not feel empathy or pity, and evil may result. Dehumanization of a persecuted group decreases the perpetrator's sense of personal responsibility and alleviates any pangs of conscience or shame, thus acting as a defense against awareness of the suffering produced by evil behavior. The perpetrator is then able to emotionally distance himself from the humanity of his victims. Therefore, those who participate in dehumanizing others are themselves dehumanized in the process.

Dehumanization is a composite of several defenses; it requires some combination of denial, repression, depersonalization, isolation of affect, rationalization, and compartmentalization.[3] One is then able to view others without the sense of empathy or identification that we usually feel for people in parlous situations. These defenses are typically used when an enemy is attacked from a distance, for example by bomber or drone pilots, and the use of neutral phrases such as "collateral damage" fosters this attitude. The perpetrator can simply tell himself he has to focus on the details of his job; this was one aspect of Adolf Eichmann's defense of his role during the Holocaust.

Nationalism and evil

Nationalism creates a sense of in-group cohesion by emphasizing the shared greatness of a people, their history, and values. At the extremes, this can produce a form of national narcissistic inflation, which is a kind of complex that grips an entire society. This inflation – as in "we are the most exceptional nation" – has the quality of a defense against painful historical truths, just as grandiosity defends an individual against shame or guilt. Mandel (2002) points out that nationalism may exacerbate the sense that a nation is threatened and may provoke hatred towards those deemed responsible for its failures. He notes that twentieth-century tyrannies "have been characterized by a combination of perceived national superiority coupled with perceived national threat and/or a collective sense of insult from the outside world" (p. 104). After 9/11, President Bush repeatedly cast the problem of terrorism as a struggle of good vs. evil, exactly reflecting Ayatollah Khomeini's description of America as the "Great Satan." This kind of oversimplified approach heightens social identification within the group, but by devaluing the other group it supports the escalation of violence.

Nationalism is one of the main factors that allow discrimination in favor of group members and against other groups (Tajfel, 1981). Nationalism fosters a strong sense of "us vs. them," based on features such as race, religion, ideology, and language. In the presence of a potent ideology fostered by propaganda, accompanied by fear of an authoritarian regime and mass mindedness, a lowering of the individual's level of consciousness occurs, so that the individual regresses and is swept up by group pressures. He or she is then no longer able to make discriminating moral decisions. The use of racist epithets such as "gook" by propagandists makes it easier to treat others in a dehumanized manner. Nazi propaganda was able to convince the Germans that they were a pure and ideal race, whereas the Jews, Slavs, and others were a contagious pestilence that was responsible for German misfortune after World War I. The pseudoscientific notion of genetic inferiority contributed to this stigmatizing, and Hitler was able to promote himself as the savior of a demoralized Germany. The notion that one social group is entirely innocent and must defend itself from other inferior groups has been a major contributor to evil behavior since the dawn of humanity.

The power of the immediate situation

Social psychologists emphasize the individual's susceptibility to the influence of the immediate situation when describing behavior, thoughts, and feelings. Thus, social psychologists are drawn to Milgram's[4] findings of the importance of obedience to authority, which is often used to explain the behavior of those who participated in the Holocaust. But is that a sufficient explanation? The situational factors described by Zimbardo[5] and Milgram (see also p. 76, note 4) are said to offer some degree of explanation for the behavior of concentration camp guards who were ordered to behave in evil ways towards others at the behest of their superiors. Milgram (1974) believed that his results suggest that human nature cannot be counted on to resist the pressure of brutal and inhumane authorities; a substantial number of people do what they are told to do irrespective of their conscience, if they believe that the order comes from a legitimate authority. An alternative approach suggests that Milgram's experiment shows that people can be put in a situation in which they are absolved of responsibility for their sadism. Or, the research subjects in Milgram's experiment were in a kind of dissociative state that allowed them to administer shocks to others because their normal conscience was not operating. From these points of view, Milgram's subjects were in a situation that was so powerful that their usual personality characteristics were overridden.

No single personality pattern seemed to be characteristic of those who resisted the authority of the experimenter (Miller, 1986), although there is some evidence that people who refuse to comply with an authority's orders are more likely to view themselves rather than external circumstances as responsible for events in their lives (Blass, 1991; Miller, 1986). This ability allows them to resist situational pressures. Fully obedient people in Milgram's experiment tended to score higher on authoritarianism and lower on social responsibility scales than did those who defied authority. In this context, some of the people who rescued Jews from the Nazis tended to score higher than non-rescuers on measures of social responsibility and internal control, so they were able to resist serious social pressures (Blass, 1993). However, Berkowitz (1999) disagrees with the belief that obedience to authority was a significant explanation for the behavior of the Nazis during the Holocaust, because obedience alone does not distinguish between the motivation of those who initiated Nazi policy and those who followed orders. The motivations of the instigators of genocide are often different from those of the lower-level perpetrators.

Most investigators agree that the violent traits displayed by the Nuremberg defendants were not exclusively attributable to gross psychopathology, psychopathy, or any other homogeneous personality characteristic. However, Zillmer et al.

(1995) point out that the leaders on trial at Nuremberg were not the concentration camp guards or SS killers; they were high-echelon bureaucrats distant from the actual killing.

The argument that evil may arise in response to obedience to authority persists. Lifton (1986) and Dicks (1972), who both interviewed Nazis involved in the Holocaust, emphasized that they were relatively normal people, not particularly pathological, and they behaved the way they did in response to higher authority. Dicks believes that Milgram's experiment helps to explain the behavior of the SS. Arendt's work on Eichmann also supports the idea that ordinary people can carry out evil. However, some of the people who murdered Jews were extraordinarily and unnecessarily sadistic in the way they behaved, so their behavior was not simply the result of dispassionately following orders.

Zimbardo's (2007) notion of the "Lucifer effect" suggests that everyone is capable of committing evil acts under the right circumstances. The willful intention behind an action is important for moral judgment of the action, but the will can be impaired by situational and psychological conditions. The Milgram and Zimbardo studies show how the will can be swayed beyond our ability to resist. Like many social scientists, Zimbardo is critical of a purely "dispositional" approach to evil, as if the individual carries the psychological disposition for evil like a disease; he argues that this view neglects the power of social and environmental forces. He believes that in the name of justice and loyalty, people will eliminate certain groups of people such as "witches" if they are believed to be carriers of evil. Zimbardo (2007) believes that George Orwell's novel *1984* reveals how ordinary people who are institutionalized by their upbringing to obey authority instead of to value freedom can be induced to commit evil.

Soldiers at Abu Ghraib[6] were obeying authority when they dehumanized their prisoners and committed human rights violations. However, responsibility was diffused, and the Bush administration tried to portray the abuse as the result of isolated incidents rather than U.S. policy, thus scapegoating the perpetrators. Zimbardo suggests that these soldiers were behaving in an evil manner because of environmental pressures, but the administration treated them from a dispositional or psychological point of view as if they were "bad apples." Zimbardo attributes these abuses to a combination of dispositional, situational, and systemic factors; for him, responsibility lies with the senior officers, civilian interrogators, and government officials who created the necessary conditions for the abuse to occur. The dispositional view allowed senior figures to avoid moral and legal responsibility. On the surface, these soldiers were ordinary people operating under extremely difficult circumstances, and they felt under pressure from senior officers to obtain intelligence from their prisoners. To the outsider, it looks as if harsh treatment of prisoners was tacitly condoned, and the soldiers believed they were acting lawfully. The psychological question is whether they had a predisposition to sadism that their circumstances evoked. The implications of this situation are serious for the question of whether evil is a proclivity common to all human beings. This issue has been heightened by the fact that modern technology permits evil to emerge that would otherwise be hidden, since people can now hide behind pseudonyms on the Internet while they behave badly.

Kelman and Hamilton (1989) describe three modes of social influence that were operating in the case of Lt. Calley, who commanded the soldiers who perpetrated the My Lai massacre in Vietnam in 1968. These modes are compliance, identification, and internalization. Compliance means following rules based on rewards and punishment, combined with social approval and disapproval. Identification means that the individual's role in the group becomes part of his self-definition. The group's values have then been internalized to the extent that they become his own. These mechanisms enforce the person's tendency to behave in accord with social expectations, even if that means behaving in an evil manner. When an organization is seen as legitimate, it is more likely to inspire obedience and feelings such as loyalty. I should add, however, that before being judgmental about the soldiers who participated in the My Lai massacre, one has to realize the kinds of pressures they were under, and acknowledge that it is difficult to imagine how one would behave under similar circumstances. We can be more critical of the attempt to cover up what happened or the attempt to justify it.

In his discussion of experiences of evil described by Vietnam veterans, Shay (1995) explores the effects of trauma on character. He identifies a "berserk" state during which veterans would perform amazing feats of mind and body, sometimes losing their humanity in this process. These states are triggered by events such as betrayal, humiliation by a leader, death of a comrade, and the sight of dead soldiers mutilated by the enemy. Shay believes that such an encounter with evil may lead to a loss of trust and innocence that may not be recoverable. He suggests that the knowledge that trusted authorities have committed evil, authorities that are supposed to be the custodians of law, produces irreversible personality change. "To encounter radical evil is to make one forever different from the trusting, 'normal' person who wraps the righteousness of the social order around himself snugly, like a cloak of safety" (p. 185).

Social psychologists such as Darley (1992) point out that individual psychopathology may not be relevant to large-scale organizational pathology within a society or institution. An institution might either purposefully or accidentally cause evil while neutralizing or suspending the moral scruples of its members. Darley points out that we might mistakenly attribute evil behavior to the internal disposition of the individual rather than recognizing that it stems from situational pressure. He takes a strong situationist position, which focuses on the social context of evil behavior. He believes that any individual – irrespective of personality – can behave in an evil way given the right social forces, even though some people are more likely than others to be so recruited if they are predisposed to do so. This socialization process can have permanent effects on the individual, making him susceptible to evil behavior in the future if social conditions permit. Darley therefore believes we are socialized into committing evil acts, and he points out that it requires great strength to resist coercive pressures. Thus, for him, the prevention of evil is best done at the level of organizations. In summary, therefore, evildoing is not confined to individuals who are evil; there is evidence that ordinary people can act in an evil way given the right social pressures. It seems clear that in social situations such as war, severe poverty and deprivation, gross lack of opportunity, and other national crises, evil is more likely to happen.

Evil as social violence

Some social scientists define evil in terms of the morally unjustified infliction of violence. People are more likely to become violent when they become part of a violent group such as a neighborhood gang. Violent groups increase their members' motivation to become violent. This is partly because of identification with the group, leading to a vicious cycle in which violence increases group identification. Motivation to be violent also results from the group's ability to remove psychological obstacles to violence, obstacles such as the individual's innate aversion to violence or distress provoked by exposure to violence (Littman & Paluck, 2015). Littman (ibid.) lists some of the motivations for joining violent groups, such as political and economic grievances, greed, the desire for revenge, protection from the violence of others, ideology, a quest for personal significance, and the reduction of uncertainty.

Athens (1997) shows that one does not need to be in combat to develop the capacity for violence. According to Athens, the process of "violentization" has four stages. The first is a stage of brutalization or violent subjugation, when the individual is forced to carry out violent actions by the group, and he witnesses the violent subjugation of other members of the group or of a close relative. An older member of the group coaches the individual in such violence, and this process fosters long-term submission to the group's leaders. In stage 2 the individual becomes belligerent; he has to find a way to stop others from brutalizing him, and he learns to violently attack others who provoke him. Gradually he becomes emotionally attached to what he is doing. In stage 3 he becomes more confident, and he begins to incorporate violence into his daily activities without any sense that he is doing wrong. He may even gain notoriety. In stage 4 he feels his violence is a good thing, and he needs to show off what he can do and move to bigger things, perhaps feeling invincible.

Collective evil

Evil behavior is not restricted to individuals; collectives, such as nations, ethnic and tribal groups, religious sects, and corporations may also behave in evil ways by being cruel, exploitative, or oppressive (Scarre, 2012). The obvious examples are groups such as the Ku Klux Klan. People in large groups may not be able to resist collective pressure, and as part of a group it is easier to diffuse responsibility for evil actions. Scarre points out that, like individuals, collectives may act out of character, committing evil out of laziness, thoughtlessness, or inertia, without intending to be evil. This may happen regularly or on isolated occasions. It is also clear that organizations and large collectives such as nations can have evil intentions and cause serious, undeserved harm. The sources of this behavior can be approached from the point of view of history, politics, economics, and social sciences, or in terms of the collective psychology of the group. Here we enter the difficult question of the extent to which theories that describe individual psychology can explain the phenomena and behavior of large groups, and whether group psychology can be understood in terms of the psychopathology of its constituent individuals. Many writers believe that these two human spheres each require their own methodology (Lu, 2013).

Writing from a Jungian perspective, Singer and Kimbles (2004) suggest that just as individuals may commit evil as a result of negatively toned complexes, large groups such as nations may suffer from autonomous cultural complexes[7] that contribute to conflicts within and between societies. This theory presumes the existence of a cultural level of the psyche, including a cultural unconscious, with its own history that is analogous to the history of the individual. This history may include the memory of traumatic events and other stressors that accumulate over time and are transmitted across generations, producing cultural psychopathology. Just as the individual ego may be overwhelmed by a complex that is activated by a current situation, so the society or nation may be possessed by the activation of a cultural complex. This activation produces a shared, intense emotional state that grips the collective psyche, often resulting in conflict, evil, or irrational behavior. An offending group becomes the container for the society's negative projections and biases. This leads to an "us versus them" dynamic. An obvious example is the anti-Muslim prejudice that arose after 9/11. The theory of cultural complexes tries to apply a mechanism that operates within the individual psyche to a large group. This notion has been challenged (Lu, 2013) because disciplines such as sociology and history must also be brought to bear to understand a culture. Even though it is true that archetypal processes can manifest themselves culturally as well as individually, the cultural and historical context of their appearance must be taken into account, because these factors radically affect the manifestations of the archetypal level. Nevertheless, Jungian theory would suggest that autonomous factors in the objective psyche interact with or contribute to economic, political, and other factors that affect the behavior of a society.

Like people, societies may have good intentions that result in actions that cause serious damage to others. A collective may irreversibly corrupt its members by referring to outsiders as enemies or as less than human, while demanding unquestioned loyalty. By participating in a collective with evil intentions, individuals are no longer autonomous moral agents. The organization thus degrades its members and subverts their conscience. An evil collective such as Nazi Germany may circumvent the moral sensibility of its members by distributing tasks in such a way that individual members do not know what other members are doing and cannot see the big picture.

All cultures contain social evils; their nature simply changes with the times. Slavery is an obvious example, but there are many others. In the nineteenth century, child labor was common; for example, young boys were commonly used as chimney sweeps, a dangerous and dirty job. The boys were whipped and driven up the chimneys from below, and most of them developed serious injuries or lung disease. The British Parliament refused to intervene, on the grounds that this was the cheapest way of cleaning chimneys (Phillips, 1949). Today, collective evil is expressed in many ways: forests and wilderness are destroyed; species are driven to extinction; rivers, oceans, drinking water, and air are polluted by our industries; but no individual is held to be responsible for this damage to the environment. Our ecological crisis is not only a matter of human greed, indifference, and unconsciousness of the interconnectedness of all species; it is a reflection of the structures of industrial civilization. Technology has in many ways freed us from being at the mercy of natural forces, but now our own technology threatens to destroy us. Because of evil social policies, many people suffer poverty and racism, and are forced to work in intolerable conditions. In the USA, gun violence is epidemic, and pervasive fear leads to the need for private weapons, disguised as triumphal adherence to an eighteenth-century situation that no longer exists. Some of our politicians seem to be prejudiced against poor people, who often suffer disproportionately from social policies. This phenomenon may be due to an unconscious terror of poverty, as if it has to be warded off externally.

Many contemporary thinkers decry our spiritual barrenness, and condemn the corruption, inequity, oppression, violence, and sheer vulgarity of modern life. Naked narcissism is fostered by our celebration of celebrity and power. We have an economic system that exploits the masses of people for the sake of a few, and we spend huge amounts of money on war. Aggressive nationalism is another obvious source of collective evil. A society is vulnerable to the atavistic violence of some of its inhabitants, and laws such as those forbidding discrimination are often ineffective because they are only a veneer over human hatreds, fears, and prejudices. It is arguable that such social problems are a function of human nature and not simply a product of our social systems, but the moral nature of a society depends on the morality of its individual people, not only on its political system. We see what lies beneath an apparently civilized surface very clearly in Golding's *The Lord of the Flies*, which depicts the evil behavior of a group of young boys stranded on a desert island, free from the constraints of a moral social structure. What gives us hope is the undoubted presence of real goodness among human beings, seen in societies such as the village of Le Chambon in France, whose occupants saved the lives of many Jewish children fleeing the Nazis.

Notes

1 Stranger anxiety is a form of distress experienced by babies about the age of 6–12 months old in the presence of people they do not know. This form of anxiety may have evolved to ensure that children would not stray far from their own social group.
2 In November 1938, thousands of Jewish-owned shops and synagogues throughout Germany had their windows smashed and their contents vandalized, and many were burned,

with the tacit approval of the authorities. Approximately 30,000 Jews were sent to concentration camps, and mob violence against Jews led to the murder of 91 people.

3 Compartmentalization is an unconscious defense that is used to avoid cognitive dissonance by allowing conflicting beliefs and values to co-exist side by side, without acknowledging any connection between them.

4 In Milgram's experiment, an authority figure ordered the research subject (the "teacher") to administer what the subject thought were increasingly severe electric shocks to a "learner," who was actually an actor. Only 35% of subjects resisted the insistence of the authority figure and refused to administer the most severe shocks, while the other subjects increased the voltage to levels that would have been lethal if they had been real.

5 In Zimbardo's prison experiment, students played the roles of guards or students. The guards wore sunglasses and uniforms and identified the prisoners by numbers, which tended to dehumanize and de-individualize them. The guards became sadistic, and many of the prisoners broke down emotionally. Zimbardo himself found that he behaved like an institutional authority figure, more concerned with security than with the needs of the experimental subjects. The experiment had to be terminated after six days. The studies of Milgram and Zimbardo illustrate how ordinary people can torture others under certain circumstances, allowing our moral convictions to fail.

6 In 2003, CIA personnel and U.S. soldiers committed human rights violations against prisoners in the Abu Ghraib prison in Iraq. The mistreatment included physical and sexual abuse and other forms of torture.

7 Lu (2013) points out that the phrase "cultural complex" is not confined to the Jungian tradition, and its origins go back to at least 1964. Lu also points out the danger of determinism if we assume that archetypal processes are somehow unchangeable or unavoidable, doomed to repeat themselves.

Chapter 4

Psychoanalytic approaches to evil

Introduction and overview

Because of the early Freudian aversion to any topic that smacked of religion, psychoanalysts have tended to avoid the subject of evil until relatively recently. Many preferred to think of evil in terms of the psychodynamics of mental states that predispose to evil, such as envy, uncontained aggression, or severe character problems, rather than grapple with the nature of evil itself. Psychoanalysts typically explain traditional notions of evil in terms of unconscious processes. For example, the notion of a devil is seen as a reification and projection of toxic internal objects or of personal evil tendencies. Another fundamental insight is that our fear of demons is based on a fear of our own repressed, projected capacity for evil.

Evil is sometimes carried out as an apparently conscious choice that is actually motivated by unconscious factors. However, the typical concern expressed about any psychodynamic account of evil is that, if we understand an evil act psychologically, we somehow imply that the act is not really evil because it has been driven by unconscious factors out of the individual's control. This fear is not realistic; we can judge an act to be evil at the same time as we try to understand its sources. To understand an evil act is not the same as to pardon it or to diminish its gravity. Psychological approaches to evil do not bypass the moral dimensions of evil, but the psychological and the religious approach to evil may differ in some important ways. Behavior that is disapproved of by our religious traditions has complex motivations that are often unconscious. For example, a lonely individual who suffers from painful internal emptiness because of developmental failures may become sexually promiscuous in his search for comfort. This behavior represents an attempt to soothe himself. Such behavior may be potentially harmful both to himself and to others, but it is not driven by a primary wish to do damage. Whether we describe this behavior as evil, sinful, or the result of an emotional difficulty is a matter of our preconceptions and the lens through which we view the behavior. Such an individual may suffer from intense shame, and moral condemnation is not helpful. The psychotherapist is able to empathically understand such behavior in a fragile personality. A more difficult problem for the psychotherapist occurs when our empathy fails us because the individual seems psychologically

intact, not suffering from serious fragmentation anxiety, and not desperately trying to hold together a fragile sense of self. This person might consciously choose
evil, even perhaps enjoying it. One then has to choose between searching for
developmental factors that help to account for his behavior or writing it off as
primary or "pure" evil, the result of a "bad seed." A case can be made for the
existence of such a personality, based on stories of children who seem to be psychopathic from infancy[1] or in the case of children who commit murder. Because
we expect children to be innocent, these accounts are particularly horrifying and
incomprehensible.[2] The press usually describes child murderers as evil monsters,
but most of them have experienced physical and emotional abuse and deprivation
(Heckel & Shumaker, 2001). Whether these factors are a sufficient explanation
remains an open question, but this kind of explanation satisfies psychologists who
do not consider "they did it because they were evil" to be a sufficient explanation.

Proponents of a bad seed[3] theory of evil, based on nature rather than nurture,
point to the behavior of children who behave in evil ways even though they were
raised in apparently average families. However, even though a family looks ordinary on the surface, it is not easy to see subtle but damaging levels of childhood
mis-attunement or micro-traumas, which may be cumulative, and the influence of
the prenatal environment may be important. As well as overt cruelty and neglect,
factors such as unavoidable parental absence, parental depression or illness, or
misguided, fallible care even with good intentions, may all lead to conditions that
allow the seed of evil to form in a child. Even the epigenetic effects of trauma may
be passed on from generation to generation. Psychoanalytic writers agree that
environmental failure in infancy is traumatic and leads to unhealthy development
of the structures of the self, but the question is whether there are *always* developmental antecedents to the emergence of evil behavior. It is, however, clear that
childhood experiences of neglect, abandonment, abuse, or deprivation gradually
accumulate, forming a personality with a monstrous potential. From this developmental point of view, evil is an emergent phenomenon within the human being
that may have a deeply tragic side. Another view would see such a person as fated
to be evil, as if this was part of the person's destiny.

Before venturing into some contemporary depth psychological explanations for
evil behavior, I should note that depth psychologists are skeptical of the claims
of social scientists that evil can largely be accounted for in terms of situational
and social factors. Psychodynamic theorists insist that something pathological
has to be going on in the minds of individuals who systematically torture, rape,
and murder innocent civilians, in particular when such people derive pleasure or
gratification from doing so. It does not seem that these kinds of behavior can be
explained purely in terms of the influence of the group. Even if we attribute terrorism to religious and political beliefs, the question that arises is why extreme
violence is so prevalent among extremist ideological believers, or why they are
attracted to ideologies such as violent *jihad*. A violent, punitive God-image combined with complete lack of empathy for one's victims and the sense that one has
the power of life and death over other people usually betoken a deeply disturbed

internal world, even if the outer world of the perpetrator condones and reinforces such behavior.

Psychoanalytic contributions to the study of evil

Freud (1915) explains evil in terms of sexual and aggressive drives. He sees aggression as linked with the instinct towards self-preservation. He is sometimes accused of demonizing the "seething cauldron" of id drives, as if these were an inborn evil that must be tamed. He believes we cannot fully eradicate evil because of humanity's instinctual, primitive impulses, including those that are selfish and cruel, and our civilization is only a thin veneer over these impulses. He writes that he emphasizes what is evil in men "only because other people disavow it" (Freud, 1915/1981, p. 146). Aggression became a derivative of his proposed death instinct (Freud, 1930/2002), which wants to oppose attachment and reduce life to a state of inertia or non-being. Freud also notes an innate hostility to otherness. This is a theory of aggression as an endogenous psychological force that seeks release; aggression is then not simply the result of frustration or deprivation. In fact, unless we can inhibit cruel behavior, it manifests itself spontaneously "and reveals men as savage beasts to whom the thought of sparing their own kind is alien" (ibid., p. 86). Freud's idea helped to move the field away from metaphysical notions of evil towards psychological explanations such as sadism. However, it would be too simplistic to try to reduce evil to aggression. Aggression may be used either destructively or constructively, and many forms of evil are not motivated by aggression but by factors such as greed or profit.

Fairbairn (1954) described the developmental sources of hateful behavior in childhood that arise when the individual does not feel that he is loved for who he is, and when his love for his mother is rejected. He may even feel that his love is harmful. Eventually he decides that all loving relationships are dangerous to himself or to others because love is destructive, so he must neither love nor be loved. In order to organize the personality, he gives himself to hating, which becomes satisfying; he thereby makes a pact with the devil. Like Milton's Satan, he says: "evil be thou my good." According to Fairbairn, it feels better to destroy by hatred and risk the accompanying depression than to destroy by love, which seems to be his fate in life.

Melanie Klein thinks that destructiveness is innate, part of the death instinct or a kind of hatred of life. Kleinians also see aggression as a reaction to or a flight from dependency and the anxiety it causes. For Klein, the loving and destructive aspects of the self are split; destructive aspects are projected into fantasy figures such as the devil or onto other people. Or the individual identifies with the destructive parts of the self, and the good parts are projected onto others.

Klein uses the phrase "bad object" to describe the subjective pressures produced by internalized early caretakers who were persecutory, abandoning, or violent. Here, the word *bad* refers to the individual's personal experience of a parent rather than a moral judgment. Such internal objects have been "metabolized" by the individual's own wishes and fears and elaborated in fantasy, so they do not necessarily correspond accurately to the reality of these early figures. For Klein, the infant's primitive inner world is dominated by persecutory figures and fantasies that are created from the infant's own frustration and aggression. These are projected outward and subsequently re-introjected, leading to guilt and anxiety. Therefore, we live on an outer plane of reality and an inner world that consists of past introjects and images. These two worlds interact and overlap, distorting reality. Klein (1927) follows Freud in believing that people are born with innate aggression and primitive destructiveness, so that criminal tendencies are a natural part of normal children. In her 1934 paper on criminality, she stresses innate aggression, persecutory anxiety, paranoid projection, and guilt as the sources of this behavior. She repeats Freud's (1916) point that some criminals suffer from a sense of guilt, so that criminal behavior may be motivated by an unconscious wish for punishment. That is, evil acts may be carried out to rationalize a preexisting sense of culpability. Freud believed that the origin of this guilt was in the Oedipal period and its murderous fantasies. The idea of original sin may originate in this early predisposition to guilt.

Karen Horney believed that human beings are born as loving and caring, but the influence of the environment produces evil tendencies. Horney (1933) believed that anxiety underlies anger and rage, which children may repress because of their fear of alienating parental support, or because they fear they will incur abuse if hostility were to be openly expressed.

Erich Fromm (1973) believes that human destructiveness and the resulting evil arise from character traits that are based in development; for him, destructiveness is not part of our instinctual endowment. Fromm distinguishes between benign or defensive aggression, which is a response to a threat, and malignant aggression such as sadism and cruelty. He leans towards a sociological and ideologically biased view of human aggression, which he does not believe is inevitable or instinctual. For him, destructiveness, cruelty, and malignant aggression are not essential aspects of human nature; they originate in social problems such as meaninglessness, frustration, poverty, and deprivation. He does not like Freud's idea of a death instinct as the source of aggression. Instead, he postulates the idea of the "necrophilous character," one who is attracted to death or the destruction of life. He believes that Hitler was a prime example. Behavior such as laziness, detachment, indifference, or the absence of effort are necrophilous traits because they are deadening rather than life-generating. (It is worth noting that merely to describe someone in this way explains nothing.)

Psychoanalysts such as Kohut (1972, 1977) who are not drive theorists usually see aggression as a reaction to frustration rather than being fundamental to the development of the self. When an individual's level of frustration is tolerable or optimal, it leads to healthy aggression or assertiveness, but chronic, traumatic deprivation produces a fragile sense of self, prone to hostility and destructiveness. Kohut believed that children who are deprived of affective resonance and empathy are more likely to become adults who treat others with indifference or cruelty, and they seem to invite cruel treatment from others. The child subject to massive failures of attunement experiences his sense of self as defective. The resulting fragile self may defend itself with aggression or it may result in malignant narcissism, leading to "demonic" behavior. (I should note here that pinning the problem of evil on individuals with malignant narcissism does not account for large group behavior such as genocide.) In other words, being exposed to hurtful behavior seems to contaminate the infant's psyche, so that he is then more likely to act in a hurtful way towards others; this behavior then acts as a defense against the feeling of being victimized.

Kohut (1972) described narcissistic rage as the result of fragmentation of the self in the face of narcissistic injury. This form of aggression is characterized by an unrelenting need for revenge in an attempt to right a wrong or undo a hurt, and it can be found in response to a perceived slight in a narcissistically vulnerable personality – road rage is a typical example. Some of the people who commit murder seem to be possessed by narcissistic rage secondary to rejection or failure. Winnicott (1945/1975) also believed that destructive aggression is essentially behavior that arises when a child's needs are met with inadequate parental responses. He believed that healthy aggression in children is a natural aspect of development, allowing the child to test the limits of its personality and the environment. Interference with the expression of aggression interferes with emotional development. Normally, Winnicott thought that the child's mother acts as a container for the child's aggression. If the environment allows it to be expressed, aggression becomes integrated into the personality, but otherwise it may become split off and destructive. He also thought that when an infant feels an urge to hurt, he feels a protective counter-urge that inhibits his aggression. For Winnicott (1957), aggression is rooted in excitement or even appetite; it is a form of connection to others, a form of self-expression, and a part of the child's life force that helps in the development of reality testing and self-realization. Aggression allows the child to discover otherness; by using the other, by destroying the other in fantasy and discovering that the other survives, the baby discovers the other as a separate entity. As the external object comes into being, so does the baby's sense of self-differentiation. The responsive behavior of the environment is important in determining the outcome of the child's aggression. Winnicott (1989) therefore sees aggression and love as inextricably linked.

Both Kohut (1977) and Winnicott (1957) believed that maladjustment in children is due to a failure of the environment to provide what the child needs at critical developmental stages. When these needs are repeatedly frustrated and the infant is abandoned and deprived, healthy assertiveness breaks down into destructive aggression. Narcissistic injury, annihilation anxiety, or separation anxiety are also likely to generate reactive aggression. This environmental failure, which may be unintentional on the part of the parents, is traumatic and leads to the potential for wickedness. The situation is made worse if such failures are not repaired, leading to deficits or emptiness at the core of the self that form the seeds of later evil. Winnicott defines *infantile trauma* as the result of a breakdown in the facilitating environment, leading to a disintegration of conscious functioning. Kohut also saw a failure of affective attunement as traumatic; both writers believed that children need help to contain the resulting painful affective states, or evil may result.

Typically, psychoanalytic writers such as Alice Miller (1991, 1996) see evil as the result of trauma that has been internalized and is then re-enacted by making others suffer in the way the evildoer suffered in childhood. The traumatic experience cannot be mentally digested or assimilated, and so it is compulsively repeated in an attempt to expel it. In these models, evil behavior is the result of prior persecutors who are living on inside the personality of the evildoer, radically affecting his behavior. Cruel parenting may lead to introjective identification with tyrannical parental objects. A failure of positive emotional nourishment leads to missing internal positive structures, and constant abuse of children is not only traumatic and terrifying but also leads to the internalization of rage and hostility. The child becomes cruel as a way of coping with a toxic environment, allowing him to transform helplessness and victimization into domination of others. In such children, empathy for others may fail to develop, predisposing them to indifference to others.

Bollas (1995) believes that the serial killer is a "killed self," a child who has been robbed of the continuity of his being by abusive parents. For Bollas, evil originates in the parental destruction of the true self of infancy, leading to pathological narcissism that wants to destroy love and trust in others, as these were destroyed in the child. The resulting false self wants to destroy anything that is life affirming. The killer wants to master the psychic death inflicted on him by the infantile destruction of his true self. Such a person goes on living "by transforming other selves into similarly killed ones, establishing a companionship of the dead" (p. 189).

Hering (1996) points out that evil that is felt to be a threat coming from the outside can be used as a container for the projection of an internal threat (such as a toxic inner object) that cannot be integrated into the self because it is too frightening and incomprehensible.[4] Hering is also concerned that the term *evil* can be used to defend against realizing how much we have in common with the perpetrator of evil. He points out that we all may discover evil fantasies, thoughts, and intentions in ourselves, perhaps as revenge for the cruelty inflicted on us early in life, and we have all been tempted to do something evil. We then become aware that these states of mind are connected to a "profound sense of having suffered unforgivable injustice and the burning desire to get one's own back and take revenge in cold blood" (p. 211). We defend against these states of mind in order to protect our mental equilibrium. Consequently, it is difficult not to retreat behind defensive disbelief or moral outrage in the face of evil, in an attempt to distance ourselves from the perpetrator of evil. Hering believes that the notion that one day Satan will be defeated is a primitive form of denial and projective expulsion, instead of acknowledging and integrating our own evil.

Hering suggests that the average individual has a conflict of conscience when he wants to carry out evil, or we repress our evil impulses so that the loving and caring part of the personality outweighs the temptation to do harm. However, in an evil person the hateful part of the personality is predominant and overrides the rest of the personality. In such a person, evil behavior can be justified and rationalized, so that the individual feels self-righteous. Hering believes that the source of this scenario is a totally negative primary object relationship, accompanied by the conviction that the individual's life has been destroyed by this early object, and the individual's only remaining mission is to revenge and destroy it, "without mercy, forgiveness, or any hope of reparation. You have ruined my life, I will ruin yours" (p. 212). The content of this "concrete dream" must be expelled and externalized; it has to be enacted because it cannot be symbolized, for example in an ordinary dream. Hering believes that Hitler was living out such a concrete dream in his "final solution," which he translated into a political ideology. These kinds of "concrete dreams," which Hering believes are born of the paranoid-schizoid position, seem to be unavailable for further processing by the rest of the personality, which they dominate and organize. The fact that so many other Germans went along with Hitler's dream must have provided a way of living out their own similar dreams.

There are childhood experiences of abuse that amount to soul murder, and Hering points out that a victim of this abuse may have no choice but to identify with the bad object and repeat his experience of his own destruction with others, in order to survive. These kinds of experiences foster hatred that becomes a *raison d'etre*. They keep the individual going by providing some coherent sense of self and identity. He also acknowledges that not all victims of evil become perpetrators of evil. The average person struggles with his evil side and understands the need to protect himself and others against it. Hering believes that psychotherapy is able to help with this process.

All these psychodynamic approaches suffer from the difficulty of explaining why people with similar psychological structures and developmental histories may or may not act in evil ways. Motivation may result from a complex of many different psychological and situational factors acting in concert, so it is difficult to tease apart a specific source of evil behavior.

The psychodynamics of sadism

Sadism involves deliberate cruelty to another person, often taking pleasure in doing so. Sadism is an evil form of predatory gratification, or a way of affirming one's own power at the expense of others. Typically, sadists have a childhood history of being humiliated, shamed, and made to feel impotent and vulnerable. This leads to a character structure characterized by defensive contempt and hostility towards others, often with no capacity for empathy, although some sadists use what empathic ability they have to enjoy their victim's pain. The sadist often degrades his victim, apparently as a way of making himself feel superior and powerful, as a defense against feeling helpless and vulnerable himself, as an attempt to master suffering rather than experience it personally. Some varieties of sadism are therefore the result of a fear of being preyed upon. Finding a helpless victim allows the sadist to feel safe, because he is then in the position of the abuser rather than the victim he used to be. At the same time, by looking at the pain on his victim's face, the sadist is able to unconsciously connect with his own abused childhood self. The sadistic treatment of another person may also act as a form of revenge against the individual's childhood persecutors. In addition, there are forms of sadism and cruelty beside the infliction of physical pain; the violation of a person's dignity and self-respect are also forms of cruelty or sadism. The use of a person as if he were an instrument or object, less than human, is a form of sadism. Hallie (1981) believes that a disparity in power is a central dynamic in the commission of cruelty. For example, the power of the majority compared to the weakness of the minority was at the center of slavery.[5]

Fromm (1973) describes the sadistic character as one who needs the "sensation of controlling and choking life" (p. 325). Fromm thinks of sadism as the passion for absolute control over a living being, which he refers to as the transformation of impotence into omnipotence. In his study of Himmler, the head of the Nazi SS, Fromm says that Himmler needed to control others in an attempt to overcome his sense of impotence, shyness, and uneasiness, and he was envious of people with more strength and self-esteem, leading to the wish to humiliate and destroy them.

As noted previously, Miller (1991) believes that sadistic cruelty to others is the result of childhood abuse and repressed trauma, and that evil people were inno-cent victims of their childhood. They feel a compulsion to avenge the abuse and neglect they suffered in childhood, combined with the need to keep these feelings repressed. The lack of acknowledgment and empathy by the adults responsible for the abuse, and by those who should have stopped it, does not allow the devel-opment of the child's capacity for empathy for others. He can only evacuate his feelings onto others by making them feel the pain he was subjected to. In this way, he unconsciously maintains connection to his own abused childhood self, which is projected onto his victims as he identifies with his abusers. In her discussion of Hitler's pathology, Miller emphasizes the importance of a long tradition of sadis-tic and cruel German child-rearing practices that tried to "tame" the child's willful behavior. According to Miller, in nineteenth-century Germany, parents sometimes tried to "break" the child in a manner analogous to breaking a wild horse, in order to ensure obedience. If the child is to maintain any positive bond to such a parent, the child must deny or repress the memories of this abuse, leading to a defensive idealization of his parents as a way of avoiding consciousness of the child's rage at the abuse.

Miller (1991) is thus in the camp of those who stress the importance of unac-knowledged hurt in the origin of sadism and other forms of evil behavior; she believes that every evil person was initially an innocent victim. The way concen-tration camp inmates were treated is an exaggeration of the way the Nazis and their henchmen were treated as children. For her, every murder is revenge for gross abuse during childhood. She believes in the therapeutic value of the recov-ery of these memories.

I should note here that there is a serious objection to Miller's hypothesis. She assumes that cruel behavior is evidence that the perpetrator suffered childhood abuse, and the absence of memory of the abuse is proof that it has been repressed. Obviously this is a circular argument, making the hypothesis, although plausible, difficult to refute. It is also true that sometimes people commit evil in an attempt to prevent the evil that they fear is about to be inflicted on them.

What helps to break this cycle of repetition is the individual's becoming conscious of the relationship between his childhood abuse and his current behavior. Miller points out the need for an enlightened witness (such as a psychotherapist) who validates the individual's rage and disappointment and acknowledges the injustice he suffered as a child, which was disguised as "for your own good." Miller insists on condemning abusive parents, although I think one also has to remember the need for understanding, since in most cases the parents were themselves victims of abuse. Whether such parents can eventually be forgiven is an individual matter. It is worth noting that some failures in development are inadvertent, more tragic than malevolent. Needless to say, none of this absolves the abusive individual from the moral or legal responsibility for his actions, even if it minimizes blame. The individual might be responsible but not necessarily blameworthy.

People who were abused as children tend to abuse their own children (Groth, 1979). Hostile, punitive parenting, harsh discipline, and physical punishment and abuse lead to a cycle of violence and aggression in children and adults (Dodge et al., 1990). A high percentage of violent adult criminals were abused as children (Lewis et al., 1989). A violent childhood environment and parental violence in childhood tend to make the child see the world as a hostile place in which force is essential. Parental violence towards children offers a model for aggression as an approach to conflict, as does witnessing parents abusing each other. Furthermore, abusive parents produce children with various failures of attachment; neglect is associated with anxious-resistant attachment, abuse with avoidant attachment, and combinations of these may also occur. These disorders of attachment predispose to aggressive behavior (Youngblade & Belsky, 1990).

Abused people who become abusers thus follow a particular pattern. The hated parent is internalized; the individual identifies with the bad object, thus escaping its persecution and its terror and helplessness by becoming one with it. The individual is then not only a victim of parental abuse or rejection; he reverses his childhood experience by becoming a perpetrator of cruelty. He projects his vulnerability and hurt onto his victims. At the same time, he may be envious of the good in others and wants to destroy it. Many such individuals devalue or scorn traditional ideas of goodness, thereby defending against acknowledging the painful absence of good internal objects in themselves. Being hated in childhood leads to self-hatred and may lead to indifference to others as a form of self-protection. Being treated contemptuously leads to contempt for oneself, and this may lead to contempt for others or for the world at large. Sometimes, having been seriously shamed in childhood, the attempt to make oneself feel better leads to an attitude of superiority and grandiosity that may allow the individual to treat others destructively, as if they were inferior or worthless.

Psychological aspects of torture

Torture is clearly a form of evil; it seems to offend our innate moral sense. Torture is defined by the United Nations as the intentional infliction of physical or mental suffering by agents of a state (Kantemir, 1994). More broadly, torture means any action that deliberately, unjustifiably, and unnecessarily inflicts unbearable mental or physical pain on any sentient being. Totalitarian societies use torture for the purposes of social control or punishment, to intimidate citizens, or simply to express the power of the state. However, even liberal democracies justify torture at times in order to prevent serious threats to the population. These societies often narrow the definition of torture in order to sanitize their behavior, by using forms of torture that do not cause obvious physical harm, such as sleep deprivation, solitary confinement, or exposure to cold or humiliation.

From the psychotherapist's point of view, it is important to note that as well as physical pain, the residual psychological effects of torture include severe mental anguish in the form of fear, psychological numbing, hypervigilance, poor sleep, nightmares, survivor guilt, suspicion, an impoverishment of psychological life, and interference with relationships. Major personality change has also been reported following torture, as well as post-traumatic stress disorder and severe depression. Other long-term effects are impaired memory and concentration, social withdrawal, and sexual difficulties (Basoglu et al., 2001). The survivor's family is often affected, and the effects of torture are transmitted to subsequent generations. Torturing other people is emotionally harmful to the torturer as well as to the victim; it has a corrupting effect on the torturer and on his society.

Many people who torture others initially feel distress, but over time they become inured to this work. Torturers are able to justify the infliction of severe pain on another person using a variety of strategies that allow them to block any sympathy or empathy for their victims. The torturer often dehumanizes his victim, justifies his actions in terms of national security, rationalizes his behavior as interrogation or intelligence gathering, or he deflects responsibility by blaming his superiors. Some torturers are merely sadists who are given an opportunity to act out their need for domination over others. It is true that liberal democracies only use torture when they feel particularly threatened, at which time it is easily rationalized. However, once torture is used, its use tends to spread to more and more situations. Many experienced interrogators believe that non-coercive forms of questioning produce better results than torture, and the information extracted by torture is often not reliable.

The therapist's countertransference reaction when working with victims of torture is typically characterized by helplessness, vulnerability, despair, overidentification, ambivalence, fear, and even a challenge to the therapist's religious faith (Comas-Diaz & Amado, 1990; Herman, 1992). That is, psychotherapists who treat torture victims are vicariously traumatized, as if trauma is contagious, and many of them feel that their usual therapeutic approach is inadequate in such situations. Boundary violations are more likely to occur when working with torture survivors. Herman (ibid.) also notes that severe grief may occur in the therapist who identifies with the victim, but occasionally the therapist may identify with the perpetrator and not believe the victim's story. She also suggests the possibility of bystander guilt as the therapist realizes she or he did not suffer.

Evil resulting from pathological narcissism

Fromm (1964) suggested that malignant narcissism represents the quintessence of evil because it is the root of the most vicious destructiveness and inhumanity. Many serial killers, such as Hannibal Lecter and Ted Bundy, fall into this category. Pathologically grandiose narcissists lack empathy for others and have an intense need for admiration. They typically need to feel powerful to deal with their childhood experiences of being shamed or treated as insignificant. To deal with their unconscious shame, they are dishonest and exaggerate their achievements and abilities. They insist on being recognized as superior to others. Because they feel special, they have unreasonable expectations of special treatment and they expect that others will comply with these expectations. When frustrated, they are prone to fits of narcissistic rage and a desire for revenge. They are often envious and willing to exploit others, at the same time as they are intolerant of otherness. They fear humiliation if their grandiosity is challenged. These are people who recapitulate with others the way in which they were treated in childhood, by making others experience the victimhood they were forced to feel as children. Many are contemptuous of social conventions. Such a personality often idealizes destructiveness, which enhances his grandiosity. He often believes he is able to decide whose life is worth sacrificing for his own goals. He may inflict evil on others without compunction, because he is hateful and contemptuous of others. Many such individuals are overtly psychopathic, able to readily manipulate and exploit others for profit or satisfaction.

Psychopathic personalities idealize destructiveness and unconsciously identify with a grandiose sense of self. To inflict suffering on others expresses a need for power and the need to completely control others, who are dehumanized. If one feels like an object because one has been treated in this way, one wants to turn others into dehumanized objects. The malignant narcissist enjoys his perverse accomplishments, and the pleasure of victimizing others is an enactment of the unconscious hope that the psychopath's early experiences of helplessness can be magically undone. Such characters suffer from unmodulated envy, greed, rage, and vengeance. Projective identification keeps negative self-representations and primitive anxieties out of awareness but leads to attempts to control the feared object and perpetuates distrust and aggression. These kinds of defenses not only impair object relations but also weaken ego functions such as impulse control and frustration tolerance.

Kernberg (1984) describes several key features of malignant narcissism, including paranoid tendencies with micro-psychotic episodes during which they want to punish enemies in order to avoid internal pain. Kernberg sees their malignant grandiosity as a sadistic attempt to triumph over authority, perhaps as revenge against an uncaring or abandoning father. Kernberg believes that they triumph over fear and pain by inflicting it on others, and this reinforces their grandiosity. He believes that when they are trapped in a crisis, malignant narcissists may commit suicide to support their grandiosity.

There has been considerable controversy about the etiology of this character structure. There is usually a childhood experience of severe narcissistic wounding, neglect, abandonment, and a complete lack of any empathic parenting. Kernberg (1997) believed that pathological narcissism is the result of pathological early object relationships characterized by the parents' callous indifference. This results in a pathologically grandiose self as a defense against a frightening world that is devoid of love. Grandiosity also defends against the child's experience of overwhelming frustration in his early relationships, which results in hatred and chronic rage. As a result, the individual suffers from unmanageable aggression combined with overwhelming dependency, which leads to intrapsychic conflict requiring primitive splitting defenses. Such an individual feels he has to rely entirely on himself, especially on his own specialness, and he can control and exploit others without guilt. His fantasies of being special and powerful compensate for his childhood experiences of severe frustration. His inflated idea of himself conceals a sense of worthlessness and shame, and his own unacceptable qualities are projected onto others who are devalued. Kernberg emphasizes the narcissist's intense envy and hatred of others who appear to possess things he does not. Kernberg (1992) believes that hatred is a form of chronic rage, and this is the core affect of these severe personality disorders.

Kohut's deficit model of narcissism sees it as resulting from serious failures of attunement by indifferent or rejecting parents, for example if parents use the child to meet their own narcissistic needs instead of responding to the child's needs. These developments lead to a fragile self-structure and poor self-esteem. The evil that results is an attempt to cope with emptiness and prevent or soothe fragmentation anxiety. Kohut believes that the child's grandiosity is actually the persistence of an archaic but normal early sense of self, not a pathological development as Kernberg suggests. The normal child also develops an idealized image of his parents. Given adequate responsiveness, these early narcissistic configurations are integrated into the adult personality; the grandiose self of childhood develops into normal self-esteem and healthy levels of ambition, while the idealized parent is transformed into an idealized superego and the development of the individual's values and sense of direction. For Kohut, pathological narcissism only occurs if these infantile configurations are not allowed to mature normally, so that they persist in some split-off fashion and continue to need expression in adulthood. The narcissistic personality maintains one or other of these early patterns to stabilize a fragile sense of self. Either the grandiose self of infancy persists, leading to a constant need for external mirroring and validation of the individual's grandiosity, or persistent hunger for an idealizable selfobject leads to a constant search for such a figure, in which case even a dangerous demagogue might be idealized.

The grandiosity of the dangerously aggressive individual should not be minimized. Hitler was extraordinarily grandiose. According to Roper (1987), Hitler saw himself as the incarnation of historical change, a kind of messiah who would lead the world into a new millennium. However, according to psychoanalytic accounts of his personality, he had an enfeebled and unformed self (Muslin, 1992). His grandiosity was an attempt to compensate for his sense of inadequacy. Narcissistic leaders of this type tend to foster a cult of personality and surround themselves with sycophantic followers who support the leader's fantasies of omnipotence. Power seems to act as a kind of drug for such a person. Most people become quickly disillusioned with this kind of leader, but those who are allowed to share the leader's grandiosity and those who share his pathology may identify with him and stay with him. Others stay either because they are dependent or because they are true believers, even defending the malignant leader to the bitter end.

The evidence clearly suggests that evil begins with early developmental failures, or with serious impingement into the baby's continuity of being in Winnicott's sense. Evil results from being seriously shamed and hated in childhood; extreme neglect, humiliation, and cruelty in childhood leads to self-hatred, which leads to hatred of others and indifference to them. Such a person can then torture others by projecting his own hated sense of self onto the one he is torturing. People who were abused and neglected in childhood tend to have both a lower level of empathy (Miller & Eisenberg, 1988) and an increased incidence of criminality (Widom, 1989). They are more likely to commit antisocial acts, including murder (Schlesinger, 2000).

If these notions are correct, the intrapsychic origins of evil begin in infancy, based on developmental failures that lead to tragic deficits in the self. These problems lead to a sense of something missing or of brokenness. Early separation and loss lead to rage and despair, which leads to destructiveness. In contrast to these severe developmental failures, both Kohut and Winnicott stress that manageable failures by caregivers in infancy facilitate emotional growth. Winnicott says that growth is "jogged along less effectually by satisfaction than by dissatisfaction" (1965, p. 181), and Kohut (1984) also points out the importance of manageable, non-traumatic empathic failures. Minor failures of attunement can be repaired quickly, but traumatic failures disrupt the child's emotional development and lead to a loss of basic trust, the sense that failures cannot be repaired, and the conviction that the world is not safe. Both Winnicott (1957) and Kohut (1984) see uncontained, destructive aggression as the result of unrepaired disruptions in early relationships.

Psychodynamic sources of murderous violence and aggression

The relationship between killers and their victims can be conceptualized in various ways. Killing can be seen as a primitive form of linking, as we see in the ritualized, magical connections between early hunting societies and their prey. Grand (2000) analyzes the inner lives of victims of "malignant trauma," who go on to commit child abuse and other forms of violence. She finds that the evildoer is often a survivor of unspeakable trauma that results in "catastrophic loneliness," which is a core experience of those who survive massive trauma: "It is a solitude imbued with hate and fear and shame and despair" (p. 4). She says that the cycle of violence occurs because of the trauma victim's desire to have his profound experience of loneliness felt by someone else; the abuse of others is the abuser's attempt to "answer the riddle of catastrophic loneliness. Unlike all other forms of human interaction, evil alone bears witness to the contradictory claims of solitude and mutuality that haunt traumatic memory" (p. 5). In other words, such a person can only connect emotionally with other people by making them suffer, which represents an unconscious attempt to undo the evil person's childhood experiences of being a helpless victim. Either one feels like a victim or one is constantly seeking revenge on one's early persecutors.

Grand believes that trauma produces the annihilation of the core self of the victim, and the perpetrator needs to be able to deny the core of humanity in the victim. The perpetrator feels internal deadness and a vacuous "no-self," a form of pathological narcissism. Such an individual tries to escape his own insularity by "inscribing its loneliness on the victim" (p. 13). Grand therefore believes there is a "relational nexus of evil," meaning that evil is a mode of relationship, an attempt to deal with loneliness: "Only in the context of evil is it possible to achieve radical contact with another *at the pinnacle of loneliness and at the precipice of death*" (p. 6; italics in original). She believes that some victims of evil become perpetrators because in this way they return to their tormentors and experience "a paradoxical form of confirmatory relatedness" (p. 7). Grand admits that she has at times behaved in evil ways in relation to her severely traumatized patients, for example in the case of a woman who raised the question of being sexually abused by her father. This made Grand anxious that the patient's father would sue her for implanting false memories of abuse, so she abandoned the patient by suggesting that her imagery could be more symbolic than real. Because she sacrificed her patient to save herself, by repudiating the patient's questions about her own history, the analyst felt "inauthentic, subtly coercive and secretly ashamed" (p. 59).

Knight (2007) also removes the notion of evil from its religious and philosophical sources and re-frames it within psychoanalysis. Basing her work on a study of serial killers, she defines evil as destructive aggression that emerges as violence against another. Knight's definition includes the component of sadistic enjoyment of inflicting pain on the victim, which she believes to be essential in her definition of evil. She believes that sexually motivated serial killers are truly evil. For her, evil is premeditated violence, but this can also be reactive to a perceived threat or sense of being in danger. She notes that these killers use aggression to protect a weak and inadequate sense of self, and they are fearful of the world, which is experienced as hateful and dangerous. Most of them have had traumatic, abusive childhoods with punitive, rejecting, hateful caregivers, or mothers who were controlling and infantilizing, and the ghosts of these early persecutors still haunt the individual. Many serial killers are the sons of prostitutes. For some killers, an attack on others is unconsciously an attack on early childhood persecutors; it is a form of revenge against childhood pain and helplessness or a re-enactment of past insults, so that the victim is a symbolic representation of those who tormented the individual in the past. The killer's fragile sense of self is rooted developmentally in early traumas, leading to hatred, rage, and the need for revenge. The sadism expressed towards others represents a symbolic expression of hatred for the world.

Knight takes the position that aggression is both innate and also reactive in the interpersonal context. She makes the point that even though serial killers are protecting a fragile and pathological sense of self, this does not legitimate their crimes even as it allows us to understand their behavior; she sees them as bad but not mad – few are psychotic.

Eigen (1984) points out that the murder victim is "a proxy for the killer's once wretchedly vulnerable baby self" (p. 111), such that the killing eliminates any external sign of the killer's own potential subjugation. The murderer is trying to get rid of his own helplessness though the victim; murder cancels dependency and also "covetous differences and inequalities." The killer affirms his own uniqueness at the expense of leveling otherness. "For the moment at least, the subject feels on top of everything, with nothing truly unknown. Murder simplifies. . . . For the moment, time stands still" (ibid.).

Gilligan (1996) found that overwhelming shame in childhood is a marker for potential violence in adulthood. Most of his violent subjects had childhood experiences of severe abuse and shaming. He suggests that shame is initially experienced as a feeling of painful numbness or deadness, to which the body responds by anesthetizing itself, leading to an icy cold feeling. The individual has no social or cultural means of warding off or expressing his shame, and this problem is often combined with a lack of the capacity to feel guilt or love. Gilligan believes that the combination of intense shame and self-hatred lead to terrible behavior. Relentlessly being shamed in childhood leads to the conviction that one is bad or defective in some way, and leads to contempt for oneself and others. However, it is also true that shame may prevent bad behavior and promote self-awareness.

Many psychopathic personalities try to avoid the experience of shame in response to threat. Their reaction is to try to become dominant and protect themselves by threatening others to hide their shame (Morrison & Gilbert, 2001). Shame often leads to hostility, and serial killers use violence to defend against their sense of a defective, empty self, "full of impotent anger and revengeful at a world which seems equally as hateful and revengeful as themselves" (Knight, 2007, p. 31). Vengeance is an important motivation for serial killing among men who hate women in general, or who are enraged with a particular woman. A less common motivation for serial killing is a perverted form of thrill seeking and the need to dominate a victim.

Goldberg (2000) suggests the following steps that may lead an individual to become acclimatized to violent behavior. Feelings of shame and humiliation as a result of mistreatment, combined with an inability to express this hurt both to himself and to others, lead to self-contempt. Self-contempt is converted into contempt for others, and the individual searches for an opportunity to express this contempt. He then finds a vulnerable victim who unconsciously reminds him of his own hurt and shame. He violates this victim, and this action is followed by a feeling of serenity and superiority. Goldberg points out that the individual who is only violent under situations of extreme stress requires additional steps to lose control of his emotions and commit violence. He is in harmony with others until some outrage to himself or to someone important to him occurs; he regards this as unjust, and he loses trust in the social order. He is unable to express his feelings of outrage in an articulate manner, leading to a feeling of self-hatred because he feels ineffectual. This is an intolerable feeling, leading to rage and confusion at those he holds responsible for the outrage or at those who did not prevent it. He justifies or rationalizes his contempt, allowing him to dehumanize those he holds responsible; this allows him to be indifferent to the violence he directs at his victims. He then feels shame, regret, and remorse.

Goldberg's approach to the psychotherapeutic treatment of destructive people is based on his idea that destructive behavior is based on unacknowledged shame and despair. Thus, he recommends seven essential steps in their treatment. The first is to help the individual recognize the presence of shame behind his distress. Shame is often misidentified as physiological discomfort, or it is misunderstood as guilt or another emotion. Goldberg traces the origin of his patient's shame based on the way the patient has been treated, leading to a punitive negative inner voice that accuses his adult behavior the way his early caregivers accused him in childhood. The patient is encouraged to discuss his shameful feelings with another caring person, allowing him to examine and repudiate feelings about himself that are unfair. The patient is helped to realize he is not alone in his distress, so that support groups are useful. The patient is encouraged to express the authentic aspects of his childhood longings and the sadness resulting from failure to achieve the intimacy he craves. He is taught the language of emotions, how to use emotionally expressive language to communicate his needs, and when it is appropriate to do so. He is taught to speak to others as if he already is the person he wants to be. These skills allow him to halt the vicious circle of being humiliated, ashamed, and weak, leading to hiding from others and feeling cowardly about dealing with conflictual material. Finally, he is encouraged to help others deal with toxic shame and despair, perhaps by engaging in altruistic activities.

In her psychoanalytic study of the sources of evil, Aragno (2013) points out that the talionic response, the notion of an eye for an eye, produces an unending chain of vengeance and destruction. She also notes the importance of "scapegoating, sibling rivalry, tribalism, the wish for dominance and power, greed, prejudice, extremism, exploitation, and, *uniquely* human, the pleasure in causing pain" (p. 103). To this list of factors that contribute to evil behavior, she adds sibling rivalry and its associated envy, as well as excessive ambition.

Superego pathology

Superego pathology produces various degrees of anti-social behavior, dishonesty, and lack of concern for others.[6] A poorly formed superego might be the result of excessive leniency in childhood, leading to narcissistic self-importance and an undeveloped moral sense. Conversely, an extremely harsh upbringing might lead to an overly harsh superego colored by aggression and defiance. Kernberg (1992) describes the relationship between the nature of the superego and the quality of the individual's object relations. He points out that a pathologically grandiose self that is infiltrated with ego-syntonic aggression leads to violence and sadistic cruelty. For Kernberg, evil behavior is a manifestation of a pathological personality organization using primitive defenses such as splitting, poorly modulated aggression, and a tendency to act out. These problems are found among psychopaths, malignant narcissists, and borderline personalities, who have poor impulse control and a pathological superego. These factors are often combined with grandiosity or omnipotence with poor reality testing, massive use of projection, primitive splitting, denial, and isolation of affect, leading to lack of concern for others and detachment from the results of their behavior.

Is aggression reactive or primary?

Given that violence, hatred, and rage may lead to extreme evil and destructiveness, it is obviously important to understand the sources of human aggression, but there exists a wide spectrum of opinions about this question. From an evolutionary perspective, aggression probably appeared as a process for managing disputes, to deal with threats to survival, or because of competition for resources, so that the potential for aggression is wired into the human nervous system. In the psychoanalytic literature, part of the debate hinges around the question of whether aggression is such a fundamental human instinct that it is central to the dynamics of the psyche, or whether aggression is largely reactive or defensive. If aggression is a primal force in the psyche, as Freud and Melanie Klein thought, then only our conscience and moral and social training can inhibit it. Evil occurs when these barriers fail.

If aggression is truly an innate potential in the child, aggressive behavior may result from an acquired failure of containment of infantile aggression. A lack of containing boundaries, a fragile sense of self that is unable to contain painful affects, or a failure to feel safely held lead to a failure to develop internal constraints on aggression. Early psychoanalysts saw evil as the result of unrestrained primitive aggression erupting through the repression barrier. Thus, for Freud, aggression is an innate drive that demands release; only civilization restrains aggression, using law and order and the superego that turns aggression against the self. For him, morality involves such self-directed aggression. (This theory does not account for why some sadistic people enjoy inflicting pain on others.) Later psychoanalysts realized that aggression might be used to compensate for a sense of internal emptiness or deadness, or to maintain self-esteem or to revenge narcissistic injury. Violence allows people to cope with feelings of humiliation, helplessness, and death anxiety, as if killing others somehow represents a victory over death, as Becker (1975) suggested. Sometimes the fantasy of conquering evil through violence contributes to further evil. Whatever its source, violence often seems to be addictive. Sometimes people take pleasure in apparently senseless destruction and violence.

Mills (2016) believes that all humans are to some degree evil. He writes that: "The evil that inhabits man . . . is a metaphysical principle that saturates the natural world." He exemplifies the notion that aggression is the underpinning of evil. According to Mills (p. 42):

> Everyone is intrinsically evil: it is a structural invariant of the human psyche. . . . [E]veryone is predisposed to aggressivity and violence, to mistreating others, to intentionally inflicting verbal, emotional, relational and/or physical pain . . . no matter how unsavory the thought, or how one vociferously objects to or disavows such characteristics or how saintly a person may appear.

Mills goes on to say that our world is a "festering cesspool of pathology," but we cannot say the same about goodness, which he believes to be a developmental achievement acquired through socialization rather than something as structurally intrinsic as evil. For Mills, humans are naturally aggressive creatures because of evolutionary and phylogenetic pressures, so that the notion that we are born good and become bad because of developmental factors is mistaken. Aggression is a natural predisposition in us that can be either activated or inhibited, and our inborn aggression leads to primary evil. He believes that "early fantasy life is dominated by evil impulses, sadistic urges, primitive affects and paranoiac anxieties we project onto objects" (p. 44). For Mills, we cannot eradicate this problem because evil is a deep structure in the human psyche; we can only mitigate it and control its enactment. The defensive containment of our innate evil, or our empathic ability, makes the difference between a civilized human being and a criminal.

Rather than seeing aggression as central to the core of the self, other theorists see it as the result of provocation or as a reaction to frustration (Mitchell, 1993). Relational approaches to aggression suggest that aggression is a response to others that is biologically pre-wired but expressed in a relational context. Mitchell (1993) points out that to characterize aggression as a response to danger or threat does not undermine its biological basis; circumstances evoke aggression when they are dangerous. Mitchell suggests that to feel endangered is a subjective experience of the self that may not be related to the actual level of danger as perceived by an external observer. The sense of danger is produced by a threat to the integrity of the self, which produces a deeply aggressive reaction.

> In fact, the pursuit of revenge generated by a need to redress past insults or humiliation often propels people into situations that are physically dangerous. Much of the political aggression and violence on the world today is connected with nationalistic and ethnic identifications that are rooted in a collective sense of endangerment and past humiliations.
>
> (p. 163)

Most relational theorists believe that such aggression would fade as the threat to the sense of self fades.

Mitchell's approach to reactive aggression is essentially the same as that of Kohut (1972), who describes narcissistic rage produced by a wound to one's sense of self, such as an experience of painful rejection or other narcissistic injury. In vulnerable people, this leads not only to depression and shame but also to pervasive rage combined with a vindictive need for vengeance. Sexual aggression is more typically about power and sadism. Sexually aggressive men feel threatened and demeaned by women, with a compensatory need to dominate and control them, or they feel they have been betrayed and deceived by women (Lisak & Roth, 1990).

The role of psychological defenses in the production of evil

To commit genocide, large numbers of a population must be at least tacitly complicit. Many of the people who committed atrocities in the Holocaust and the Rwanda genocide[7] also had families and led otherwise ordinary lives. How is this possible? Were all those who participated intrinsically evil people, or were they capable of massive defensive operations that split off any awareness of what they were doing? According to Lifton and Markusen (1992), they deployed a variety of defenses to defend against consciously experiencing the harm they were inflicting. These include splitting, dissociation, numbing, blunting of feelings, and what he refers to as "doubling," an unconscious mechanism whereby the person such as a Nazi doctor developed a kind of part-self or "Auschwitz self" that could function within the concentration camp according to its values, while also having access to a prewar personality and a family life. For example, the head of the Auschwitz death camp, Rudolf Höss, was said to have had a normal family life at the same time as he was perpetrating atrocities in his daily work. Another example is the atrocities committed by Bosnian soldiers who participated in murders and sexual assault and then returned home to their ordinary lives. Doubling means that the self divides into two functioning wholes, so that a part-self acts as an entire self. Lifton suggests that among the Nazi doctors: "The Auschwitz self had to be both autonomous and connected to the prior self that gave rise to it" (Lifton,

1986, p. 419). This defense allowed Nazi doctors to behave in extraordinarily evil ways without falling apart psychologically; one part of the self disavows the other. The original self repudiates what the Auschwitz self was doing; the Auschwitz self violated the Nazi doctor's previous self-concept, "requiring more or less permanent disavowal" (p. 422). The individual's conscience became disconnected from his previous self and attached to the ideals of the Nazis – Lifton calls this a "transfer of conscience" (p. 423). He believes that doubling is motivated by the experience of death anxiety and is a "form of psychological survival in a death-dominated environment" (p. 419), but it also involves the avoidance of guilt – although he points out that it does not absolve the individual from responsibility for moral choice. In Peck's terms, this splitting or disavowal was a form of radical self-deception and an avoidance of self-examination. The major critique of Lifton's notion of "doubling" is that it assumes that the Nazi doctors realized that what they were doing was evil. In fact, most of them were rabidly anti-Semitic before the war, and they believed that the extermination of the Jews was necessary and good. Some of them may have had to disavow or deny the suffering they were causing, but the notion of two separate selves seems to be an exaggeration. Furthermore, it is doubtful that the doctors he interviewed were honest witnesses to their behavior.

We see defenses against acknowledging the presence of evil in nations as well as individuals. It is difficult for some Americans to acknowledge both the genocide of the American Indians by early American settlers and the role of slavery in the development of the USA. The cultural myth around the Thanksgiving festival is still taught as the truth.[8] The Turks still insist on denying the Armenian genocide. In France, collaboration with the Nazis is sometimes minimized, and the genocidal massacres in Algeria still haunt the French, some of whom express little remorse. Many Japanese prefer to ignore the atrocities perpetrated by Japanese soldiers in World War II. The damage done by British and other colonial powers was enormous, but few of these powers acknowledge the harm they have caused.

Evil due to dread

Based on interviews of 68 people, both free individuals and prison inmates, Alford (1997) suggests that moral evil is rooted in the experience of dread, pain, abandonment, and meaninglessness. Evil behavior is a strategy for dealing with these feelings; evil is an attempt to master the experience of dread by inflicting it on others. Alford says that "dread is a fear of a living death" (p. 53). He explains the infantile origin of dread in terms of the experience of formlessness and loss of the boundaries of the self, during what Ogden (1989) describes as the autistic-contiguous position.[9] This idea suggests that dread is produced by the sense that the self is leaking away. This dread cannot be symbolized and contained, so it is evacuated into others in the form of violence or sadism, making them feel dreadful. For Alford, evil is a paranoid-schizoid attempt to evacuate the formless dread of the autistic-contiguous position by violently intruding it into another's body in an attempt to give it form. Or, by destroying the other, we destroy our dread. Paranoid-schizoid anxiety "expresses and defends against autistic-contiguous dread" (p. 43). For Alford, therefore, dread is the ground of evil – the dread of being human, vulnerable, alone, and doomed to die. Doing evil tries to transform the "terrible passivity and helplessness of suffering into activity" (p. 3). His incarcerated respondents were at one time victims but then acted out in an evil way to gain emotional distance from their abuse: "Evil inflicts pain, abandonment, and helplessness on other so that the evildoer will not have to experience them himself. It is that simple and that complicated" (p. 52).

Alford tries to understand what evil means to his informants, and concludes that evil is "that which threatens to obliterate the self, overcoming its boundaries" (p. 38). He says that evil is about nothingness, the dread of boundlessness, the "loss of self, loss of meaning, loss of history, loss of connection to the world itself" (p. ix). Doing evil tries to transform the passivity and helplessness of suffering into action.

Alford believes that our ability to avoid dread depends on the ability to symbolize it, and the capacity to symbolize only occurs in the depressive position. Alford (1999) believes that some individuals lack the capacity to express their dread in narrative form because they do not have sufficiently differentiated social roles, or adequate self-representations, which would allow them to participate in story lines about evil. One such role is that of a "meaningful victim," exemplified by Primo Levi, whose role in life was to remind people of the Holocaust; this role gave his life meaning.

For Alford, society and culture ideally provide symbolic resources that enable people to manifest their experience of dread in a harmless way. Symbolic expressions of dread allow people to give form to their dread and so limit the expression of their evil. The symbolic process allows the dread to be formed and reformed by an image. Alford uses the example of Picasso's 1937 painting *Guernica*, representing the carnage done by Franco's bombing of a Spanish village during the Spanish Civil War. Alford quotes Mary Gedo, one of Picasso's biographers, who says that Picasso had experienced an earthquake when he was 3 years old that coincided with the birth of his sister, and he believed he was responsible for the earth shaking because of his rage at her birth. This rage had been re-kindled in his domestic life just before he painted *Guernica*. Thus, the painting combines the private and public into a new symbol. Such symbols and narratives provide the forms within which we can contain dread; we can then organize our experience into categories that can be symbolized. Murderers and rapists are stuck in their bodies, more likely to physically inflict unbearable feelings on others than to put these feelings into words. The capacity to imagine doing evil to others is an alternative to doing evil. Ideally, we can project our dread into cultural symbols such as words or media rather than into the bodies of victims.

Alford suggests that evil is attractive because it is about the transgression of boundaries and the violation of taboos. Ricoeur (1967) also describes evil as a loss of boundaries between inside and outside, producing dread and horror. He too suggests that the primordial experience of evil is an experience of dread. However, Levine (2000) criticized Alford on the grounds that it is too reductive to account for all evil in terms of dread; there are many other ways of accounting for it. Levine points out that reductive accounts of evil, like the psychoanalytic and the religious (evil as disobedience to God), are attractive but simplistic, because evil has many causes. Evil might be the result of fear rather than dread, or it may occur because of other psychological, physiological, and social problems. In response, Alford (2001) says that his was a phenomenological study of the way in which people *use* the term "evil," what the word means to them.

Predatory identity

Prince (2016) uses the notion of predatory identity to discuss evil. He points out that although identity is no longer a popular subject of psychoanalytic study, because it is seen as a superficial or conscious level of the mind, identity has a major influence on life and relationships. People are motivated by identity based on race, religion, nationality, and ethnicity, which form important components of our belief systems, which in turn help to organize the sense of self. Group membership, belonging, and affiliation are important components of identity, as Erikson (1950) pointed out. Group and individual identity are inextricably intertwined; the superego is formed through identification with group and family values, and superego lacunae may produce evil. Prince points out that even the most "absurd, extreme, and demonstrably false ideas" (2016, p. 109) persist in the face of contradictory evidence because they are intertwined with the dynamics of identity. (This mechanism may help to explain some of our contemporary political allegiances.) Thus, "the most hideous prejudices persist and justify horrific acts because they support identity" (ibid.). He notes that an identity based on an evil ideology, such as Nazism, may constitute a powerful way of making sense of the world, even though it does not correspond to reality.

Prince postulates that predatory identity directs itself against the other, or wants to destroy the identity of the other, and sustains itself by predation. Such an individual believes that he can only exist if he destroys the other person, or "my destruction of you is who I am." Predatory identity "may contain, express, or emanate from well-known dynamisms including sadism, malignant narcissism, and envy" (p. 112). Examples range from schoolyard bullying to racism. Other belief systems produce reactions ranging from rage to violent persecution of others. Examples of this kind of identity are people such as Josef Stalin, Pol Pot, Saddam Hussein, and a long list of similarly evil dictators. The relationship between such predatory leaders and their followers, and the reasons that these individuals become dominant, has been the subject of much debate. It may be that the leader is able to sense and evoke the unconscious needs of his followers because they are similar to his own. Prince believes that some predatory identity is defensive, a reaction to threats to identity or a repair of inadequate identity among narcissistically vulnerable individuals. The power to hurt others then shores up the perpetrator's sense of self.

Another way of discussing the issue of identity is to see it as a matter of identification with nation, religion, or ethnic group. Ordinary respect for these factors is not problematic, but overidentification can become so and is reinforced by governments with strategies such as vows of allegiance, national rituals, a mythic national history that ignores the society's shadow, and lies about other societies. Such intense identification predisposes people to in-group/out-group psychology. In particular, wars release our latent potential for predatory identity.

Notes

1 Rarely, children as young as 3 years old have been noted to be callous and unemotional, with lack of guilt and no capacity for empathy.
2 Fortunately, these instances are rare, but they happen. In 1993, in Liverpool, England, a 2-year-old boy, James Bulger, was abducted and murdered by two 10-year-old boys. Both of them were seriously emotionally disturbed children. Although most young murderers come from disturbed families, there remains the constant problem that not all young people who commit serious crimes have been abused, and not all children who have been abused commit crimes. The question of a genetic component to evil therefore remains (Heckel & Shumaker, 2001).
3 In a 1956 movie with this title, based on a novel by William March, an 8-year-old child who looks angelic and innocent turns out to be a cold-blooded, psychopathic killer. This was a "nature" rather than "nurture" account of evil, since the child seems to have inherited her evil nature from a grandmother who had been a serial killer.
4 This means, for example, that the fear of terrorism, and some kinds of overreaction to it such as the invasion of Iraq, is the result of our internal terrifying objects projected outwards onto a real enemy, thus magnifying the actual danger.
5 Parenthetically, he believes that the antonym of cruelty is not kindness but hospitality. It lies not simply in the absence of cruelty but in unsentimental, efficacious love.
6 Most writers today believe that human morality cannot be accounted for entirely in terms of superego or ego functioning. Moral dilemmas are more complex. Morality is said to have sources in evolution, culture, and brain structure.
7 Hutus in Rwanda killed 800,000 Tutsis in 1994, which the rest of the world did nothing to prevent.
8 The story is traditionally told as if the local Indians and the Pilgrims sat down for a happy meal together. The reality is that the Massachusetts Bay Colony declared a day of thanksgiving after English and Dutch mercenaries had brutally murdered hundreds of Indians. Other days of thanksgiving were declared when local Indian villages were repeatedly attacked, with the result that many Indians were sold into slavery or massacred.
9 The autistic-contiguous position (Ogden, 1989) is a primitive mode of being in which the contact of two skin surfaces creates the experience of one shared skin; the infant is unaware of where his surface ends and his mother's surface begins. This boundary is an experience of the other that is at the same time an experience of oneself. This position may transform into dread if the experience becomes an experience of loss of self; this anxiety is caused when the self feels as if it is dissolving into unbounded space. In this position, there is no symbolization; there is experience without boundary. The infant

attempts to organize and structure tactile sensations of the skin that constitute bounded surfaces. These tactile impressions at the skin surface constitute the earliest experience of the self and are forerunners of later internalized self- and object-representations. Failure to establish a secure, lasting sense of a bounded sensory contiguity leads in turn to pre-symbolic anxiety, involving the terror of "impending disintegration of one's sensory surface or one's 'rhythm of safety' resulting in the feeling of leaking, dissolving, disappearing, or falling into shapeless unbounded space" (ibid., p. 68). That is, a loss of boundaries occurs, or inside and outside are not distinct, which produces dread.

Chapter 5

Jung and Jungians on evil

Introduction: Jung's view of evil

Jung saw good and evil as a manifestation of "opposite poles of a moral judgment" that originates within human beings (CW 11, para. 247). He felt that we could not have one pole without the other; for him, good and evil are part of the inevitable tension of the opposites in the psyche. In his view, we call certain things good and evil based on our view of the world. This is often a subjective judgment, since we do not know the deepest qualities of good and evil, or what their essential natures are. If we think we know in advance whether something is good or not, we behave as if we are gods, but in fact we are limited; we do not always know what is good or evil in a given case. We form an opinion, but we don't know if it is valid. Ideas about morality vary with the culture one is in. We have to judge by the way something appears to us, and our values are relative, even though we cannot abstain from judgment. Because we only know the surface of things, the way they appear to us, we must be modest in our appraisal of them. Jung argues that human beings can never know when evil may be necessary to produce good; what at first appears to be evil may later prove to have been a positive force. An example is the Christian notion of the *felix culpa*;[1] we have to take into account such paradoxes, and see what the concrete situation demands.

Jung (CW 10) points out that the psychotherapist has to take an empirical attitude toward good and evil, hoping that we are correct in the individual case, realizing that we cannot always say what is good or bad for the individual. Something may be evil for a person at a certain time, while at another stage of development the same thing may be good for him. An apparently good thing at the wrong moment in the wrong place may turn out to be bad, just as what seems to be evil may later prove to be positive; we never know when evil is necessary to produce good. Perhaps the patient has to experience evil, and suffer accordingly, in order to make him change. Accordingly, Jung believes: "Often we cannot say in such situations how the problem of good and evil will work out. We have to put our trust in the higher powers" (CW 10, para. 883).

What we label as good or evil is often the result of our conditioning and preferences, determined by psychological and cultural factors. Sometimes the attribution of good or evil is really a way of making ourselves feel self-righteous, or it is a way of projecting our own shadow. Sometimes we need to struggle with evil for the sake of the development of the personality. Evil can exert a kind of secret attraction, presumably because it connects us with shadow aspects of ourselves or with depths of the soul with which we have lost contact. In *The Red Book*, Jung notes that a confrontation with the shadow may be necessary for psychological transformation because it dissolves the structures of the personality such as ego and persona, in a way that opens us to change. In fact, Frey-Rohn (1967, p. 185) believes that "there can be no self-realization without the experience of evil," and that recognizing the reality of evil is the first stage in establishing a relationship with the Self.[2] Facing evil may open the way to spiritual renewal or to higher levels of meaning.

Jung believed that the archetypes have the capacity for both good and evil. Because they have both a light and a dark side, they may produce positive or negative effects from the point of view of the ego. Jung warned that the ego must not identify with or too highly regard any archetype, and he did not advocate moral relativism. For him, moral evaluation is the concern and the responsibility of the ego; ethical behavior is the product of conscious reflection. Jung (CW 10) believed that we have two forms of conscience, or a sense of inner guidance about right and wrong. One corresponds to Freud's superego, which is internalized from the values of our family and culture, based on local notions of right and wrong. The other is the innate voice of the Self, part of the self-regulating function of the psyche that emerges spontaneously. This voice may at times conflict with the opinion of collective morality about what is right and wrong, and this tension is one of the eternal themes of literature and philosophy.

Jung on the *privatio boni*

Jung strongly criticizes the Christian idea of the *privatio boni*, which is the notion that evil is the absence of good and only has a relative existence, whereas good is something positive. (This idea is discussed further on p. 61) He says he came across this idea in a patient who was involved in morally dubious practices that the patient justified with this doctrine. Jung points out that if evil is not substantial, good cannot be substantial either, and if good is substantial, so must evil be (CW 11). Good and evil imply each other; one could not speak of good if there were no evil. He thinks that the attempt to deny the substantial reality of evil is apotropaic. He also thinks this doctrine is morally dangerous because it trivializes evil.

In Jung's view, the *privatio* doctrine gives a too-pessimistic view of the human soul. He thinks that Christianity wants to minimize the importance of evil by exclusively blaming humanity for evil, rather than acknowledging that the divine has a dark side. The doctrine probably began as a way of preserving the Christian idea that God is all-good. Jung thinks the doctrine is an attempt to save Christianity from dualism, or the Manichean idea that there could be two equal spiritual powers in the universe, one good and one evil. However, Jung believes that if

Christianity is to be truly monotheistic, all the opposites must be contained in its image of God, so we need a God-image that includes a dark side. Jung (CW 9, ii, para. 19) wrote of "absolute evil," which can be read to imply that there is a level of evil that is beyond its personal dimensions. In the Christian tradition, evil is given substance by lodging it in in the figure of the devil, but Jung notes that if evil is only a *privatio*, the devil too cannot be substantial.

Evil and the shadow

Jung's concept of the shadow is broad, with a range of meanings. The shadow can refer to the dark or evil side of the personality (CW 9, ii) or to positive aspects of the person that are not conscious or not claimed. The shadow is therefore not entirely evil; it may consist of aspects of the personality that are simply undeveloped or childish. The term *shadow* can also refer to the whole unconscious (von Franz, 1995).

Jung (2006) believes that neglect of the shadow opens the individual to becoming an instrument of evil, and he notes that "human nature is capable of an infinite amount of evil" (CW 9, ii, para. 97). He believed that Christianity tells us to eschew or suppress evil, but this only makes us try to drive it away like the scapegoat in the Hebrew Bible.[3] Instead, we have to come to terms with the shadow, and here there are a variety of strategies. We can try to suppress or repress the shadow by going along with collective morality, using willpower, but then the strength of the shadow tends to build up in the inner world. Preferably, the reality of the shadow must be acknowledged and accepted before it can be changed, which takes courage and often a grief process when we acknowledge this aspect of our nature. Jung recommends self-knowledge; he says that we must know how much good we can do and what crimes we are capable of; both are potential elements in us. He recommends that we become as conscious as possible of the shadow because consciousness allows the shadow to have less hold over us. We can try to integrate the shadow where possible, so that we do not project it. Integration means for example that aggression becomes appropriate assertiveness, vulnerability becomes sensitivity to others, or the drive for power becomes reasonable ambition. Such integration may indeed transform the shadow. However, in practice, the notion of the integration of the shadow can be problematic, for various reasons. The shadow often cannot be integrated because it is affectively too intense, and then the best one can do is to depotentiate it. We might try to develop an opposite quality to a shadow problem, such as humility instead of arrogance, or it may be possible to try to soften the shadow by depriving it of some of its emotional intensity, which may happen if one becomes conscious of it. We can also sublimate the shadow, as in the case of the surgeon who sublimates his sadism and aggression into a healing vocation. In the end, we may have to give up the need to be only good and allow the shadow a certain right to live in us. Neumann (1990) speaks about the ego entering into a kind of "gentleman's agreement" with the shadow, as opposed to trying to be perfect. A degree of empathy for and understanding of oneself is required, and people who suffer from self-hatred must learn to value themselves instead of castigating themselves for having a shadow. Humor is helpful; to make fun of our shadow loosens it a little and takes some of the shame out of it. Often, when we laugh at jokes we are acknowledging the shadow element that the joke depicts. I should point out, however, that it is not necessarily true that consciousness of the shadow prevents one from acting it out or projecting it. Not surprisingly therefore, when trying to help an individual with a shadow problem, Jung admits that there may be:

> nothing I can do except wait, with a certain trust in God, until out of a conflict borne with patience and fortitude, there emerges the solution destined – although I cannot foresee it – for that particular person. Not that I am passive or inactive meanwhile: I help the patient to understand all the things that the unconscious produces during the conflict.
>
> (CW 12, para. 37)

To use the word *shadow* is to paint with a very broad brush, without providing all the details we need to understand it. As noted, the shadow may be thought of as the whole unconscious, but even if we restrict it to discrete problems such as envy and hatred, the relational and developmental sources of these difficulties and their therapeutic management are very complex. What we call the shadow in its negative aspect overlaps with negatively toned complexes that are hateful, destructive, sadistic, abusive, and so on. To understand such a complex fully, we need both Jungian theory and some kind of detailed personalistic or psychoanalytic theory. Jung's work is essential for recognizing the archetypal core of the complex, and relational theory is helpful for understanding how the human shell of the complex developed.

The archetypal core of the complex may be positive or negative; the fact that the dark side of the archetype is so numinous helps to explain the gripping power of evil that results from complexes that form the shadow. We see mythological representations of archetypal evil in dreams, in the form of figures such as demons or vampires. The collective shadow manifests itself as either an evil leader or a mass phenomenon such as Nazism.

Neumann's new ethic

Neumann (1990) pointed out that whereas traditional ethical systems based on Judeo-Christian teachings were once the source of moral behavior, these systems now fail to contain or transform human evil. This was clearly the case at the time Neumann's *Depth Psychology and a New Ethic* was first published in 1949. The world had just seen a terrible war and persecution, which the traditional ethical system had not prevented. Neumann therefore believed that the traditional Judeo-Christian ethic is incapable of dealing with human destructiveness. Something new is needed, and Neumann thought that a depth psychological approach to ethics would be an improvement.

Neumann says that the traditional ethical system depends on repression, suppression, sacrifice, asceticism, projection, and scapegoat mechanisms. The individual is therefore split between ego and shadow, and society is split between an ethical elite and those who are unable to conform to its standards. In contrast, according to Neumann, the new ethic, based in depth psychology, encompasses human wholeness because it takes into account the unconscious. The new ethic acknowledges the shadow without trying to repress it. In fact, acceptance of one's own shadow is the essential basis for the development of an ethical attitude towards others.

We have a subliminal awareness, according to Neumann, that we are not good enough. If we consciously reject or repress forbidden impulses or the negative aspects of the personality, we lose touch with these parts of ourselves and so lose control of them. The negative shadow material then functions independently of consciousness and becomes more primitive. Disowned contents may then be released in a demonic way, or they are projected onto an outside enemy or a scapegoat. It is preferable to recognize and accept aspects of the personality that do not conform to our overall ethical standards, containing them as much as possible.

Neumann thinks that in the collective the new ethic appears as a concern with social evil, and in the individual the new ethic appears as the responsibility for consciousness to come to terms with the unconscious. The new ethic requires us to become conscious of the evil within ourselves, in our relationships, and in our social roles. Each person must be conscious of his or her own darkness and live it consciously. The new ethic is therefore very individual, and one cannot evade it by becoming part of a collective or by following a leader.

The new ethic presupposes that the person is moral by the standards of the old ethic. Neumann says that only a person who is loyal to the values of the old ethic is in a position to live the new ethic. (Here he seems to want to have it both ways.) In Jung's foreword to Neumann's book, Jung says that the new ethic is a development or differentiation within the old ethic, and at the moment it is confined to uncommon individuals who try to bring conscious and the unconscious into a responsible relationship. This implies that a new type of ethical elite will develop. An interesting comment appears in the preface to the Spanish edition of Neumann's book (p. 21):

> One of the main lines of argument in this little book has been the attempt to establish the necessity for a hierarchical ethic – that is to show that for men with different types of psychological make-up, different types of ethic are appropriate.

Accordingly, different psychological types require different ethics, but a conscious relationship to the shadow is the essential common factor.

The dark side of the self

Jung maintains that the Self is an *a priori* intrapsychic image of God, or an expression of the divine in the psyche. We do not know how that image relates to the divine itself, or to the transcendent God of theology, but the Self "constitutes the most immediate experience of the divine which it is psychologically possible to imagine" (CW 11, para. 396). Jung believes that the Self must contain all the opposites, including justice and injustice, good and evil, masculine and feminine, because the Self is the totality of the psyche. Many characters in the Hebrew Bible, such as the biblical Job, experience divine savagery and ruthlessness, and their experience is a mythic paradigm for the human experience of the dark side of the Self.

Jung emphasizes the difference between the psychological *experience* of the Self, which includes a dark side that causes evil and suffering, and traditional Christian doctrine in which Christ is only good and evil is split off and projected onto the Antichrist or Satan. The ego experiences the dark side of the Self, or the archetypal shadow, as unfathomable destruction, chaos, physical or mental suffering, negative synchronicities, and evil – much more than just an absence. This form of archetypal evil cannot be integrated or treated in the therapeutic sense; at best, it can only be held at bay or coped with. Here we are talking about events such as the Holocaust, which is certainly an example of human evil but also raises major questions about the relationship between evil and the divine. This kind of questioning has arisen before. The Lisbon earthquake of 1755 killed tens of thousands of people and forced a radical re-thinking of the problem of evil in relation to the divine. In our era, the Holocaust is one of the events that forces us to the realization of a new God-image, because an all-good God-image can no longer be sustained. Here, Jung's notion of the dark side of the Self becomes important. This idea has the advantage of approaching the problem of evil psychologically and spiritually at the same time.

The Self is not only the principle of order in the psyche; it may produce suffering that is beyond human understanding. At these times, one often has to accept uncertainty and persevere in patience without trying to control or explain what is happening. This requires both faith and a sacrifice on the part of the ego, or a process of radical acceptance. We have to decide to live despite our suffering at the hands of the Self, as we try to relate to its dark side. This does not mean acceptance in an attempt to change the situation, which would not be true acceptance; it means acceptance based on the realization that what is brought about by the Self is a necessary part of our lives. We thereby acknowledge our connection to the transpersonal dimension and our participation with it. What this might mean is that it is therapeutic to live in harmony with one's fate, in accord with the *telos* of the personality.[4] In this view, the suffering produced by the dark side of the Self forces us in a direction that we would otherwise not take but that is essential. Healing may sometimes require that we consciously accept a difficult destiny. Needless to say, such acceptance does not mean abandoning personal responsibility or avoiding necessary action; it means that the action arises from acceptance rather than from anger or bitterness. As Jung says (CW 11), rather than trying to escape the sense of being attacked by God, one has to allow oneself to be affected by the Self so that in knowing it one may transform its violence into further knowledge of the Self, as Job had to do.

If Jung is correct to insist that the Self has a dark side, evil is more than purely human. The evil that results from the dark side of the Self is therefore a spiritual problem. However, a major drawback of the concept of the dark side of the Self is that it mythologizes evil and reduces our ability to understand it. We face serious difficulties if we have to contend with a God-image that includes evil, including the moral implications that would result. This idea undermines morality if the wish to align with the divine means we can align with its dark side, and thereby legitimize evil. As well, we don't know what aspects of scripture or which commandments were given by the dark side of the divine. This notion leaves open the question of God's total righteousness, which is so central to the monotheistic traditions, which would have to radically re-evaluate their theology and liturgy that insists on the exclusive goodness of God.

The notion of the dark side of God has other doctrinal implications, for example in relation to the notion of a Trinitarian God. Jung (CW 11; CW 12) believes that the unconscious uses the quarternity, an image with a four-fold structure, as the best symbol of wholeness. He therefore tends to see the Christian trinity as an imperfect symbol of wholeness (CW 12; CW 9, ii). One solution to this would be to add the dark side of the Self to the trinity, producing a quarternity.[5] Importantly, however, Jung often admits that we can know nothing about the divine nature, so that even though he believes that empirically the Self often assumes quaternary symbolism in the psyche, this structure may not apply to the divine itself. Jung also wants to incorporate the feminine aspects of the divine, and matter, into the Self, which would produce an impasse if he insists that the Self must have a quaternary structure.

Not surprisingly, the notion of the dark side of the Self is controversial. But it is consonant with many mythologies that describe opposing light and dark divinities, such as Set and Osiris in Egyptian mythology, Loki and Baldur in Norse mythology, or Ahriman and Ahura-Mazda in Zoroastrianism. The dark side of the God-image is well known in the Hebrew Bible, for example when Amos (3:6) says that evil does not befall a city unless the Lord wills it. Proverbs (16:4) says that God has "made all things for himself, even the wicked for the day of evil," and Isaiah (45:7) tells us that God both makes peace and creates evil. Jeremiah (28:8) says that God's judgment will take the form of war, famine, and pestilence. Here, God is clearly a warrior who promotes military destruction, and defeat in battle is a reflection of the wrath of God. We also see Christians who admit that the divine has a dark side, who agree for example that the handiwork of God can be seen in the atomic bomb (Garrison, 1983). However, the idea of the dark side of the divine is antithetical to the more traditional Christian insistence that God is only good and loving. For example: "God is light and in him there is no darkness" (1 John, 1:5).

Jung recognized that the dark side of the Christian God-image appears in the form of the avenging angels of the book of Revelation, but collectively Christianity has tended to ignore the dark aspect of the God-image. However, the dark side of the Self cannot be repressed. Perhaps its effects can be tempered by a conscious personality or a conscious society, but we cannot eliminate the suffering produced by the dark side of the Self, and there is not always a resurrection following a crucifixion. One has to find a way to live with the divine darkness that causes suffering, and relate to it, which may allow peace rather than the sense of being a victim.

The very notion that the divine has a dark side that is responsible for evil is frightening. But divine darkness may not mean evil in the sense of a moral defect in the divine nature itself; it may simply mean that suffering is caused by the ways in which the divine nature manifests itself to us. If categories such as light and dark do not apply to the divine, we may be merely dealing with the projection of the human shadow onto the divine by attributing a dark side to it.

In the debate about why God allows suffering and evil, the view from process theology suggests that God is not really in control of everything that happens; although God is on the side of goodness and hates evil, he cannot always stop evil – he is not in fact omnipotent. However, this approach, and that of Jung, both have problems; one might not wish to worship a less-than-omnipotent God or a dark God.

If there is an archetypal shadow, or a dark side of the Self, it is not clear whether it could be affected by human consciousness. If Neumann's concept of the ego-Self axis is correct, we might be able to develop a relationship to it, or perhaps by becoming conscious of the personal shadow we might actually redeem a fragment of the transpersonal shadow that is incarnate within the individual human personality. But that is a metaphysical proposition; what matters in practice is whether the personality can contain and relate to the dark level of the Self. One can think of emotional disorder as the result of the difficulty that the ego has in relating to the dark side of the Self.

Here we must be humble and conscious of the intensity of the numinous energies involved; identification with or possession by the dark side of the Self may lead to great evil. The inflation produced by identification with the archetype is very dangerous, as we see among all historical demagogues. There is also a human dimension to this feeling of being very special; it may either be due to untempered infantile grandiosity, or it may occur as a defense against being hated or envied. Grandiosity may arise as a defense against narcissistic vulnerability and shame produced by relational traumas in childhood, leading to narcissistic character pathology. Such grandiose characters often commit evil, as discussed in Chapter 4. From an archetypal perspective, these dynamics allow the incarnation of the dark side of the Self into the empirical personality in the form of the human shadow and dangerous complexes. The important implication of this process is that archetypal evil cannot be fully realized without the complicity of human evil, and only the human moral sense stands in its way.

If the Self has a dark side, evil is more than only human malevolence. Does that mean that evil has a kind of ontological essence to it that is independent of human beings? Evil would then be an *a priori* archetypal potential that may or may not be realized in an individual's life. Perhaps the childhood environment determines whether the light or dark side of the archetype incarnates in us. In a childhood full of abuse and pain, evil is more likely to incarnate, because the personality is full of rage, envy, and other destructive emotions. These live within the personality in the form of negatively toned complexes; their archetypal core is a fragment of the dark side of the Self.

Evil, suffering, and the transformation of Job's shadow

Almost by definition, evil results in suffering. Evil and suffering are so intimately related that we often cannot tease them apart. Their relationship is nicely illustrated within the biblical book of Job, in which an apparently innocent and pious man suffers undeservedly, partly as a result of natural evil when a storm kills his children, and partly as a result of human evil when marauding robbers steal his flocks. The important point is that all this occurs with divine approval. In his *Answer to Job*, Jung believes this story indicates the need for the canonical God-image to change, since the suffering and evil that Job experiences emanates from the dark side of the divine.

On closer examination of the story, we see that Job had distinctly narcissistic traits in his personality (Corbett, 2012). He was spiritually asleep and rather smug. Jung's analysis, however, focuses on the transformation of the canonical God-image and ignores the personal level of the story, which depicts the way in which Job's narcissistic shadow is transformed by his suffering. This transformation leads to the development of authentic compassion and empathy for the poor. It is therefore possible that what Job went through was a form of the dark night of the soul, leading to necessary spiritual transformation. In that case, from a teleological point of view, what seems to be transpersonal evil, or the dark side of the Self, may produce transformative suffering that plays a part in the individuation process.

Evil, suffering, and the incarnation of the self in the complex

Jung believes that the Self forms a kind of blueprint or archetypal basis for the development of the personality. During development, the archetypal potentials that act as deep structures within the personality gradually embody themselves and become humanized within the empirical personality. In this way, the potentials of the Self are increasingly lived out in time and space. Jung believed that this process of incarnation inevitably involves suffering; the individual suffers "from the violence done to him by the Self" (CW 11, para. 233). However, this incarnation is a necessary part of the individuation process. As Edinger (1973, p. 153) puts it, we may "recognize experiences of weakness and failure as manifestations of the suffering God striving for incarnation."

The mechanisms by which the archetype incarnates are important in understanding human suffering and evil. One way the Self incarnates is in the form of the emotion or affect associated with a complex. Complexes cause suffering and evil when their emotional tone is painful and negative. Complexes are always affectively laden, and emotion is felt in the body, so the complex incarnates or embodies itself in the form of the emotion associated with the complex. At the core of the complex lies an archetype, so that when the complex is activated, the archetype associated with it also embodies. This is why Jung (CW 11) says that suffering is the ego's experience of the incarnation of the Self during the individuation process. This suffering forces us to a new consciousness of the Self, as Job discovered, and this new consciousness is itself a form of incarnation. The process of the incarnation of the Self is continuous throughout our lives.

The complexes that form the personal shadow, with their archetypal core, represent the incarnation of a fragment of the archetypal shadow, or a fragment of the Self. The archetypal source of evil therefore lies beyond the personal psyche, since it arises from the dark side of the Self, but it is up to the individual human to wrestle with it. We may incarnate more or less of the dark side of the Self, depending on how we deal with the personal shadow. The complexes that form the shadow, problems such as envy or hatred, have an archetypal core, but whether the archetype manifests its positive or negative aspects depends on developmental, cultural, or other human factors that form the human shell of the complex.

Evil behavior is often driven by a complex. Most of us have occasional impulses that could be damaging or hurtful to others or to ourselves. Our therapeutic task is to understand the dynamics that give rise to these difficulties and find ways they can be contained or redeemed without being acted out. Because complexes may be associated with unbearably painful affects such as rage, depression, or envy, the issue of working with the shadow is connected to the individual's capacity to contain painful affects, and this development is an important function of psychotherapy. Children need help containing painful affects in order to develop the capacity for self-regulation of intense affect, and if this is not achieved, it is harder to restrain shadow material, and the dark side of the archetype is then more likely to incarnate. Since the Self has a dark and a light side, when the Self incarnates into a human being, that person is presented with a conflict of good and evil, and only the human capacity for consciousness and discrimination can resolve this conflict.

To illustrate how both human and archetypal factors combine to produce evil, I'd like to use a biblical example of possession by an emotionally overwhelming shadow complex containing an element of the dark side of the Self. This is the story of King Saul and David (1 Sam. 18:10). When David defeated Goliath, Saul had an attack of envy and paranoid rage, as a result of which he threw a spear at

David, because "an evil spirit from God rushed upon Saul." This description of an evil spirit represents an experience of the dark side of the Self; it is the archetypal core of the complex that made Saul envious. But difficulties such as envy and rage can also be understood at the ordinary human level; Saul was narcissistically vulnerable; he was afraid that David was becoming too popular because of his victory over Goliath. Envy is a toxic and often unconscious state of mind that wants to destroy the goodness it feels it cannot have. This state of mind often begins by comparing oneself with others, leading to shame and feelings of inferiority, combined with the sense that the gap between the individual and the envied one is unbridgeable. Developmental difficulties in childhood contribute to the human shell of such a complex. Chronic rage resulting from early abuse or severe frustration of a child's needs may harden into a complex that becomes permanent structure within the personality, turning into intense hatred or the wish to destroy. These affects are so intense that the incarnation of the dark side of the Self within a human being leads to evil that is often beyond the ego's ability to control.

An entire society may be subject to possession by a complex with an archetypal core based on the society's mythology. Jung's essay on Wotan[6] (CW 10) suggests that social and historical conditions in 1930s Germany were such that this hitherto dormant archetypal image was able to surface, generating irrational enthusiasm for war. Jung believed that the population was possessed by this archetype, such that their normal judgment was in abeyance, leading to large-scale evil.

Can the self be unconscious of itself?

Jung suggests that the Self consists of a "*complexio oppositorum*" (CW 11, para. 1640), a mixture of opposite qualities, which include good and evil. The Self is therefore not wholly good, but it is not fully conscious of the opposites within its own nature, so that sometimes the Self behaves lovingly and sometimes tyrannically. Since the Self is not aware of these internal opposites within itself, it is amoral. According to Jung, the Self requires the reflecting consciousness of a human being for the Self to become aware of the opposites within its own nature, and even to know that it exists. Therefore, Jung believes that the Self needs to incarnate in human beings in order to become conscious: "God becomes conscious in the act of human reflection" (CW 11, para. 238). Jung points out that Yahweh's unconsciousness of his own dark side became a problem for Job. Job had to accept this burden, and by standing his ground Job rendered Yahweh the service of making him conscious of his dark side by acting as a reflecting consciousness for the divine. Not until Christ experienced the suffering of the crucifixion did God fully realize what it feels like to be mortal and what suffering he put Job through.

This is an area in which it is important to make Jung's distinction between the Self as a God-image and the divine itself. Jung believes that the Self (qua image) is unconscious of its own dark side and needs human consciousness to become conscious of its own shadow. However, Jung often writes as if he is talking about the divine itself, not just its image, and he is often understood by writers such as Edinger (1973) to mean that the divine itself is unconscious. I find this idea of an unconscious God very problematic, since I do not think we can distinguish between the divine and its expression in the psyche. Jung believes that we cannot distinguish between the manifestations of the unconscious and the experience of the divine, and in practice many Jungians use the term *psyche* as a God-term. So, to say that the divine consciousness needs something extra to become conscious is rather like saying that the sun needs light to allow it to shine. I cannot see how we could distinguish between the psyche and consciousness. I prefer to think of Jung's notion of an unconscious God as a reference to the fact that the Self may be in an unconscious condition within the individual – the ego is then unconscious of the Self – rather than seeing the Self as unconscious of itself or as unaware of its own internal antinomies. In several Eastern non-dual traditions, the divine, whether referred to as the Self, the Atman, or the Purusha, is *identical* with pure Consciousness, so it cannot be unconscious of itself. The notion of the unconscious would only be true from the ego's perspective, not from the perspective of the Self. I would therefore dispute the notion that the Self needs a reflecting human consciousness to make it more conscious of itself.

Jung believed that consciousness and the unconscious form a totality, which is a non-dual approach to consciousness (Corbett & Whitney, 2016). From the non-dual point of view, archetypal images arise from pure Consciousness, which is the level beyond name and form. The dark side of the Self is simply part of this totality. From this non-dual perspective, whatever happens is a manifestation of the Self. Evil is then a part of what-is, an aspect of reality that is unpleasant for us because it causes suffering. The Self simply is what it is, while good and evil are human value judgments.

Jung's complex

Jung admits that his *Answer to Job* is a purely subjective reaction to what happened to Job, which he says produces a "shattering emotion" because of the "unvarnished spectacle of divine savagery and ruthlessness" (CW 11, para. 713). Jung believes that statements about God are based on psychological processes, so we might ask what processes in Jung account for his intense emotional reaction to the story of Job? What clues do we have to answer this question? In a letter (1975, p. 112), Jung says that the book was "a drama that was not mine to control." Writing to Henri Corbin, he says that the book came during the fever of an illness; it "came to me . . . as if accompanied by the great music of a Bach or a Handel. . . . I just had the feeling of listening to a great composition" (ibid., p. 116.). In a letter to Aniela Jaffe in July 1951, he says: "If there is anything like the spirit seizing one by the scruff of the neck, it was the way this book came into being" (ibid., p. 20). Jung's sense of being possessed, and his emotional reactions in the book, are so intense that it seems he wrote it in the grip of a complex, and he interprets what happened to Job through the lens of this complex. Which complex? In a letter of 1955 (ibid., p. 257), he says that he saw his father "cracking up before my eyes on the problem of his faith and dying an early death." In *Memories*, he says that his father had a wound that would not heal, and as a child Jung was a witness of this sickness, and speech failed him. It was obviously very painful for him to see his father suffer so much. I suggest that Jung was influenced by his father complex as he writes *Answer to Job*, because just as Job is angry with God, so Jung is angry with God about his father's struggle with his faith and the lack of help from God. We see Jung's anger throughout the text, for example when he accuses God of cruelly needing a human sacrifice in the form of Jesus in order to appease him. This would not be the usual Christian understanding of Jesus's sacrifice; it's a bitter interpretation of the story.

Jung describes a primitive, brutal, unconscious image of God that has to evolve by incarnating in human beings, which he needs in order to become conscious of his own shadow. Jung always insists that our God-image is only subjective, but here he formulates a God-image that he believes to be generally true. He often says he is talking about the God-image rather than the divine itself, but he attacks this image as if he were speaking about an actual being. Several authors (e.g., Weisstub, 1993) have pointed out that Jung becomes God's analyst who is more conscious than God.

Although Jung admits he was seized by intense emotion when writing this book, he does not analyze these emotions – he does not analyze the source of his transference to the material he is discussing. Furthermore, by projecting the whole problem onto God, he ignores Job's obvious narcissistic shadow;[7] before his tragedy, Job was too morally self-righteous or pious in a pretentious way, as William Blake pointed out (Raine, 1982). The figure of Satan at the beginning of the story, who accuses Job of not being as pious as he seems, seems to represent the personification of Job's internal self-doubt. However, Jung ignores all Job's personal material and instead focuses on God's shadow.

Other people have noticed this omission. Victor White (1959) asked whether we can transfer our personal problems to the archetypal level and ignore our personal psychology, as if Jungians are so possessed by the archetypes that they ignore ordinary psychology. In response, Jung (1975) acknowledges White's insinuation that Jung is ignoring Job's shadow by appealing to the archetypal level. Jung acknowledges that, according to personalistic theory, appeals to the archetypes are only an escape and camouflage. Jung says that we can assume that Job is neurotic with a lack of insight, and he undergoes a kind of analysis by listening to the counsel of his friend Elihu, but all he would hear from such an analysis is his own shadow material and not the divine voice. The shadow is the block that separates us from the divine voice. However, Jung says, if Job has his shadow analyzed, he would be deeply ashamed of what has happened, he would accuse himself of complacency and self-righteousness and assume that this is what brought disaster down on him. He would realize that he has ignored his own shortcomings and instead accused God. He would then despair, feel inferior, and have to repent. He may even doubt his sanity to think that his vanity had caused divine interference. Jung goes on to say that after such an analysis Job would be less inclined than ever to think he heard the divine voice. To see himself only in terms of personal psychodynamics would end in disillusionment and resignation. In other words, Jung says that to focus on Job's shadow is a dead end, but the hypothesis of the archetypes is an answer to the problem of the shadow because looking at the material archetypally is better than despair and resignation and truer than rationalization. That is, it was more important for Job to listen to the voice of God or to the archetypal level than to have his personal shadow analyzed. However, it is indeed possible to avoid the personal shadow by defensively focusing on archetypal material, and there is no reason we cannot look at both levels – in fact, that combination is part of the value of Jung's psychology.

In a review of *Answer to Job*, White (1955) accuses Jung of having an immature reaction to God's apparent injustice to Job, as if Jung was having a temper tantrum about it, thereby concealing his grief and resentment. Although White is exaggerating because of his own annoyance at Jung, White clearly senses that Jung is writing out of a complex. White is responding in part to Jung's arrogance in accusing God. White may realize that Jung may be projecting the shadow of humanity onto his God-image when he accuses God of being amoral, ruthless, and lacking in compassion. Instead of protesting that God must change, surely humanity must change to make sure that the innocent stop suffering. Worrying about making God more conscious is not our problem.

Finally, it is important to remember that Jung's notion that the God-image is evolving only says something about the God-image in the psyche, or our understanding of the divine; it says nothing about the nature of the divine itself. As I noted earlier, although Jung often makes this distinction, he seems to forget it at times as he writes *Answer to Job*. For many of us, the notion that the human ego is somehow equal or superior in its consciousness to the divine consciousness is ludicrous on its face and does not bear scrutiny, which is why I suggest that a reasonable reading of Jung's notion of an unconscious God would say that the God-image in us is in an unconscious condition. We do become more conscious of it, for example as we experience God-images in dreams – a process that Jung refers to as the transformation of God. He writes that as we penetrate further and further into the unconscious, we are going to contact "spheres of a not yet transformed God" (1975, vol. 2, p. 314). Even in this letter it is not clear whether he is talking about the God-image or the divine itself. I think the idea of the transformation of God is important only if it refers to the evolution of the God-image. We do not know if the archetype itself evolves, or whether only its collective and personal image evolves. The divine itself may be unchanging, as traditional theology insists, or it may be evolving in the way suggested by process theology, but there is no doubt that it is time for our collective God-image to evolve.

Evil in fairy tales

It is axiomatic in Jungian psychology that myths and fairy tales reveal both the dynamics of the psyche and a response to typical human situations, and indeed these stories offer a range of suggestions about coping with evil. Von Franz (1967, p. 83–120) even claims that most fairy tales "hinge on the struggle between good and evil" (p. 85), because these stories tend to have black and white, good and evil oppositions, although within the hero there is no conflict. Fairy tale protagonists are rigid and unchanging, each personifying a particular archetypal quality such as kindness, malice, courage, or cowardice. Evil is usually punished by destruction, or it is driven away with supernatural assistance. The evil principle often condemns or does away with itself at the end of the story.

Based on her study of both fairy tales and dreams, von Franz concludes that the unconscious has a form of morality, but the ethics of the unconscious are highly contextual; they are not about justice as much as they are about appropriateness. Fairy tales contain a natural morality; they are not about action as much as they are about process. Accordingly, one cannot discover general rules of conduct from fairy tales. What rescues the hero or heroine from evil varies from one situation to another. According to von Franz, the right action in a given context might be "courage, flight, naiveté, guile, kindness, hardness, pious gravity, or frivolity" (1967, p. 92) or some combination of these. As a result, von Franz suggests that, in addition to becoming attuned to one's conscience, the process of moral development involves learning to value two types of morality: the rule-oriented morality of collective consciousness and the context-oriented morality of the collective unconscious.

Kast (1992) also shows that fairy tales exhibit a variety of ways of dealing with evil, and she contends that they all offer hope if one can find the right approach, which is the hero's task. Based on a range of folkloric approaches to evil, Kast believes that it is fundamental to respect the power of evil and acknowledge one's fear of it, allowing it a place in one's life. One might be able to hold one's ground against evil, but when the adversary is stronger than the ego's capacity to cope with it, one might have to distance oneself from evil with no attempt at rapprochement. At times, combat or trickery might be required. When dealing with evil, it helps if one knows and accepts one's own evil, which allows empathy into the strategy of the adversary.

Notes

1 The phrase *felix culpa* means "happy fault"; in Christian theology, it refers to the Fall of Adam, which eventually brought goodness to humanity in the form of Christ.
2 I am choosing to capitalize the word Self to distinguish it from the personal self, as understood in personalistic theories such as psychoanalytic self-psychology.
3 In the book of Leviticus, the sins of the people are loaded onto a goat that is banished into the desert, symbolically removing these sins.

4 Jung believes that the personality has a *telos*, or goal towards which it is developing. The major events of our lives move us in that direction.

5 However, in other places, such as his essay on the Trinity (CW 11), he refers to the Trinity as an image of three stages of a historical developmental process that is complete in itself, with no need for the addition of a fourth. To reconcile this difference, Edinger (1973) suggests that the symbol of quarternity represents the psyche in its structural, static sense, while the trinity symbol expresses a dynamic, developing aspect of the psyche. In dreams and religious imagery such as the mandalas of Tibetan Buddhism, quarternities represent stability. Trinitarian imagery is associated with creative movement and opposites united by a third factor.

6 Wotan or Odin was an ancient Germanic god of war and frenzy as well as wisdom and healing.

7 I'm referring here for example to Chapter 29 of *The Book of Job*, in which Job gives a long list of how rich and important he was, and how he was revered in the community. Self-importance is a particular impediment to spirituality.

Chapter 6

Biological factors that predispose to evil

Evil from the viewpoints of evolutionary biology and evolutionary psychology

Evolutionary biology assumes a biological basis for human behavior. This field assumes that we can explain behavior by understanding the ways in which our species adapted to changing conditions over the course of our evolution. Behavior that has survived must have had adaptive value for the species in the Darwinian sense – it promoted survival in a competitive environment. In this vein, Jonason et al. (2012) suggest that narcissism, psychopathy, and Machiavellianism – often seen as the dark side of human nature – are not necessarily inherently maladaptive, because these personality traits can confer reproductive and survival benefits for the individual. These traits are moderately correlated with each other, and they have in common disagreeableness, dishonesty, aggressiveness, and a short-term mating style. Such individuals have a life strategy based on immediate rewards and gratification, often combined with impulsivity. From the point of view of evolutionary biology, these traits may be maintained in the population if they accrue some benefits; they evolved to enable tactical exploitation of the environment and of other people.

Evolutionary psychology evolved out of evolutionary biology. Evolutionary psychologists suggest that human nature, based on our brain architecture, evolved to solve problems of adaptation to the environment in which our earliest hominid ancestors developed. This field assumes that the brain evolved systems for behavior such as kinship, mating, and coalitions with others (Tooby & Cosmides, 2005), and these systems developed to cope with selection pressures in early hominid hunter-gatherer societies.

Evolutionary psychology tries to explain social evils in a variety of ways. For example, war is said to have evolved as a result of a crisis of resources produced by population growth (Henson, 2006). Some evolutionary psychologists suggest that natural selection has produced behaviors that are crimes in our society, such as assault, murder, rape, and theft. These strategies can be traced back to conflicts among our hominid ancestors; they may have originally given some individuals an advantage when competing for the scarce resources needed for reproduction (Duntley & Shackelford, 2008).

Evolutionary theory suggests that human social and cognitive programs began to evolve during the Pleistocene age, about 2.5 million to 11,500 years ago, and *Homo sapiens* appeared about 150,000 years ago. During the Paleolithic or Old Stone Age period, our ancestors lived in small, nomadic groups of up to 200 people, many of whom were closely related. Although our modern culture is very different from theirs, our brain is thought to be not so different, so there is a "misfit" between our brain structure and modern life, and hence arise some of our societal problems (Hamilton, 2008). This idea is said to explain human evil because it bases human irrationality within our evolutionary history. For example, Friedman and colleagues (2012) use ideas from evolutionary psychology to explain child murder, which may have evolved in response to some of the adaptive pressures of our evolutionary past, when resources were too scarce to care for all the children in a group.

Many writers question this biological approach, which is based on gene-centered thinking and the notion of an innate, biological basis for human nature. Hall (2012) points out that biological explanations of human nature advantage certain people in terms of race, gender, and sexual privilege. She believes that the turn to biology in the humanities, especially towards evolutionary biology, constitutes an "epistemology of ignorance" that "contributes to a climate of hostility and intolerance regarding feminist insights about gender, identity, and the body" (p. 30). Hall points out that although a scientific or evolutionary explanation of human nature is possible, that does not mean it is the best or most accurate explanation.

Evolutionary biology has been criticized on many other grounds. It is possible that there has in fact been an evolution of the brain in the last 11,000 years, due to the development of agriculture and industry, so that modern brains may actually be different from those of the Paleolithic period. Furthermore, the human capacity for culture may be more important than evolutionary pressures. Evolutionary explanations of behavior have to speculate about conditions in the past and the nature of selective environmental pressures on our early hominid ancestors. We have no idea of their forms of communication or their social organization or the specific ecological problems they faced (Richardson, 2007).

The basic assumption that underlies sociobiology seems to be that the main reason for our existence is to perpetuate our genes, so our most persistent social behavior is ultimately related to its reproductive advantages during human evolution. This notion is debatable for many reasons, such as its assumption that we can generalize from animal behavior to human behavior, which is much more complex psychologically and culturally. Evolutionary psychology assumes that human beings have evolved sexual strategies that are mainly designed to enhance reproductive success; in this account, all evolutionary selection is based on sexual selection, and the most important motivation of all social behavior is reproduction and maximizing the number of one's offspring. For example, there is a controversial evolutionary psychological explanation for rape as a reproductive strategy, since it was said to increase men's reproductive success among our early ancestors (Apostolou, 2013). However, this belief cannot be tested or falsified, and this is a typical criticism. Furthermore, it may well be that factors other than reproduction that also improve overall survival are the main drivers of evolution – these include traits such as tolerance of adverse climatic conditions, competitive ability, and resistance to pathogens (Mayr, 1997). Furthermore, traits that promote the success of the group may be more important than those that favor individual selection. Evolutionary psychology has also been criticized because it does not take development into account, suggesting it falls into the phylogenetic fallacy, which assumes that the organism's phenotype is independent of developmental processes. A further assumption of evolutionary biology is that the brain has evolved innate computational mechanisms, or modules, which allow psychological adaptations to specific situations. For example, there are supposed to be cheat-detection modules, fear-of-snakes modules, and so on. However, the same areas of brain may serve different cognitive functions, and the same cognitive functions may involve different areas of the brain. Ultimately, the brain works as a whole. Panksepp and Panksepp (2000) point out the absence of credible neural perspectives to support the evolutionary perspective on psychology. There are many other critiques, in particular that evolutionary psychology is too anecdotal, it is not falsifiable, it is a-historical, and it ignores a multitude of complex factors that affect human behavior, such as language, empathy, and societal pressures. Evolutionary psychology often seems to be based on ideological convictions (e.g., Grossi et al., 2014).

Despite these criticisms of evolutionary psychology, it is easy to imagine that our early hominid ancestors had to compete for food within a shared territory and that this competition probably led to violence. For some anthropologists, therefore, the origin of human violence is related to the phylogenetic evolution of our species from early primates. Pre-human hominids (such as *Australopithecus* or *Homo habilis*) gradually changed their diet as they evolved; early primates began as vegetarians, but as the brain evolved and climatic changes occurred, they had to hunt for meat to meet their caloric needs, so they developed weapons and warfare, with all the strategies this demands. Behavior that we now refer to as evil seems to have been an inevitable concomitant of this evolution. The evidence for this view is found in the discovery of cannibalism and injuries made by stone axes and arrows in the skeletons of early hominids, as well as the battle scenes depicted in Mesolithic and Neolithic rock paintings (Eibl-Eibesfeldt, 1979). However, other anthropologists believe that very early hominids lived in cooperative, largely harmonious groups, and true wickedness developed much later with the beginning of agriculture about 10,000 years ago. The evidence for this latter position is that, as Montagu (1957) points out, in non-literate societies a great deal of sharing and hospitality are found, and hunter-gatherer societies such as the Australian aborigines, Eskimos, and South African Bushman Hottentots are not warlike. However, the anthropological evidence is mixed; other hunter-gatherers such as the Pygmies of Central Africa and the Bushmen of the Kalahari are indeed warlike. On balance, it appears that there are peaceful and warlike cultures among both hunting and agricultural societies.

Neurological correlates of evil behavior

Reimann and Zimbardo (2011) believe there is a unique neural framework that underlies the mechanisms of human evil. This work focuses on the neuroanatomy of aggression and anti-social behavior, pointing out that decreased activation of prefrontal lobe structures, temporal lobe lesions, and abnormalities of subcortical structures such as the amygdala are associated with aggression. In this vein, Stein (2000) distinguishes between the neurological basis of banal evil and sadistic evil; banal evil may involve a dissociation of cortico-striatal processing from limbic input (disconnecting reason from passion), whereas sadistic evil may involve a dissociation of limbic processing from frontal controls – passion without reason. This kind of research raises important questions; if the brains of violent criminals are different from normal brains, or if injury to the frontal lobe may contribute to violence, we must ask whether such individuals should be held responsible for their behavior.

According to Peck (1983), self-deception allows the evil individual to deny the emotional consequences of his actions. Evolutionary psychologists have suggested that self-deception may have evolved to produce adaptive advantages and survival value. Based on neurobiological studies of psychopathy, narcissism, and sadism, Stein (2005) suggests that accounts such as that of Peck may not be complete. According to recent accounts of the affective neuroscience of evil, such people have major deficits or lacunae in their cognitive and affective processing. Psychopathic people have a disturbance in moral processing because they do not have the necessary frontal-amygdala circuitry required for the empathic processing and assessment of emotions. Stein also notes that early abuse leads to later antisocial behavior, and he believes that this effect is moderated by a functional polymorphism in the monoamine oxidase A (MAO-A) gene. However, he adds, we are loath to label such behavior as *mad* rather than *bad* because we want to emphasize these individuals' moral responsibility for controlling their violent behavior. Stein also points out that even if we have normal cognitive-affective processing, based on adequate frontal cortical activity, we may still engage in questionable behavior such as eating animals raised in cruel conditions, so a neurological explanation cannot be a complete one. Not only is there evidence that psychopathy is associated with neurological dysfunction, but there is also evidence of an association between disturbed serotonergic functioning and impulsive aggression. At least it can be said that in some perpetrators of evil, biological factors interact with social, psychological, and political factors.

Using single photon emission computed tomography (SPECT[1] imagery), Amen and colleagues (1996) studied the brains of murderers and other violent felons, who all showed reduced prefrontal activity (involving judgment and planning), overactivity in the anterior cingulate gyrus (which allows the brain to shift from one thought to another), and abnormalities of the left temporal lobe involving mood and impulse control. His clinics now use this method to study disorders such as depression and obsessional states. However, the American Psychiatric Association has published two skeptical reports about the value of this research, because there is doubt about whether specific scan patterns reflect specific clinical problems in a reliable way. Amen claims to be able to choose the correct treatment based on scan results, but his evidence is still considered anecdotal and based on testimonials. The safety of the radioactive nucleotides used in SPECT scans in children and adolescents is not yet clear.

Note

1 SPECT scans indicate blood flow in different areas of the brain; they require the injection of radioactive material. Areas of low blood flow appear as "holes" on colored images of the brain.

Chapter 7

Religious, mythological, and philosophical views of evil

Do we need a spiritual approach to evil?

One of the great divides in the debate about the nature of evil depends on whether we view human existence from a purely materialistic point of view or whether we adopt a spiritual or religious attitude. Atheists who see the universe as neutral or indifferent to human beings tend to see evil as simply a matter of unpleasant reality, just a part of the way things are. For these individuals, terms like *evil* are merely mythological or superstitious. Natural disasters are part of the natural order, and they have no moral qualities. The word *evil* is a personified way of talking about horrifying behavior. For some writers, therefore, the word *evil* in its theological sense has today been replaced by a set of socially or personally harmful behaviors. For many psychologists, "evil" behavior has become a set of symptoms. In contrast, religious people often believe that mythic notions of evil, such as the Christian devil, may be necessary to convey its intensity. For some people, notions of a supernatural source of evil may give it special meaning or may allow reflection on it in a way that captures the imagination and preserves the element of mystery. In this view, mythic imagery about demonic forces is emotionally powerful and takes us beyond what can be expressed using rational thought. There is some concern that if we try to be too scientific in our account of evil, without invoking such mythological metaphors, we may end up being too reductive about evil, especially if it turns out that there is no rational explanation for it. The current profusion of movies about vampires, the demonic, and the un-dead are modern mythic representations of evil, in which evil is depicted as a kind of non-human, independent power. Perhaps these images fascinate people because they appeal to an archetypal predisposition in the psyche, or perhaps we are fascinated by stories about the darkness that lies dormant in the unconscious.

The combat myth

Traditional theistic religions assume that there is a background moral order in the universe, but some kind of evil power, such as the devil, interferes with this goodness. At the same time, these traditions assume that human beings behave in evil ways as a result of their free will, although their will may be influenced by malevolent entities such as Satan. In such mythological systems, evil is seen as an alien power that can control people. Obviously, any such metaphysical view would be rejected by non-religious thinkers, who would see it as an avoidance of human responsibility for evil and a form of denial or magical thinking. They point out that the metaphysical approach fails to offer any mechanism by which the devil influences the individual and does not explain why the devil affects some people and not others.

There are various mythologies of the universe as a battleground between good and evil powers, a conflict that is sometimes called the combat myth. One of the earliest of these is found in the *Enuma Elish*, the creation story of ancient Babylon that is as old as or older than the Hebrew Bible. In this story, the primeval gods fight with each other and with the subsequent generation of gods they create. The gods of chaos fight with the gods of order, and both sides display hatred and envy. The world is created out of the dead body of the mother goddess Tiamat, who was killed in combat with Marduk the creator, so that the world arises out of conflict. This ancient mythic intuition suggests that evil is an inevitable part of the initial material of creation, and evil is a cosmic force beyond human control.

The classical dualistic view of evil, found in traditions such as Gnosticism and Zoroastrianism, talks of two fundamental principles that conflict. In Zoroastrian mythology, Ahura Mazda was the good god of creation, and Angra Manju or Ahriman was the evil god of destruction and death. In that tradition, the universal opposition of good and evil is a first principle of the cosmos, and the human experience of good and evil is only one instance of the tension between these powers. The human task is to work with Ahura Mazda to resist and defeat Ahriman, by means of correct thought and behavior. Zarathustra taught that this conflict would reach an eventual climax in a perfect world order, a hope that is also found in Christian eschatology.

In other words, the problem of the relationship between the divine and evil is ancient. Plato writes that God is good but is not responsible for everything; he cannot commit evil because it is not part of his nature, so we must look elsewhere to find the responsibility for bad things (*Republic*, 379c). The Neoplatonist Plotinus believed that only the divine itself is perfect; the divine emanates itself through nature into matter with decreasing degrees of perfection, becoming less perfect as it descends into material existence. Human beings are caught in the tension between the pull towards the divine and the evils of physicality.

Theistic approaches to evil: theodicies, or the justification of God in the presence of evil

Theistic religious traditions have long struggled with the problem of why a loving, benevolent God would allow evil, and whether such a God is worthy of devotion. The argument is that if God could prevent evil but does not do so, then he cannot be all good, and if he cannot prevent it, then he cannot be omnipotent. For some writers, this represents an unresolvable problem for traditional theism (Mackie, 1971). The existence of evil is one of the sources of atheism because evil constitutes evidence against the existence of a perfectly good God. Even if moral evil is attributable to human sinfulness, at least it seems that God could prevent natural evils such as earthquakes and volcanoes that are not the result of human activity. Given the apparently unfair distribution of good and evil, the universe does not seem to have a moral quality, much as we would like it to do so. This problem was recognized by biblical books such as the *Book of Job* and by the psalmist: "For I was envious of the arrogant; I saw the prosperity of the wicked. For they have no pain; their bodies are sound and sleek. They are not in trouble as others are: they are not plagued like other people" (Psalm 73).

Despite the threat that evil poses to theism, most traditional theists insist that even in the face of evil and suffering, God is good, although the word "good" may not mean to God what it means to humans. However, given the amount of suffering and evil in the world, some authors believe that to defend the goodness of God actually dishonors the victims of evil. There is also a risk that to insist that an omnipotent God could prevent evil but does not do so undermines the necessity for humans to prevent evil. Nevertheless, there are defenses of God that insist that the existence of evil does not rule out the existence of God, and there are a variety of theodicies, which are justifications of God in the face of the evil in the world (Scott, 2015). Classical Christian ideas describe evil as the result of a fallen world resulting from the Fall of Adam; his rebellion spoiled an original perfection and brought evil into the world. But today only fundamentalists believe this story is an adequate explanation for evil. A more typical theodicy is based on the need for free will; in this account, the presence of evil is necessary so that we can have the freedom to choose between good and evil. This view holds that moral values could not develop without the existence of evil and suffering. For many people, however, this is a weak argument because of the overwhelming amount of evil and suffering in the world; surely it would be possible to develop a morality based on a choice between lesser degrees of evil or different degrees of goodness. Another problem with the free-will defense is that serious suffering and evil actually interfere with our ability to exercise free will, assuming we ever had it.

Adams (1999) deals with what she refers to as horrendous evils, meaning those that make a person doubt that his or her life could be a great good on the whole. She believes that God's power can defeat even horrendous evils. She asks in what way God is good to people who suffer such evils, and whether a victim of horrendous evil can make enough sense of his or her suffering to defeat the evil that caused it. For her, divine goodness involves the distribution of harms and benefits within the individual's life, and God defeats evil by giving it "positive meaning through organic unity with a great enough good *within the context of his/her life*" (p. 31; emphasis in original). She believes that one way that God is good is by guaranteeing that a person participates in important values. Evil is defeated when the positive and negative aspects of life are woven together in such a way that life is of great good to the individual. Those who are the victims of evil can identify with the suffering of God, receive divine gratitude, and be intimate with God. She claims that God's goodness guarantees a meaningful, worthwhile life, and relationship with God "confers significant meaning and positive value even on horrendous suffering" (p. 220). She believes that there is an enormous gap between God and humanity, so the idea that sin is defiance of God's will is like blaming a baby for having dirty diapers.

Another strand of Christian theodicy suggests that human beings are imperfect or incomplete creatures, and evil and suffering are necessary for their development, or for "soul making." Even if this were the case, it does not account for the suffering of animals or why God created a world with so many dangers in it, or why it has taken 2 million years of evolution to arrive at our species, or what Auschwitz has to do with human development. Another typical theodicy is to insist that we cannot know the mind of God, or God's ultimate purposes, so we have to trust and accept what seems to be the divine plan; when the Eschaton arrives, all will be well. Belief in an afterlife is also invoked as the way in which the books will be balanced. In the attempt to preserve an image of God that is all good, some traditional religionists adopt the notion that evil is only created by human beings, while still others fall back on the notion that Satan is responsible for evil.

It is often argued that human beings have a limited perspective on reality; we cannot see the world from God's view. But to a suffering person, evil and suffering are personally real, and it is not much help to be told that there is a larger perspective that we cannot see. Nevertheless, many writers insist that we could not enjoy perfection unless we knew imperfection; without evil, we could not reflect on the perfection of other aspects of existence; without evil and suffering, there is no struggle or accomplishment. Hick (1977) claims that God uses what we call evil as an instrument to make us more like him; God is perfecting us in this way by allowing us to develop forgiveness, mercy, and compassion. Because there is sin and evil in the world, we have the opportunity to experience God's forgiveness and mercy and to practice these virtues. God transforms evil by suffering it in the form of the crucifixion and then releasing it through forgiveness. This is a version of the idea that evil is necessary for bringing about a greater good. The "greater good" argument says that given the complexity of human consciousness, the development of pain in the course of evolution was inevitable and perhaps necessary. The suggestion is that some greater good always comes out of evil, as if that goodness somehow outweighs the horror of an evil act, but given the sheer intensity of suffering and evil in the world, it does not seem to most of us that the ends justify the means. It has long been suggested that this world is arranged as well as possible, but from our human point of view this is clearly not the case. We wonder if all the death, destruction, and suffering in the world are worth whatever good may come of it. For many people, these are not satisfactory responses to the problem of evil because they do not offer hope to people who suffer from it.

Theodicies are often unhelpful to victims of evil, and they are often unconvincing to many theologians, who prefer to see evil as a divine mystery that cannot be explained. From a psychological viewpoint, theodicies tend to sound like rationalizations, or defenses against the sheer horror of evil and a way to preserve an image of God as all good, based on an urgent need to believe that God is really in charge. Many theodicies are too intellectual and do not address the suffering individual's actual pain. As a result of evil, so much damage and suffering has occurred that it seems impossible to ever make sense of it. There are instances of evil that have absolutely no redeeming features that we can detect, and the process of trying to find such a feature risks diminishing the gravity of an evil event. There is even a risk that theodicies will somehow legitimate evil, for example by suggesting that the individual's suffering is somehow deserved or that there will be an eventual happy outcome even though we cannot see how that could happen. These are some of the reasons that some writers such as Emmanuel Levinas insist that after Auschwitz there can be no theodicy.

There are other approaches to the problem of why God allows suffering and evil. Views of evil based on process theology, such as that of Kushner (2004), suggest that God is not really in control of everything that happens; although God is on the side of goodness and hates evil, he cannot always stop evil; he is not in fact omnipotent, because there are forces of nature that are independent of divine will. He may try to persuade people to be good, but apparently his persuasive powers are less powerful than human malevolence. Just as process theology lets go of the idea of divine omnipotence, an alternative approach to the problem of evil abandons the notion that God is all good. Jung believes that the divine has a dark side and is not entirely good, a view that is also found in the Kabbalah. This approach makes the problem of evil and suffering less problematic, but it is not acceptable to traditional Christians. The notion that the divine has a dark side that is responsible for evil is frightening, although this may not mean evil in the sense of a moral defect in the divine nature; it may mean that the ways in which the divine nature manifests itself to us causes suffering. Evil is mainly a problem for the traditional Christian image God, and Jung's project is the beginning of the emergence of a new God-image that takes into account divine darkness. (This is discussed further on p. 106.)

Biblical approaches to evil

Evil in the Hebrew Bible

The Hebrew Bible raises many questions about the problem of evil. In the book of Genesis (25:19–34), the story is told of how Esau was Isaac's first-born son, and so he was entitled to the rights of the eldest son, but with the blessing of his mother Jacob deceived his blind father into bestowing the paternal blessing onto Jacob. In order to maintain the notion of God's righteousness, rabbinic commentators insist that Esau was in fact an evil man, but this sounds like an attempt to rationalize the fact that Jacob blatantly cheated Esau. In Genesis 22, Abraham was told by God to sacrifice his beloved son Isaac, a manifestly evil act. At the last moment, an angel intervened and a ram caught in a nearby thicket was sacrificed instead. The Bible describes multiple mass murders that are commanded by God, as if this makes them justifiable.[1] Mass murder is apparently not evil if God commands it, and this has been a license for many religiously based massacres.

The problem of evil and suffering has been important for Jewish and Christian theologians, because when God created the world he said it was good (Gen. 1: 31). Nevertheless, soon after the creation, people behaved in evil ways. Even though God created humanity in his own image, and initially pronounces that creation is good, it does not take long before God decides that "the wickedness of man was great in the earth, and that every imagination of the thoughts of his heart was only evil continually" (Gen. 8: 21), so that God is sorry that he created humanity (Gen. 6: 5–6). The implication is that he had not foreseen how people would turn out.

The creature that God created in his own image is obviously very flawed, so within the biblical tradition the problem became how to explain this discrepancy. One solution was to insist that human evil is only an aspect of human nature, not an expression of the divine. Jews and Christians alike regard evil as a consequence of human sin and insist on free will, so that evil occurs when we resist the will of God. However, to attribute evil entirely to humans in this way ignores the fact that evil is part of the fabric of creation in the form of the serpent in the Garden of Eden, and God seems to set up the situation so that Adam and Eve will be tempted. The potential for disobedience is therefore present at the beginning, and it is not entirely the result of human actions. The serpent tempts Eve, saying that if they eat the forbidden fruit they will be like God, knowing good and evil. Why it is a problem to know good and evil[2] is not clear, unless it means that Adam and Eve will have some absolute truth that should be the exclusive province of God, but the implication is that their sin is a combination of arrogance and disobedience. Rebellion against God is a common theme in the Hebrew Bible. The biblical story of Adam and Eve does not directly identify the serpent as Satan, although later tradition assumes this identity, but the Qu'ran explicitly says that "the Shaitan made an evil suggestion to them" (7: 22).

The next episode of evil occurs when Cain, a farmer, kills his younger brother Abel, a shepherd (Genesis 4).[3] Cain resents and is envious of Abel because Abel's sacrifice (an animal) is accepted by God, while that of Cain (the fruits of the field) is rejected. We are not told why God sets up this opposition or why Cain is shamed in this way. Perhaps Abel made much more effort than Cain, since the text says that God respected Abel but not Cain. God tells Cain to examine his behavior and exhorts him not to be overcome by sin. God also asks Cain why he is angry, so it may be that killing Abel was Cain's way of dealing with a narcissistic injury leading to rage and a need for vengeance. What is striking in the text is Cain's lack of remorse. We might imagine the situation as the result of intense sibling rivalry, guessing that Cain believed that Adam, their father, prefers Abel to him. Perhaps Abel was more successful in the eyes of their parents, leading to Cain's envy, but we have no indications in the text of such family dynamics.

The Hebrew Bible is replete with many other instances of human evil. King Solomon used slave labor in his construction projects (1 Kgs. 9: 15–24). King

David arranges for Uriah to be killed in battle so that David may possess Uriah's wife (2 Sam. 11: 2–27). The dark side of the Hebrew God-image is very obvious, since there are many episodes of large-scale murder, rape, and other atrocities commanded by God (e.g., Deut. 3, Joshua 6, Judges 21.) It is clear from the first two chapters of the book of Amos that God personally engages in military destruction: God says he will send fire onto several cities and destroy their palaces. Jeremiah says that God's judgment will take the form of war, famine, and pestilence (28: 2). Elsewhere, God condones slavery (Exodus 21: 1–11) and child sacrifice (Judges 11: 29–40, Isaiah 13: 16). He issues commandments to kill people who work on the Sabbath (Exodus 31: 12–15), to kill those who worship other gods (Deut. 13: 7–12), to stone to death a woman who is not a virgin on her wedding night (Deut. 22: 20–21), to kill adulterers or homosexuals (Lev. 20: 10 & 20: 13), and so on. The influence of this kind of biblical law on modern fundamentalist believers is rarely discussed openly today, but it seems to be in the background of some of their attitudes. What is striking in the Hebrew Bible is the level of violence it justifies when dealing with evil. Thus, when the people worship a golden calf while Moses is receiving the law on Mount Sinai (Exodus 32), this wickedness requires the death of 3,000 people for its expiation. God blesses this act of devotion.

The problem of why an omnipotent, all-good God would either create or allow evil came to a head following the destruction of the temple at Jerusalem in 586 BCE. Following this catastrophe, the people of Judah were exiled to Babylon, and this experience cast doubt on the reliability of their covenant with God, who was supposed to protect the righteous and punish the wicked. The exile was assumed to be the result of the people's idolatry, but many righteous worshipers of God also suffered, and not all the wicked were exiled. This kind of dilemma eventually led to the *Book of Job*, which depicts the theological problem caused by the suffering of an innocent, pious man. Suffering had traditionally been seen as a punishment for sin, and the advice given to Job was that he should confess and repent. However, Job disputed this orthodox wisdom because he believed he had not done anything to warrant the degree of suffering inflicted upon him. He pointed out that evil people do well and the innocent suffer. The book offered no solution to this reality, except to say that the problem of suffering and evil is a mystery that must be faced with personal integrity and faith. The subsequent *Book of Ecclesiastes* is a rather skeptical, even bitter comment on the problem of evil. This text points out that not only do righteous people suffer, but all human attainments are ultimately futile and vain, leading to nothing but dust (3, 20).

Just before the Christian era, the rabbinic tradition developed the idea of the *yetzer ho'rah*, or the evil inclination, which is based on Genesis 8: 21, where God realizes that "every inclination of the human heart is evil from childhood." The rabbis of the Talmudic tradition decided that the evil inclination is not something demonic, but part of our essential life force that urges us to marry, build houses, and work; it is the source of healthy self-interest, properly applied. However, it was created so that it could be mastered, and it becomes evil if it is not mastered or if it is misused. In the traditional view, at Mount Sinai the people were given both a moral law and a set of commandments, as well as the freedom to obey or disobey them, so good and evil in this tradition are defined in terms of whether one is obedient to God (Deut. 30: 16). Evil is very much a matter of the human will, a challenge that requires spiritual development. However, to many people this does not seem to be an adequate account of horrors such as the Holocaust. The rabbis also postulated an inclination to goodness, but the evil inclination seems to be more demanding. (Christian theologians also adopted the idea of an innate, natural inclination to virtue that in their view becomes weakened by original sin.)

The rabbinic tradition could not tolerate the idea of evil as the result of a source other than God, since they wished to preserve the unity of the divine. Somehow, therefore, God creates evil and tolerates its existence. The rabbis also insisted on divine justice and ultimate goodness, so that no suffering is ultimately undeserved and no sin or evil act goes unpunished. Essentially, they adopted a reward-punishment psychology, falling back on the notion that where necessary the apparently unfair distribution of suffering and evil would be balanced in the next world.

Various theologians, both Jewish and Christian, have tried to come to terms with the evil of the Holocaust and its implications. For most people, the Holocaust was such an enormously evil event that no explanation, whether theological, psychological, or sociological, seems adequate to understanding how it could have happened. Rubenstein (1992) wrote that the mystery of the Holocaust means that traditional Jewish ways of understanding God no longer work, because we can no longer believe in a just God keeping a covenant with his people. Accordingly, either this God is dead or the Jewish people are not chosen. For him, Jews have to question their traditional ideas about God and decide how to rethink them. Other writers, especially within the orthodox Jewish community, preferred to insist that belief in God, God's role in the world, and traditional Jewish practices must still be affirmed despite the Holocaust. Cohen (1988) suggested that God was not responsible for the Holocaust because God is transcendent. For him, rational thought cannot comprehend the enormity of the Holocaust, which defies explanation, although God must be acquiescent in it. For him as well, the image of God that the Jewish people have worshipped now seems to be only a fabrication.

Kulka (2013) offers a response to the question of where God was in Auschwitz, which for some sincere believers has been a forbidden question. Kulka's response is based on a dream he had more than 50 years after being in Auschwitz as a 10-year-old child. He dreamed he was inside crematorium number 2, and there was God, also:

At first I felt Him (only) as a kind of mysterious radiation of pain, flowing at me from the dark void in the unlit part of the cremation ovens. A radiation of insupportably intense pain, sharp and dull alike. Afterwards He began to take the shape of a kind of huge embryo, shrunk with pain. . . . He was alive, shrunken, hunched forward with searing pain . . . a figure on the scale of His creatures, in the form of a human being who came and was there . . . as a response to "the question they were forbidden to ask there," but was asked and floated in that dark air.

The dream says that God was present in the ovens, took human form, and suffered accordingly. To me, the appearance of God in the form of an embryo suggests the incipient birth of a new God-image as a result of the Holocaust.

Evil in the New Testament

St. Paul (Rom. 7: 19) complained that "I do not do the good I want to do, but the evil I do not want to do, this I keep on doing." That is, even though he wanted to do good, he saw in himself "another law at war with the law of my mind and making me captive of the law of sin which dwells in my members" (Rom. 7: 23). Paul did not have the concept of the unconscious, but he obviously realized that something else was operating in him apart from his ego, and this produced an internal conflict. Paul saw the body, or at least human passions, as irredeemably corrupt and a source of evil. He recommended that we "walk by the spirit and do not gratify the desires of the flesh, for the desires of the flesh are against the spirit, and the desires of the spirit are against the flesh" (Gal. 5: 17). He goes on to say that "those who belong to Christ Jesus have crucified the flesh with its passions and desires" (Gal. 5: 24). These comments indicate a radical matter-spirit split in his psyche, which was to affect subsequent thinking for a long time because of the implication that the body is somehow evil.

For Christian theologians, since the initial creation of human beings was good, human nature must have become corrupted, and the obvious candidate was the Fall of Adam, who ate the forbidden fruit. Because of Adam's disobedience, sin is said to have come into the world, and his sin was said to have corrupted human nature (Rom. 5: 12). This idea was developed into the doctrine of original sin by St. Augustine, who also found bodily desire a great problem. Augustine was pre-occupied with finding the origin of evil, and he decided it was the sin of Adam and Eve that was transmitted to all subsequent generations. Not just sexual lust but also pride, and the soul's self-centered desire for wealth, power, and position are sinful. Of the seven deadly sins of the Christian tradition, four of them – lust, glut-tony, greed, and sloth – involve the need to curb the appetites of the body. Today, different Christian denominations have different views about what is sinful – birth control is a good example; it is allowed in some but not in other denominations.

The doctrine of evil as *privatio boni*

Theological approaches to evil are of two kinds, depending on whether evil is seen as a positive force such as Satan or as something negative, exemplified by St. Augustine's notion of the *privatio boni*, which says that evil is the privation or absence of goodness. (The same idea is found in the Jewish tradition in the work of Maimonides.) Augustine did not want to accord evil an active or positive ontological status, because that would make it a kind of divinity. He wanted to maintain the idea that God's creation was entirely good, whereas if evil was a substance it would be part of God's creation. Therefore, for Augustine, consistent with Plato's notion that evil has no essential being in itself, evil became the name for the absence of goodness, something entirely human. Augustine considered evil to be the result of the limitations of creation and human frailty. According to Augustine, the original source of human evil was Adam's disobedience to the will of God in the Garden of Eden. All subsequent human beings are tainted by this sin in a kind of Lamarckian inheritance,[4] so that after the Fall of Adam, humans are prone to sin. This doctrine raised the questions of why God did not create Adam in a way that made him freely choose goodness, and how it can be that for the rest of eternity people can be punished for a sin they did not commit.

The doctrine of *privatio boni* says that evil is not an active principle or force, but a lack of the capacity to restrict desire to things pertaining to the perfection of God, such as peace and love. Evil exists as an absence, like holes in the fabric of creation. Augustine claimed that if evil is really nothing, then sinful people are perverted towards wanting nothing. Their lives are aimed at things that are meaningless, even if what they want has the appearance of something good. He does not believe that anyone would do something purely because it is evil; in his mind, people stray from goodness because they cannot see that what they are doing is bad. In his *Confessions*, he compares his act of stealing pears from a tree during his youth with the monstrous evil of the Roman tyrant Sulla, who executed thousands of people he considered to be enemies of the state, or sometimes for the sake of personal enrichment. Surprisingly, Augustine says that his own act was worse because it was irrational, while Sulla's cruelty at least had the goals of wealth and power.

Augustine was not trying to dismiss the reality of evil, only to make a metaphysical point about its origin. However, many people point to the fact that to carry out evil such as the Holocaust, a great deal of positive action must be taken in terms of planning and execution, so that evil must be a real power or an ontological reality, not simply an absence. Many post-Holocaust theologians now agree that evil is too serious to be defined purely in terms of a lack of goodness. It does not seem that events such as the Holocaust, or characters such as Pol Pot, can be reduced to the mere absence of good, any more than illness can be seen as only the absence of health. It seems that evil is a real presence that actively opposes or destroys goodness. A further problem with the *privatio* doctrine is that it is no help in dealing with evil.

For some theologians, the *privatio* argument is best seen as a way of asserting the goodness of God, and it does not really deny the destructiveness of evil. However, as Hannah Arendt (1994) points out, notions such as the *privatio*, or the idea that evil is a part of a divine plan that moves us towards greater moral development, may obscure the terrible reality of evil. Arendt refers to such theodicies as "dialectical acrobatics" based on a superstitious belief "that something good might result from evil" (p. 570).

Despite such objections to the *privatio* argument, some writers still adhere to it. In his attempt to reconcile the God of traditional theism with the presence of evil in the world, Kerr (2011) argues on the basis of Aquinas's thought that there is no such *thing* as evil; that is, evil is not a substance. Evil is not something created by God. He argues that in Aquinas's metaphysics, anything that God creates is other than God, and so must be limited in its goodness. It is therefore impossible for God to create a universe without evil, since this demand would mean that he creates a universe with no limitations, which is absurd – creation has necessary limitations.

Traditional Christian doctrine was much focused on the problem of human sin, which was understood as a disregard for the will of God. To insist on suffering as a punishment for sin at least gave believers a sense that their suffering is meaningful. It was assumed that human beings are incapable of dealing with evil on their own; divine grace was required to free the person from sin. Traditionally, only those redeemed by Christ could be saved, while the rest were condemned to eternal damnation.

Modern Christian thinkers and theologians continue to struggle with the problem of evil, and some of them have tried to develop a Christian response to the Holocaust (Davies, 1993). Paul Tillich (1936), a Lutheran theologian, believed that sin is an active energy with its own givenness; it is not simply an absence of goodness. For him, sin means estrangement or alienation from God understood as the Ground of Being, or sin results from a failure to recognize our dependence on God. Tillich suggested that there is a tension between the creative and destructive forces in creation. One of his signature ideas is the notion of the demonic, which is a perversion of creativity that corrupts what is holy. In contrast to the demonic, the Satanic represents pure destruction with no positive or creative aspect. A major problem with his notion of the demonic is that radical evil seems to be much more than a perversion of creativity.

For Tillich, the Nazi era was an eruption of the demonic. Tillich believed that throughout history there have been charismatic personalities who were filled with demonic energy, as if a power from the abyss had possessed them. Tillich believed this happened when the individual became inflated with self-importance and had the idolatrous desire that Tillich describes as "the creative ambition to be like God." He is clearly referring to malignant narcissism, which he believes always contains the seeds of its own destruction.

The Calvinist theologian Karl Barth was an important opponent of the Nazis. He sees such radical evil as grounded in what he refers to as the "nothing," which God did not create and does not will, something on the margins of creation that threatens and corrupts it (Barth, 1994). This "nothing" is not nothing in the ordinary sense of the English word; it is a form of radical evil, or evil as an end in itself. It is the shadow side of creation, a remnant of the primitive chaos mentioned in Gen. 1: 2, when creation was "without form and void." This nothing wants to reduce everything else to nothing. Barth rather overoptimistically insists that Christ defeated this nothing, even if appearances suggest otherwise. Barth seems to disregard, or is in denial about, historical events, which suggest that evil is manifestly out of control, and this is generally regarded as a weakness of his approach to evil.

Reinhold Niebuhr (1996) suggested that sin and evil are intrinsic to the human condition. They are an inevitable consequence of the way we were created, and we have failed to pay attention to the implications of this original sin. For him, there are two sides to human nature. Human beings are finite and mortal, with free will, but we also have a spiritual nature – in fact, we stand "at the junction of nature and spirit" (p. 17), which causes tension since we are neither pure nature nor pure spirit. This combination, our ambiguous, contradictory nature, causes anxiety because we will die, and anxiety leads to the temptation from which evil arises. He believed that human beings have free will, and we are fated to sin, but he has no explanation for why some people sin more than others or why we sometimes do not commit evil.

Alvin Platinga (1979) argues that it is logically impossible for God to control all the world's evil. As long as there is free will, there could not be a world with less evil than our world. God cannot create every logically possible world, and so cannot eliminate evil. Platinga argues that in any of the worlds God might have created with free agents, there will be individuals who freely chose evil. Platinga calls this transworld depravity.

In the Gnostic tradition, the high God was not involved in the creation of the world, which was made by the God of the Bible, who is a lower-level divinity. In this mythology, creation is evil and Christ is necessary to lead people back to the original high God. Humanity lives in this world but does not belong to it; the Gnostic feels alien to the world and cannot be content with it, because he constantly feels a yearning for the eternal realm. The sense that there is something wrong with the world, or that the human spirit is obsessed with evil, seems to go back to this early Gnostic myth. Traditional Christian theologians could not accept this Gnostic account of evil, which goes back to an idea of Plato in the *Timaeus*, which claims that the Demiurge who created the world tried to eliminate the world's evil but was not powerful enough to do so.

In the Hindu tradition, evil is an aspect of the divine itself (Cenkner, 1997). This tradition would have no problem with Jung's notion of the dark side of the Self, because Hinduism does not try to preserve a God-image that is all good and loving; in the Hindu pantheon, many gods and goddesses are destructive, albeit for the sake of new creation. According to the Kabbalistic Zohar, the powers of God consist of love and mercy on one hand and wrath on the other; when his wrath operates independently of his loving side, evil appears. Other traditions, such as Buddhism, see evil behavior as the result of ignorance or a faulty perception of reality. Abe (1989) says that Zen sees the problem of good and evil as a problem confined to the discriminating mind, and we must awaken to No-mind, which transcends discrimination. He says that the cause of suffering is not rooted in a substantial objective entity but in our ignorance of the non-substantiality and impermanence of things to which we are attached. This emptiness is prior to the opposition of good and evil, and the realization of true emptiness allows freedom. However, even if the phenomenal world is an illusion, it is the one in which we live, and at that level evil cannot be dismissed. Even if reality is empty, as Buddhism says, and even if good and evil are only epistemological illusions and not substantial, objective entities, this does not mean we can avoid discussing the difference between good and evil as unreal or pointless, because they are experiential realities. As Kim (1998) asks, would the individual awakening to the ontological non-existence of good and evil be sufficient to solve the problems in the world? Would "illusory phenomenal matters such as social justice" (p. 90) be dissolved into emptiness if each of us awakens to the illusory nature of the need for social peace? Kim points out that the Buddha did not stay in nirvana but turned back to the phenomenal world to help others. He also points out that the *Dhammapada*[5] teaches the importance of practicing goodness and avoiding evil, and Buddhism has moral teachings that are not to be taken as mere illusory fabrications of the mind.

Psychological interpretations of religious views of evil

Religious views about evil are amenable to psychological understanding. For example, classical psychoanalysts assume that notions of demons and devils result from the projection of human aggression onto fantasy figures. Freud believed that such beliefs are superstitions derived from repressed hostility and cruelty; a person might want to do evil to others but be unable to bring himself to do so because of childhood training. He then expects punishment for his unconscious evil in the form of external misfortune, personified as the result of the devil. In other words, the notion of a demon is a scapegoat for unacceptable human impulses or reprehensible wishes. Or as Jung (CW 6, p. 109) put it, demons are "intruders from the unconscious" or the eruption of complexes into consciousness.

Psychologically we could see the mythological figure of Satan as the projection of a negative internal object or a complex that attacks or criticizes the individual. Destructive complexes try to destroy any loving parts of the self or life-affirming relationships. These complexes also attack the psychotherapeutic process, leading to suicide, depressive shifts, and self-destructive behavior. When such a destructive complex grips the person, it may feel as if he or she is in the grip of an external power or that there is something alien within the self.

Cooper-White (2003) points out that both Kohut's model of psychopathology and Augustine's notion of evil as the *privatio boni* are deficit models. Both conceive of the origin of evil behavior in terms of something missing. Psychoanalytic theory sees the *privatio* argument as analogous to a failure of care in infancy, because both are the result of an absence. She invokes Kohut's notion of a vertical split in the psyche to discuss the words of St. Paul in Romans 7: 19: "I do not do the good I want, but the evil I do not want is what I do." A vertical split may lead to behaviors that are compulsive but feel alien to the personality, some of which lead to evil. Vertical splits lead to denial and disavowal of affect, and they allow untamed grandiosity to express itself, while the underlying need for love and approval remains unconscious. A vertical split may be associated with various forms of destructive acting out, originating from early narcissistic deficit or injury. One side of the split is associated with problematic behavior that results from a desperate attempt to fill a sense of painful inner emptiness or to soothe fragmentation anxiety. This behavior, such as promiscuity, has only a transient effect; only a new relationship that allows the development of the necessary internal structure can heal the deficit. Cooper-White also believes that, since most of us do not escape childhood without some kind of deficit in the sense of self, this sense of deficit corresponds to the theology of original sin, which theologians attributed to the Fall of Adam. The idea of original sin implies that human nature is radically sinful, a notion that is fostered by harsh parenting leading to a sense of personal badness.

Cooper-White points out, however, that to understand psychopathology due to serious trauma, we need more than a deficit model. For her, evil is the result of active, persecutory internal figures or presences within the personality. (These form complexes in Jung's terminology.) This approach results in a concept of evil behavior as something positive rather than the result of an absence, and this corresponds to the idea of evil as an ontological force rather than an absence. She points out that the cultural narratives with avenging characters such as Buffy the Vampire Slayer and Xena the Warrior Princess are of interest because they resonate with the trauma victim's internal battle between good and evil. Cooper-White also points out that institutionalized and corporate forms of evil do not fit with a deficit model, which would also not account for cultural problems such as racism, war, and sexism.

Notions of sin in the religious traditions may be approached from other psychological points of view. For example, certain aspects of the self are felt as good or bad, depending on how they were received in childhood. This tension is painful, so we tend to identify with the good pole and split off the other, often projecting it into other people, who then embody disavowed negative aspects of oneself. The projection of problematic aspects of the self gets rid of internal danger but generates persecutory anxiety, as we then seem to be in danger from others. These shadow or bad parts of the self are labeled as sinful when they correspond to traditional prohibitions. The tradition might call them immoral, even if they are not actually destructive.

Goldman (1988) believes that a core sense of personal evil is the psychological equivalent of the idea of original sin. She points out that there are no children in the Garden of Eden, and the man and woman form a perfect union. Children then appear, but the pain of childbirth is seen as a punishment (Gen. 3: 16) for disobedience. In the post-Eden world, therefore, painful childbirth is associated with all that has gone wrong between the originally perfect parental couple. This mythic image depicts a child born into a world that is in mourning for the lost experience of wholeness. To make matters worse, Adam and Eve experience massive shame because of God's punitive attitude. Refusing to take responsibility for their actions, Adam blames Eve and Eve blames the serpent, so that the bad self is projected. More splitting of good and evil then occurs in the story of Cain and Abel. Cain acts out the role of evildoer, while Abel represents the innocence of the original harmony, which is now fragmented. Goldman points out that the story would be very different if Adam and Eve had been able to admit what they did, take responsibility, and apologize to God, pointing out that what they did was part of their nature. Tragically, they could not hold the opposites of good and evil together, so they had to be split and projected. Goldman believes that this ancient split is one of humanity's most fundamental problems. She sees the story of Adam and Eve as a mythic story of fundamentally split parents who cannot tolerate their internal badness, and so project it onto their children, who then take responsibility for everything that is wrong around them because of a combination of infantile omnipotence and a lack of differentiation of self and object representations. The child in such a situation feels responsible for the parent's misery, as if there was an initial paradise that was spoiled by the child being born. The child feels responsible for tensions in the family and for having caused these problems through his or her existence. Hence arises the notion of original sin. Such a child feels constantly judged and may constantly strive to do penance for a vaguely perceived sense of badness. In response, such an individual might go into a helping profession, taking care of others' needs, or he might live the life of an impaired narcissistic personality disorder.

The devil

Human evil has often been attributed to the influence of a supernatural power. Zoroastrianism, Christianity, Islam, and the ancient Hebrew tradition, although not modern Judaism, personify evil in the form of the devil. Buddhism has a tradition of the mythological Mara, the Evil One who tempted the Buddha to abandon his mission. Other traditions have demonic forces but no one specific devil. Apparently the mythic or archetypal notion of a specific personality that is hostile to goodness and holiness addresses our sense of the ultimately mysterious nature of evil, which seems to be something beyond the human realm.

The notion of the devil attributes evil to a supernatural being, partly in an attempt to make evil "other," or at least to externalize it and tell a meaningful story about it when it seems to be more than human. Many, if not all, religious traditions assert the reality of demons or evil spirits that personify evil, and the concept is found in folklore going back to Egypt and Babylon. The English word "Satan" comes from a Hebrew word meaning something that obstructs or accuses. The words "devil" and "diabolical" are derived from the Greek *diabolos*, which means to tear apart; it is the antonym of the root of the word symbol, which means to join together. Its original Greek meaning referred to a slanderer.

According to Pagels (1996), a *satan* was originally an angel or celestial messenger sent by God, with a specific task, and was not necessarily malevolent. The term referred to a kind of spiritual energy that gradually became anthropomor-phized into an entity that opposes the will of God, or even one that tries to rival God. Medieval theologians derived the image of Satan with goat-like or horned features from a ritual in Leviticus 6: 21–22, in which the sins of the people are transferred onto a goat that is banished into the wilderness.

Satan makes only a few appearances in the Hebrew Bible. In the *Book of Job*, Satan appears as a son or servant of God, part of the divine court who is allowed to torment Job and tempt him to be less good (1: 6–12). Satan tries to prevent the high priest Joshua from carrying out his priestly duties (Zechariah 3: 1–2), and in his last appearance, Satan provokes King David to sin so that God sends a pes-tilence against Israel (1 Chronicles, 21:1).[6] However, there is some debate about whether in these stories the Hebrew word *satan* is really being used as a proper name, to indicate a specific personality, rather than to simply infer the presence of an adversary or accuser. Accordingly, the notion that Satan is a discreet character in the Hebrew Bible has been challenged (Breytenbach, 1995). In later Judaism, Satan is seen as a being created by God, and working for God, in order to test or tempt people. He appears in the form of an evil inclination.

In the Christian tradition, Satan was thought of as a fallen angel, a very distinct personality who was banished from heaven because he rebelled against God by refusing to bow before newly created humanity. His disobedience is motivated by pride and resentment. In the New Testament, the devil appears frequently as an active force that competes with God for human souls; he undermines the spir-ituality of Christians by deception and seduction. Thus, 1 Peter 5: 8 says that: "your adversary the devil, as a roaring lion, walketh about, seeking whom he may devour." There is a strong sense of the presence of demonic powers throughout the New Testament; Jesus often contends with them, and he attributed some of his healings to the casting out of Satan or demons (Luke 13: 16; Matt. 9: 32–33; Matt. 12: 22–33; Matt. 17: 18). Christ was tempted by the devil, who offered him worldly power (Matt. 4: 8–9), and many Christian saints, ascetics, monks, or desert anchorites were regularly tempted by the devil, who would appear in the form of a voluptuous woman or with offers of riches and delicious food. The New Testament speaks of the devil as "the ruler of this world," (John 14: 30) the "god of this age" (11 Cor. 4:4), and even that "the whole world is in the power of the evil one" (1 Jn. 5: 19). The devil says he has control over the kingdoms of the world (Luke 4: 5–6). Women in particular were considered by the church fathers and by medieval Christians to be potential tools or aids of the devil, luring men to bad behavior, and occasionally indulging in coitus with the devil himself. Christian theologians saw the devil as an active adversary who will not be con-quered until the Eschaton (the divinely ordained end of time), but meanwhile he is allowed by God to cause trouble. This theme is found throughout the gospels, but it comes into sharp relief in the book of Revelation, which focuses on combat between the forces of evil and the goodness of God.

For many Christians, the concept of evil as the result of demonic influences or fallen angels is still very much alive. For these believers, the devil seems to have a degree of autonomy even if he is ultimately under God's control. Many other more liberal Christians take the Bible very seriously as divine revelation but cannot believe in the existence of Satan or evil spirits, and they may be somewhat embarrassed by the fact that Jesus took the existence of such spirits very literally.

As the Christian tradition developed, the term *devil* was increasingly used in a pejorative way to denounce the enemies of Christianity, or it was used as a description of other Christians with whom particular groups disagreed. The term is distinguished from the notion of the *daemon* or *daimon*, which in antiquity referred to an invisible spiritual power that affected the individual's behavior and destiny. The daemonic, according to Plato in the *Symposium*, bridges the gap between the mortal and the immortal realms, acting as a medium of communication between gods and humanity. Gradually, with the ascendancy of the Christian tradition, the Greek notion of the daemon deteriorated into the notion of the demon as entirely evil, so that especially since the Enlightenment the real nature of daemonic reality was radically misunderstood, and Western culture has lost touch with it. May (1969, p. 123) used the classical Greek idea of the daemon to describe "any natural function which has the power to take over the whole person," such as sex, rage, or the craving for power – essentially, archetypal aspects of the unconscious that cannot be eradicated. (May's approach is discussed further on p. 53.)

Ancient Manichean theology says that there are two powers or gods, good and evil, which fight each other, and human suffering is the result of the evil power. Christianity could not accept the Manichean idea that there are equally powerful forces in the universe, one good and one evil, constantly competing with each other. The notion of the devil or the Antichrist is a kind of residue of this idea within the Christian tradition, except that the devil is not considered to be as powerful as God. Augustine, for example, understood Satan as rebelling against God but ultimately under God's control. Christian thinkers of the scholastic period, such as St. Anselm and St. Aquinas, were very concerned with the study of the devil. Anselm believed that the devil has bottomless desires that can never be satisfied, and this makes Satan miserable. Aquinas believed that Satan rebels against God because of resentment that God is superior. Satan wants to be like God, and he wants to attain happiness through his own efforts rather than as a gift of God.

Many contemporary fundamentalist Christians, consciously or not, seem to either subscribe to a dilute version of the Manichean view or they are tempted by it; they commonly believe that the devil is constantly trying to subvert the goodness of God's design, so they must be spiritually prepared to struggle with Satan.

In the Islamic tradition, the Stoning of the Devil during the Hajj[7] is a symbolic re-enactment of the devil's appearance to Abraham in an attempt to prevent him from sacrificing his son. This ritual is an expression of the participants' hostility to the devil. The Qur'an tells the story of Iblis, a rebellious spirit or Jinn, who is asked by God to bow to Adam. Iblis refused because he considered himself to be superior to Adam. For this he was cast into hell. Islam teaches that Satan regretted his disobedience to God and his sin of pride, but he lost faith in God and instead turned to hatred, seeking vengeance against humanity, which he saw as the reason for his fall from grace. He tries to tempt people into evil by means of deception, to prove that he is better than humans and to justify his defiance of God. This story, which is similar to the Christian idea, raises the obvious question of exactly where responsibility for evil lies.

The devil has been thought of in very literal ways; demonic covenants were offered as evidence in the trials of witches in medieval Europe, which arose in part because Christians believed they were under serious attack by Satan.[8] The notion of a devil is still very prevalent – one still hears it invoked by fundamentalist Christian preachers. When the World Trade Center collapsed, some people reported seeing the face of Satan in the clouds of smoke that emerged from the destruction. Presumably this was a projection, or a form of pareidolia,[9] in an attempt to make sense of the indescribable in terms of a pre-existing belief system. It may be that such evil is spoken of in terms of a devil because it is so hard to understand at the human level, making it seem more than human. Ricoeur (1967) warns that myths and symbols are resources that aid us in our understanding of evil, but myth must not be used as an explanation for it.

The mythic attributes of Satan include a willingness to grant people their hearts' desire in exchange for the human soul. The notion of a pact with the devil is found in many plays, operas, films, paintings, and literary works. The image is also found in musical compositions such as Tartini's *Devil's Sonata*.

Omnipotent fantasies tend to produce evil; it is not surprising that the devil is said to suffer from the sin of pride – for example, Isaiah accuses Lucifer of thinking: "I will exalt my throne above the stars of God. . . . I will be like the most high" (Isa. 14: 13–14). Satan even offers Jesus "all the kingdoms of the world" if Jesus would worship him (Matt. 4: 8–9). As in the case of Lucifer, arrogance is often accompanied by envy of others. The striving for power and the wish to control and dominate others are clearly a source of evil. Totalitarian societies are particularly concerned with omnipotent control of others, and so are psychopathic personalities. Brennan (1997) believes that omnipotence is the "keystone holding together the other negative traits of the psyche" (p. 223) and is central to the understanding of evil. She understands omnipotence to be the denial of the rights of others or even of the separate existence of others "in favor of the wish to dominate and control them" (p. 212). She points out that in mythological accounts of the devil he always desires control, and "he feasts on power and the prospect of power. It is this that leads to his famous sin of pride, *superbia*" (p. 210). She sees the devil as driven by envy and by the "desire to be boss" (p. 211). She links omnipotence to the envious need to possess the creativity of the other, either to control it or to obliterate it. Control of others, or the lack of such control, is also important in our understanding of paranoia; for such individuals, losing control feels as if it risks self-annihilation. "The paranoid's projected fear is that just as he sought to control the other, so the other will seek to control him. One fears that what one wants to do to the other will be done to oneself, leading to paranoia" (ibid.).

Demonic and spirit possession

The folklore of many cultures and religions teems with stories of possession by demons, or the notion that spiritual presences may take over the personality (Prins, 1992). This leads to behavior that is inexplicable from the point of view of the individual's ordinary personality. During the episode, the individual is said to exhibit altered speech patterns and a change in his voice quality. The body twists into incredible contortions, and the individual exhibits facial grimaces, seizures, howling and growling like an animal, blasphemous utterances, and similar behavior. Sometimes the possessed person craves disgusting food or shows extreme physical strength. Stories of such possession go back to antiquity; in the fourth century BCE, the priestess of Apollo at the Temple of Delphi was said to be filled with the inspiration of the god, allowing her to make oracular predictions. In the Jewish tradition, the Dybbuk was considered to be a wandering soul or demonic spirit that could enter a living body. Christ exorcised evil spirits (Luke 8: 26–30; Mathew 8: 28–32), and since then the Christian church has regularly practiced exorcism. A variety of herbs, symbolic formulas, or amulets have been used worldwide to protect against demonic intrusion.

A residue of the belief in literal possession is found in the colloquial phrase "what got into me?", which is uttered when we behave in a way that is out of character. Jungians believe this phenomenon to be the result of the personality being temporarily overwhelmed by an autonomous complex. This produces the subjective experience that something alien or "not me" is gripping the individual and compelling his behavior (CW 8, p. 93). From the point of view of object relations theory, this state of mind can be understood as the result of possession by persecutory internal objects. A milder form of possession manifests itself as an obsessional state, in which a particular thought or impulse keeps intruding into the subject's mind, against his or her will. The obsessional thought or action is seen as invasive, unwanted, and often radically opposed to the subject's usual personality. One can metaphorically refer to states of mind such as depression or attacks of panic or rage as the result of possession by a force outside of one's conscious control. Because of the archetypal basis of such a complex, Jung (CW 13, para. 54) wrote that the gods of antiquity have in our time become diseases. In its positive form, "possession" by the unconscious is felt as inspiration, mystical experience, divine guidance, or falling in love. Some cultures, such as the practitioners of shamanism or voodoo, deliberately invoke the daimonic or archetypal level of the psyche, which they describe in terms of invisible spiritual forces. These are invoked for guidance, or they may spontaneously take possession of a troubled individual. Among medieval Christians, mental illness was seen to be the result of demonic intrusion, and in the New Testament Jesus is reported to have healed several people suffering from possession by devils (Mark 1: 32). Today, among some Christian groups, possession by the Holy Spirit is encouraged and valued for its healing powers.

Only with the advent of Charcot and Freud was the phenomenon of possession seen to be a psychological rather than a metaphysical problem. They decided that states of "possession" correspond to neuroses. Freud's (1923/1981) essay "A neurosis of demoniacal possession in the seventeenth century" analyzes a medieval account of demon possession that occurred after the death of a patient's father. Freud assumed that the devil symbolically represented the man's father.

The International Classification of Mental and Behavioral Disorders has a diagnostic category titled "Trance and possession disorders,"[10] in which the individual behaves as if he has been possessed by a spirit. An example is the Malayan *amok* syndrome, in which the individual is taken over by irresistible rage and indiscriminately attacks others. After the attack is over, the individual has no memory of what happened to him. It is not difficult to see such an event as the eruption of long-repressed rage in a personality prone to dissociation, and some people so afflicted are actually psychotic. In retrospect, it usually becomes clear that the victims of such attacks are chosen for some clear reason, such as infidelity.

Some religiously oriented psychologists consider the possibility of possession in their differential diagnosis of extreme mental states (Cramer, 1980; Keener, 2010). Peck (1983) distinguishes between human evil and metaphysical or "demonic" evil, which he believes produces genuine possession that can be distinguished from true mental illness. He believes that one can be both mentally ill and possessed at the same time. It is also true that mentally ill people may have the delusion they are possessed by a demonic force. The subjective experience of schizophrenia may include passivity phenomena in which the individual feels controlled by outside influences, especially when the phenomenon of possession is part of the individual's pre-existing belief system. From the point of view of depth psychology, the psychotic person is at the mercy of archetypal or daimonic levels of the unconscious whose affective intensity overwhelms the ego. Presumably the attribution of demonic influence is an attempt to make sense of, or symbolize, a terrifying experience.

The belief that human beings can be taken over by demonic entities has not fully disappeared. The ancient practice of exorcism is still performed. Ellenberger (1981) points out that exorcism is an early form of psychotherapy, and one might consider psychotherapy metaphorically as a form of exorcism of the patient's emotional "demons." Diamond (1996) and Peck (1983) provide comprehensive discussions of the similarities and differences between psychotherapy and exorcism. Whether one considers seriously disturbed people to be afflicted by literal demons or by the archetypal level of the psyche depends on one's metaphysical commitments. If the psychotherapist has a religious commitment, he might color his assessment of the patient's condition accordingly.

The direct experience of evil

For Freud, a demon is a personified aspect of one's own mind that has been repressed and projected onto this mythological figure. The projection of one's own evil onto the devil prevents the guilt and shame involved in recognizing that the evil is a part of oneself. Another psychological approach to "demon possession" is to see it as the result of the personality being overwhelmed by toxic subpersonalities. (These are complexes in Jung's sense.) The personification of such material may appear in the form of images of demonic figures that may emerge during psychotherapy. Berkowitz (1968) reports the cases of four analysands in whom the image of the devil appeared. All of these individuals were well educated and sophisticated, and incredulous at this appearance. One woman reported that something was "growing" inside her, like a baby, taking the form of a little black devil with horns and a tail, about six to twelve inches long. It looked like a statue and was felt to be a part of her although also alien. The image disappeared during the therapeutic session. Another woman experienced the hallucination of a disembodied male head that grinned and leered at her triumphantly and sarcastically. A young man experienced his "other self" as an ugly monster with a dark head, small pointed ears, wide lips, and sharp, bat-like pointed teeth. A woman dreamed of a tiny black devil with horns. Berkowitz believed that these images represent ego dystonic images of the self that had been repressed, or, in the case of the dream, the figure represented a negative father image. From a Jungian perspective, these are archetypal images of evil. Their emergence during a psychotherapeutic process indicates that a particularly toxic complex has been activated. The unconscious usually produces this kind of symbolic material in a dream, but such imagery may appear spontaneously in the waking state as a form of active imagination, a manifestation of the *mundus imaginalis* described by Corbin and Jung.[11]

A large collection of personal encounters with demonic entities has been described by Jakobsen (1999), reported on the website of the Alister Hardy Religious Experience Research Unit at the University of Lampeter in Wales. Sometimes these take the form of the sense of an evil presence in the room:

> I could feel this sense of evil enveloping me. I had the terrifying impression that this evil force or presence was bent upon taking possession of me. . . . I only knew that I was enveloped by this revolting force – so vile and rotting – I could almost taste the evil. I was in terror – so much so I could not call out or move.
>
> (p. 9)

Or:

> A year and a half ago I was asleep in the night, and woke very suddenly and felt quite alert. I felt surrounded and threatened by the most terrifying and powerful presence of Evil. It seemed to be localized within the room. It seemed almost physical and in a curious way it 'crackled', though not audibly. It was also extremely 'black' and I felt overwhelmed with terror.
>
> (p. 10)

At other times the subject actually sees a demonic figure:

> I awoke in the night with a terrible feeling of oppression in the room and my heart seemed to stop beating when I saw hovering near the ceiling in a far corner a luminous, grinning, grimacing gargoyle-like face, not static but pulsating. I was instantly wide awake and filled with terrible fear and anger that this thing should come and manifest itself to me. I remember picking up anything within reach and flinging it at the grinning evil face and like a flash it darted to within inches of my face. I was petrified and felt as if I was suffocating in a blanket of evil.
>
> (p. 11)

Or:

> Then a little figure manifested itself. It was like a sitting dog with a curly tail, large ears up-pointed, a man's face and had horns curling forward. It spoke to me in a high pitched unpleasant voice saying 'You are afraid of us but you cannot get rid of us. We are going to stay with you and we can come nearer.' It did and I felt a great fear, I felt that Evil spirits had come close and made themselves visible to me.
>
> (p. 12)

Typically, the individual is able to get rid of such visitations by the use of prayer. Jakobsen's subjects all believed that their experiences occurred in the waking state and were not dreams. It would of course be easy to dismiss these accounts as hysterical, illusory, hallucinatory, or the projection of negatively toned complexes. However, if one accepts the existence of a spiritual dimension, then the ontological status of these experiences is not so clear. Believers in spirits see the reported images as self-existent entities rather than personal contents of the psyche. We are dealing here with an area of human experience that defies explanation in the materialistic scientific sense, yet is not uncommon and cannot be proven to be illusory. These experiences do not allow for unambiguous or categorical analysis unless one is a confirmed materialist. In this debate, we tend to take positions based on our own metaphysical commitments. Pre-existing belief systems and biases clearly affect both our perception of reality and our interpretation of it. My own inclination is to take seriously William James's point that our normal, waking consciousness is only one type of consciousness, and we are separated by a thin screen from other forms of consciousness that are entirely different from ours. In his words: "No account of the universe in its totality can be final which leaves these other forms of consciousness quite disregarded" (1902/1958, p. 298).

In the 1980s and 1990s, there was widespread concern about satanic cults engaging in various forms of evil behavior. Many people claimed to be victims of Satanic Ritual Abuse (Smith & Prader, 1980), which for a while became a diagnostic category in its own right, based on the testimony of children or the memories of adults during psychotherapy, which were often recovered under hypnosis. This anxiety was consistent with the fear of Satan among evangelical Christians. However, a storm of controversy arose about whether these accounts were realistic or whether they were a cultural phenomenon analogous to medieval anxiety about witches. Skeptics pointed out the lack of forensic or legally acceptable evidence for these cults and insisted on the gullibility of therapists who were too ready to accept such stories. Skeptics believed that the reliability of recovered memories of abuse is often questionable, typically attributed to suggestion by a charismatic therapist or simply the result of confabulation or fantasy. Therapists who accepted the reality of these events pointed to the similarity of the stories, the social need to deny unpleasant truths, and the fact that a severely traumatic memory may be forgotten, but it is embedded in the body and appears in the form of flashbacks. Other therapists took the position that whether or not the stories were real, it was helpful to treat their patients as if their memories were valid.

One way to approach an individual who claims to have been a victim of satanic ritual abuse is to think of it as a narrative attempt to construct coherent meaning, to make sense of otherwise inexplicable feelings. Narrative truth differs from historical truth that is subject to factual confirmation, and a drawback of the narrative approach is that it can be too relative and too subjective; facts are important. Nevertheless, even if the therapist does not know the facts, it is important to pay attention to the personal meaning of the patient's story. The therapist can work with the patient's subjective reality while suspending judgment about its objective reality. The argument about the reality of these events seemed to center on radically different worldviews as much as on technical differences of opinion. Presumably, whether or not satanic ritual abuse occurs in the way some people claimed, the stories took hold because there is a need to believe in the reality of evil. (A summary of the debate is found in Van Bernschoten [1990].)

There have been various attempts to explain beliefs in satanic magic. One is based on the dynamics of the narcissistic personality, who is particularly prone to identification with internal bad objects, leading to contempt for others and an attitude of superiority – behind which is an empty, hungry, envious, core self. Ivey (1993, 2002) points out that participation in satanic cults and satanic magic helps to counter this painful feeling by inducing a sense of power. The idealization of destructive parts of the personality occurs when a malignant, sadistic aspect of the self is fused with a bad internal object. Ivey believes that Satanism is attractive to these individuals because it gives them a mythic and ritual structure that resonates with a destructive sub-personality; they identify with a mythic representation of the internal persecutor (Satan), which is thereby befriended and supplicated. There is no need to be afraid of monsters if you become a monster yourself. This identification creates the narcissistic illusion that the demonic powers are one's own, leading to inflation and the belief in supernatural powers. All of this is actively facilitated by ritual and cult activity such as the black mass. Ivey believes that these rituals are a regressive resurrection of infantile omnipotence, which equates thought and action. Psychotic or magical thinking does not distinguish between a symbol and that which is symbolized. It is better to be evil and strong by bonding with the bad object symbolized by Satan than to be innocent but vulnerable.

Ivey (ibid.) suggests that the psychological purpose of participating in satanic cults is to dethrone the Christian Father-God and try to create what has been referred to as an anal universe, where everything is fecal. These cult members usually have childhood histories of rejection, abuse, and neglect by parents. They are children who rebel against an unjust father, living out the myth of the ejection of Satan from heaven.

In other sectors of the psychotherapy literature, the treatment of people claiming to be survivors of ritual abuse was viewed using the language of spiritual warfare and literal confrontation with the demonic. Friesen (1992) used this terminology to address what he saw as a conflict between the kingdom of God and the forces of Satan. He worked with people claiming to be survivors of satanic ritual abuse, and he believed he could differentiate between true possession by evil spirits and multiple personality disorder. He suggested that demonic entities can disguise themselves as sub-personalities. In his opinion, ego-dystonic personality traits, aspects of the personality of which the person is aware but does not like, tend to become ego-syntonic during the course of psychotherapy if there is no evil spirit present. If an evil spirit is present, the personality state remains ego-alien. He coined the term Oppressive Supernatural State Disorder for this presence, which he believed produces revulsion towards Christian symbols, the presence of supernatural powers such as telepathy or levitation, and a counter-transference feeling of an evil presence. From a psychoanalytic perspective, this approach literalizes and reifies intrapsychic configurations and then projects them into mythological categories.

An apologist for the notion that evil has an ontologically real dimension – rather than being exclusively a form of human behavior – will point out that if there is a spiritual level of reality that affects us, there is no reason to assume that this level is entirely benign. There is a long biblical history of the discernment of spirits, the attempt to discover whether an experience truly comes from the Holy Spirit. Yet, since the Enlightenment, many Christians have given up belief in spiritual entities such as angels and devils, ignoring the fact that the New Testament contains many accounts of different types of spirits.[12] Some theologians wish to explain away the Bible's accounts of demons as merely superstitious vestiges of the worldview of an earlier time that distract us from the New Testament's ethical teaching. However, the notion of a struggle between the reign of God and the reign of Satan has long been central to Christian thinking. This idea is found in the writing of many of the early Church Fathers, not to mention Luther and Calvin. Jesus obviously believed that people can be influenced by spiritual (non-material) powers. If the New Testament accounts of Jesus's exorcism of demons were to be ignored, a large component of his ministry would be discounted.

In part, modern disbelief in spiritual entities has been a reaction to the abhorrent witch craze of medieval times, followed by the positivist, materialist turn in mainstream culture that does not take seriously the idea of a reality that cannot be touched and measured. This turn also helps to account for the resistance to Jung's notion of the archetypal level of the psyche, which is really only a new way of talking about its spiritual dimension, or a way of saying that there are non-material levels of reality.

The Antichrist

In Christian lore, the Antichrist is a completely evil human being who is an enemy of Christ and hostile to all forms of goodness. In contrast to the devil, who is super-natural, the Antichrist seems to personify absolute human evil (McGinn, 1994). He is a prominent figure in Christian eschatology or apocalypticism, the doctrine of the End Times, which have been thought to be imminent for a long time. In legend, the End Times will be heralded by the Antichrist's attempt to bring about the victory of the powers of evil, although he will be vanquished by Christ at the Second Coming. Many Christians have believed that this battle will be necessary to finally establish the reign of Christ on earth. It is hard to say how many people other than fundamentalists still believe in this figure, but in the course of history various figures have been declared to be the Antichrist; Napoleon, Luther, Mus-solini, and some popes are only a few examples. Another school of thought sees this figure subjectively, as something in the individual that resists faith in Christ. The mythic notion of the Antichrist, like belief in the devil, seems to be based on the projection of human anxieties about evil. The idea has other important psycho-logical functions; McGinn (1994) suggests that apocalyptic eschatology provides believers with a ready-made structure of meaning for dealing with the presence of evil and the absence of meaning they perceive in the world. Apocalyptic hopes are based on belief in divine vindication and the expectation of the ultimate tran-scendence of death.

For Jung, the idea of the Antichrist is an "inexorable psychological law" (CW 9, ii, p. 43), because Christianity has split its God-image by making it exclusively light, so the dark side of the Self has to be projected onto the Antichrist. There seems to be no analogous human figure in Islam or Judaism.

Philosophical approaches to evil

The problem of evil has engaged philosophers since antiquity. In an extensive scholarly review of philosophical approaches, Neiman (2015) has suggested that "the problem of evil is the guiding force of modern thought" (p. 2), and even that "the problem of evil is the root from which modern philosophy springs" (p. 13).

Philosophers of antiquity

Most of the classical Greek thinkers believed that reason and rational judgment should rule our behavior. For them, evil tends to be seen as a product of the mate-rial world and human desires, passions, and impulses. Socrates believed that if we can discern what is good we will inevitably act rightly; we only act wrongly when we are confused about what is good – we mistake an evil act for a good one because of ignorance. Lack of knowledge of what is virtuous leads to evil; we do not willfully act in an evil manner; we choose what we think is good without realizing it is evil. Socrates insists that human nature has the innate ability to distinguish between good and evil. However, while this might be true for children who do not know better, the notion that no one intentionally chooses evil has often been challenged and does not hold up to scrutiny.

Plato believed that human existence is ordered rationally by forces that aim at balance and proportion; if these are in correct measure, goodness results. In his *Republic* he develops a character called Thrasymachus who believes that justice is based on the interests of the strong. Such a ruler only follows the law to the extent it is advantageous to him, and he is only interested in dominating others – a type of tyrannical personality that is obviously still with us. In the *Phaedrus*, Plato gives us a mythic image of the duality of good and evil in human nature. He depicts the soul in the form of a chariot drawn by two horses, one noble and the other ignoble and hard to control. The charioteer represents reason or intellect, which has to act as a guide. The Platonic notion is that no one does evil intentionally, but people have mistaken ideas about what is good, so that evil is the result of ignorance. However, it is obviously implausible to suggest that just correcting mistaken thinking or providing more accurate information would lead an evildoer to desist. Such an individual might well insist that his own welfare or that of his cause requires him to act as he does. Nevertheless, the belief that morality conforms to reason has been influential in the Western intellectual tradition, but as Kekes (2005) points out, the problem with this view is that evil has a thrill of its own, and it is not unreasonable to opt for a life of evil as an alternative to a life of boredom. Some people do evil because it is evil; evil is their motivation and they do it knowingly. Evil is much more than a mistake.

Verene (2010) uses Plato's story of the Ring of Gyges as a way of thinking about the concerns raised by the psychopathic character. To imagine what would happen if we were free of any concern about being caught and punished, so that we could do as we wished, Plato tells the story of a shepherd who found a ring that allowed him to become invisible. Using the power of the ring, he was able to seduce the king's wife, kill the king, and become ruler of the kingdom. Plato asks what the difference would be between a just and an unjust person who wore such a ring. He suggests that no one would be so incorruptible that he would not commit evil acts under such circumstances. Verene believes that this story "captures the essence of the sociopath" (p. 204). This personality type knows that he possesses the ring of Gyges; he is invisible owing to his command of rhetoric, lying, deceit, and dissimulation. The sociopath masquerades as an ordinary person while manipulating others to attain his own ends, while avoiding any penalties for doing so. Sociopaths lack the necessary emotions that are the seat of moral sensibility and obligation, so they impersonate ordinary human beings. They feel superior to people who are governed by a sense of virtue and justice; they regard the emotions and morality of others as weaknesses that make them vulnerable to the power of the sociopath.

Aristotle discusses evil in the form of weakness of the will (*akrasia*), which means giving in to actions about which we feel guilty, as if the intellect or reason cannot control these actions, so we act against our better judgment. Either we do what we know we should not do, or our desire interferes with our perception of what is right. Aristotle's view assumes we are free to make the necessary choice.

Later philosophers

In his *Leviathon*, Hobbes suggests that good and evil are not metaphysical or naturally occurring categories; they are decided upon by the consensus of human communities, and they reflect our desires and aversions. He describes the "state of nature" as the human condition in the absence of civilizing influences and socially determined moral norms. In that condition, we are selfish; we would all try to meet our basic needs, and we would be afraid of others because we know they could be dangerous. We would then be in a paranoid state of "war of all against all," and no one could really be trusted. Therefore, to have a civilized society we cannot rely on human decency; we have to have laws, and we must acknowledge our tendency toward savagery. Hobbes believes that our moral codes and ethical systems are the result of collective agreements – we are not naturally moral. We therefore need strong social authority to ensure good behavior, or human life will be reduced to being "solitary, poor, nasty, brutish, and short." We can hear an early presentiment of Freud's *Civilization and Its Discontents* in Hobbes.

In contrast to Hobbes, Rousseau (in his *Discourse on the Origins of Inequality*) believed that the natural state of human beings is peace and harmony. In his view, people are naturally born good, and we are restrained from hurting others by a natural sense of pity for others, but we are corrupted by society, for example when competition for land and property creates inequality and injustice. He is generally considered to have too romantic a view of human nature.

The problem of evil was central to the work of the philosopher Leibniz. In 1709, in his *Theodicy*, Leibniz tried to defend God in the face of evil. He suggested first that the creator was limited by the possibilities available to him; finite existence is imperfect, but because of God's goodness he created the least imperfect world, or the best of all possible worlds, and any other world would be worse. (This idea raises the question of why God would create imperfect creatures, but Leibnitz does not think that God is an underachiever.) In 1755, a devastating earthquake shook the city of Lisbon and almost completely destroyed it, killing tens of thousands of people. This example of natural evil led philosophers such as Voltaire to radically question Leibniz's idea, which in the face of such a disaster seemed far too optimistic. Voltaire pointed out that it is useless to try to justify or make sense of these kinds of disasters, and the attempt to do so merely distracts us from the practical problem of dealing with them. It does not seem plausible to insist that this world is the best of all possible worlds, since we can easily conceive of a world without the level of evil we see all around us.

In his *Dialogues Concerning Natural Religion*, Hume pointed out the difficulty of believing in an omnipotent God who could prevent evil but does not, while claiming that this God is entirely good. If he could prevent evil but does not, he cannot be all good, and if he cannot prevent evil he cannot be all powerful. Given the amount of evil in the world, the most we can infer is that God is morally neutral. Hume pointed out that we have no way to know whether God will ultimately rectify the obviously unjust distribution of evil and suffering. To prove the existence of God, the believer would have to show that all the evil and suffering in the world is somehow necessary and unavoidable, which we cannot do. Hume also points out that God could have made things easier for his creatures, with less pain and without the extremes we see in natural phenomena.

Kant believed that human nature is essentially good, but we also possess an inexplicable propensity or predisposition towards evil. In his *Religion Within the Limits of Bare Reason*, he asserts that radical evil is found when our will wants to privilege itself over the general good. For Kant (1998/1793), the misuse of free will leads to evil; good and evil are rational choices. He denied that there could be people whose reason is entirely exempt from any moral law – he did not think people would knowingly do evil for its own sake, because human beings cannot be truly devilish. Most critics point out that this attitude ignores the non-rational, emotional aspects of human nature, and also ignores the fact that sometimes evil is outside of human control, either because of circumstances or because of unconscious factors. Other critics point out that it is by no means certain that human nature is essentially good; Kant does not take into account the fact that there are people who simply enjoy inflicting pain on others, even when this is not necessary.

Kant suggested that evil is actually a form of self-indulgence, and when this leads to evil behavior, it is the result of weakness in the personality. Wicked people know that what they are doing is wrong, but they are too frail to resist. Kant believed that we can be motivated either by our desires or by our principles. We can determine whether a principle is right if we try to universalize it and see the consequences. For example, if everyone were to lie, no one would believe anything anyone said, leading to chaos, so we can derive the moral principle that lying is wrong. A moral principle is therefore one that can be generalized so that everyone acts in accord with it. In his view, evil arises when we adopt a principle that subordinates morality to self-interest; we then live by an evil maxim. According to Kant, it is our responsibility and part of our freedom to deal with evil (Dews, 2012), but we cannot ultimately solve the problem of evil, and we cannot decide about the role of God in the production of evil.

Schopenhauer regarded nature as the product of a blind will, which is manifest at all levels of existence. In human beings this appears in the form of desire and craving, so that our lives are a continuous series of frustrations, and in the end life is futile and wretched. One way out of this is by means of aesthetic experience, such as art; another is achieved through compassionate action that relieves the suffering of others. For him, most evil is due to selfishness; it is a problem of human nature. The ascetic struggles against human nature, and he resolves the problem of evil by the negation of desire and the extinction of the will.

In *The Genealogy of Morals*, Nietzsche writes that those in power determine our definitions of good and evil; powerful people assume they are good, and they define others with less power as evil or bad. That is, evil is in the eye of the beholder. He believed that Christianity promoted a "slave morality" invented by priests and those envious of more powerful people. This morality advocates meekness and the mistaken notion that all human beings have equal value; notions of good and evil were invented by weak people as a way of criticizing their powerful oppressors. What strong people do to promote their own lives is defined as evil by the weak. Nietzsche pointed out that merely to submit to collective morality is not itself moral; we are only genuine when our morality is determined by our feelings and our will to live. What the collective considers to be evil may be good for the individual and vice versa. He would prefer to get rid of notions of good and evil and replace them by asking whether an action promotes life. For him, whatever strengthens us is good, and whatever weakens us is evil.

For Marx, evil lies in our social structures, especially the unequal distribution of wealth and other inequalities, which make people behave in evil ways. Evil is therefore contingent; if we had a more egalitarian social system that would allow people to develop themselves and exercise their talents and skills, evil would be less prevalent. For him, only the necessary change in social conditions could eliminate major evils such as war and slavery, because the basic cause of these problems lies in the discrepancy of wealth in our society. By emphasizing social conditions so much, this approach does not take into account the sources of evil within human psychology.

In *The Gospel of Suffering*, Kierkegaard accepts the idea that evil is a result of divinely given human freedom. He believes we have to accept the existence of evil as a necessary side effect of this freedom. However, Kierkegaard points out that we are fearful of our freedom, since it makes us anxious about what we think and what we do. The fact that we have freedom makes us radically responsible, and this produces dread. At the same time, we are proud creatures, and our sinfulness is a result of this combination of fear and pride. That is, fear and despair are at the root of evil. But he believes that evil is essential for human development, especially spiritual development.

It is not surprising that during the twentieth century many philosophers were reluctant to discuss evil because it seemed to be a theological idea. An important exception was the work of Camus. In *The Plague*, he uses the allegory of a plague infecting a city to describe the way in which evil (in this case, fascism) corrupts a society. Early on, many people in the city refuse to recognize the real nature of the plague. It takes some time to overcome their resistance to its reality. Then they try to find a cosmic explanation for the plague, perhaps an act of God. Finally, they realize that they can never answer questions about the cause of the plague, and the attempt to do so actually distracts them from the reality of its evil; they must band together and bear witness in order to respond to it.

There has been a resurgence of interest in evil among contemporary philosophers (e.g., Dews, 2012), who tend to see evil in radically immanent terms, without invoking anything supernatural. Thus, Svendsen (2010) insists that evil is about human relationships, not about a supernatural force, so it is a mistake to call evil inhuman, because evil is all too human. Svendsen believes that theology is irrelevant to our understanding of the problems posed by evil, and evil "should only be considered as a human, moral problem" (p. 77).

Taylor (2000) argues that there is nothing transcendent or objective about good and evil or moral values, and nothing is intrinsically good or evil. Notions of good and evil originate because human beings have desires and felt needs; a thing is good only in relation to someone who wants or desires it, and something is only evil to one who is averse to it. If we had no desires, we would not have values such as good and evil. Right and wrong are socially determined rules and practices for behavior, based on common goals and interests. A practice that promotes cooperation towards meeting our desires or resolving conflict is good, and practices that prevent cooperation and conflict resolution are wrong. Taylor therefore believes there is no absolute standard to decide whether something is good or evil apart from human desires. Goodness is that which satisfies our desires, while evil is that which frustrates them. In this view, reasoning about good and evil themselves is secondary to the fulfillment of desires. The obvious problem with this argument is that it implies that the desire to inflict pain for no reason on another person would not be considered to be evil, since it is good for the sadist because it satisfies his desire, as if the desire itself is neither good nor bad.

Ward (2002) believes that evil behavior is actually behavior based on principles of which the actor is unconscious, and basing behavior on principles gives their behavior a moral aspect. Ward relies on Peck's notion that malignant narcissists will not submit to anything higher than themselves, so they are governed by a narcissistic self-image regardless of the effects on others. Peck suggests that evil people act on unconscious maxims, such as "protect your self-image at all costs." Ward points out that they behave as if such an unacknowledged, irrational maxim is a moral principle that is universally valid. This principle acts as a hidden source of power. Its development was necessary for the person to survive in childhood, but it later drives adult behavior. This maxim also makes their behavior inexplicable to others and to themselves, and makes them lie to themselves. It sounds as if Ward is describing the notion of unconscious organizing principles – themes within the personality that unconsciously organize emotional and relational experiences. According to intersubjectivity theorists, these are pre-reflective principles that are the basic building blocks of character structure. These principles might sometimes be components of a vertical split in the personality, which is the result of disavowal. The material in the split-off segment manifests itself in behavior or compulsions that feel alien or inconsistent (Kohut, 1979). The split results from selfobject failure in childhood, leading to a fragile sense of self, sensitivity to criticism, or a painful sense of internal emptiness. This fragility may be disguised by a persona of self-importance or grandiosity and entitlement. On the healthier side of the split, the individual may be successful, and this is the side with which the individual identifies, but on the problematic side of the split, the individual may experience inexplicable rage, depression, or compulsive behavior in an attempt to fill the sense of emptiness. Sometimes this may lead to destructive behavior, either to oneself or to others.

Horne (2008) eschews any "foundational" explanations of evil, meaning knowledge based on secure, basic beliefs, such as the notion of evil as a kind of force. Horne suggests that to derive knowledge of what is evil from *a priori* postulates without reference to historical or contemporary contexts is to give that knowledge "the cloak of universality and permanence" (p. 670). In contrast, he wants to conceptualize evil hermeneutically and phenomenologically, such that understanding evil emerges by means of interpretation within its cultural and historical contexts. For him, such understanding is always provisional and context-dependent.

An alternative to all these views is the notion that evil is truly beyond comprehension; it is mysterious, rationally and emotionally impossible to understand. As Verhoef (2014) suggests, because of the gap between our experience of evil and our ability to understand it, there is always "something more" to evil (p. 263), in which case there is a need to speak about evil in a transcendental sense, and we might need mythological representations of evil. She notes that Levinas describes evil as something that cannot be integrated into the world because it does not fit into our attempt to grasp the world as a whole; for him, evil is something radically Other.

Ricoeur (1967) also believes that evil is inaccessible to philosophical reflection and is irreducible, and we need the language of myths and symbols to describe evil. He believes that the concept of evil is primordial and coexistent with the divine origin of things. Human beings encounter evil, for example in the myth of the Garden of Eden where evil is present at the beginning in the form of the serpent, and then people continue to commit evil acts. For him: "Evil is not nothing . . . it is the power of darkness . . . something to be taken away" (p. 155). He believes however that evil is subordinate to original goodness.

A coda on evil and religion

Why did Jesus say "resist not evil" (Matt. 5: 39)? Perhaps he thought we cannot focus on evil without being affected by it or without becoming evil oneself. A crusader against evil becomes preoccupied with evil, and it might do more damage to be against the devil than to be for God. However, Christians often ignore this teaching. Although there is a long tradition of Christian non-violence, there is also a long-standing association between Christianity and violence, exemplified by the Crusades, the Inquisition, and the historical persecution of Christians who were considered to be blasphemers or heretics. In modern times the notion of a just war was applied to the invasion of Iraq by Christian leaders.[13]

Krueger (2013) notes that to view Jesus as a sacrifice for sin depicts a violent God-image. Apocalyptic imagery, found in the Book of Revelation and the notion of a final Battle of Armageddon, is extremely violent. Religions often justify violence, and this is especially true for the three major monotheistic traditions, each of which believes that God especially favors them. The texts in the Hebrew Bible that justify mass slaughter (e.g., Joshua 11: 20) are obvious examples. The Exodus story of the delivery of the ancient Hebrews from slavery in Egypt depicts the death of the innocent, first-born children of the Egyptians. Nevertheless, the Exodus story has inspired many movements of political liberation, such as the African American struggle against slavery, but it has also justified the violent white settlement of the American West. Thus, the New England Puritans of the seventeenth century imagined themselves as the "new Israelites wresting control of a promised land from the evil Canaanites" (Krueger, 2013, p. 247). Native American Indians were considered to be less than human devil worshipers. The rhetoric of Manifest Destiny appeared during this period, teaching that God had "destined the nation to expand across the continent" (ibid.), so that it was a duty to exterminate American Indians.

There are spiritually motivated, non-violent alternatives to fighting evil with evil. Mahatma Gandhi demonstrated non-violent power as an alternative to the use of physical violence, although he also advocated extreme behavior such as prolonged fasting and harsh physical discipline, which could be seen as coercive. Today, Gandhi's attitude is seen as too utopian and politically ineffective, and we seem to be resigned to the notion that violence is inevitable. But civil disobedience, demonstrations, and other forms of non-cooperation that Gandhi called "soul force" have been effective, although they may require sacrifice of the self and great courage. Many spiritual leaders have demonstrated the capacity to endure personal suffering for a greater good. There are many examples besides Christ; Martin Luther King Jr., Nelson Mandela, and Aung San Suu Kyi come to mind. Skeptics, however, point out that their kind of non-violence would not work in the case of ruthless authoritarian governments with no scruples.

Notes

1 I'm referring to events such as the killing of the inhabitants of 60 cities in Deuteronomy 3, the killing of the men, women, and children described in Joshua 6 and Kings 10: 18–27, the murders and rapes told in Judges 21, and so on.
2 "Knowing good and evil" may refer to sexuality.
3 This story may be an allegory of the ancient competition between nomadic tribes and settled agriculturalists. The ancient interpreters have many "explanations" of God's preference for Abel, including the idea that Cain was the son of the devil or an angel, or that his offering was inferior or that he was a wicked individual.
4 Lamarckian theory said that acquired characteristics can be transmitted to the individual's offspring.

5 *The Dhammapada* is a collection of teachings of the Buddha and an important Buddhist scripture.
6 One of the difficulties here is that there are ideological mistranslations of the Hebrew Bible, so that the figure of Satan as Christianity understands it may have been developed at a later time for doctrinal purposes and retrospectively inserted into the original Hebrew text. The biblical Satan was originally a divine messenger who carries out the will of God, and his behavior has very little in common with later theological descriptions of him. The figure of an evil messenger of God seems to have gradually become more and more independent of God, evolving into the figure of an independent entity named Satan (Russell, 1992).
7 The Hajj is an annual pilgrimage to Mecca. It is a mandatory religious duty for Muslims at least once in the individual's lifetime.
8 Accusations of witchcraft were also a convenient way of enforcing the ideology of the Church, demonizing people the authorities could not control, and scapegoating devalued groups when things went wrong in the community.
9 Pareidolia is the experience of seeing images such as faces in clouds or on the moon.
10 F44.3, in the section under dissociative disorders.
11 The term *mundus imaginalis* is used by the Islamic scholar Henri Corbin. Following a Sufi tradition, Corbin believes that the imaginal realm is a spiritual order of reality, and imaginal cognition is a faculty that perceives this dimension. It corresponds to Jung's active imagination.
12 In Matthew 13: 39, angels gather the children of God and take evildoers away to perdition. There are many references to unclean spirits, such as Luke 4: 33, Luke 7: 21, and Luke 8: 2. In Matthew 16: 27 the Son of Man will be accompanied by his angels when he comes. See also Mark 13: 27, Luke 9: 26, Matthew 25: 41, the book of Revelation, and many other instances of the appearance of angels.
13 In October 2002, the Southern Baptist Convention sent a letter to President George W. Bush endorsing his call for an invasion of Iraq.

Chapter 8

Psychological aspects of religious fundamentalism and terrorism

Religious fundamentalism

Fundamentalists of all religious traditions believe that theirs is the only true religion or the only path to salvation. They usually believe that they have special knowledge of the divine intentions, because their sacred texts are infallibly true divine revelations. At the extreme, a text such as the Bible is believed to take priority over scientific authority in matters such as evolution or the age of the earth. The fundamentalists' belief that they have special access to sacred knowledge often leads to a sense of superiority and self-righteousness. Members of other faiths, or more liberal people within their own tradition who do not share the fundamentalist's beliefs, are either devalued or even demonized. Many fundamentalists believe that their tradition should adhere to its original founding principles, and later innovations can only be a departure from an original purity. Fundamentalists often reject modernity because of its moral relativism and its tolerance of alternative lifestyles. Instead, they embrace a fervent absolutism that includes a punitive, judgmental, even sadistic image of God and a preoccupation with religious purity and the control of thought and behavior. Their pursuit of purity often involves struggling with an internal sense of badness or bad feelings, which they sometimes attempt to get rid of through a ritual process. If the badness is projected onto others, they may be attacked or even killed.

Some Christian fundamentalists have a genuine fear that people who do not believe will suffer eternal punishment, so evangelizing is crucial. Other groups such as ultra-orthodox Jews prefer to remain insular and isolated from mainstream society. Many Christian fundamentalists suffer from a conflict between belief in a God who is said to be loving but also angry and punitive if they misbehave. Fundamentalists of all types are often dangerously militaristic and quite willing to impose their own structures of law and behavior onto others. There is a well-known relationship between violence and fundamentalism, and this becomes a particularly toxic brew if fundamentalist religion becomes intertwined with politics.

Despite the intense piety often found among fundamentalists, and their explicit desire to save souls, many of them are also very interested in territory and the acquisition of money; in particular, their leaders are often inordinately interested in wealth and power. Thus, we often find that some fundamentalists have considerable expertise in fund-raising, marketing, social media, and advertising.

Fundamentalism is often seen as a reaction to factors such as globalization, science, the rise of feminism, and the decline of religious belief (Armstrong, 2001), but these societal factors do not take into account the inner world of the fundamentalist and his psychology. Psychological factors help to explain the research suggesting that reactionary religious systems tend to flourish more than religions that are more liberal and accommodating to modern life (Berger, 1999). Fundamentalists prefer to avoid complexity in their understanding of their religion, perhaps because a clear set of beliefs soothes important anxieties such as the fear of death. The simplification of complex situations into binary oppositions such as good and evil creates order out of chaos, reduces uncertainty, and allows for a predictable worldview free of doubt. The fundamentalist then feels a sense of mastery and clarity instead of feeling powerless. Not surprisingly, the fundamentalist usually devalues the present situation of the world and hopes for a glorious, often messianic future era.

Partly because they need certainty, fundamentalists typically reject any symbolic, metaphorical or allegorical interpretation of their sacred text, insisting on its literal meaning, or they only allow interpretation of the text from a doctrinal viewpoint. Instead of understanding the truth that a religious symbol is pointing to, or what the symbol means psychologically, they take the symbol literally and freeze its meaning. They prefer that truth be single, and they are intolerant of any questioning of their beliefs, sometimes leading to hatred of non-believers that may lead to violence. Their antipathy to non-believers occurs partly because to listen to criticism or the doubt of unbelievers would stir up any latent doubt of their own, so the non-believer has to carry the projection of the fundamentalist's own religious doubt. Non-believers also carry the projection of the fundamentalist's internalized toxic objects, contributing to an obsession with purity. Any sense of personal badness can be evacuated onto unbelievers and fought out there, rather than within the self.

Fundamentalism has a seductive quality to people looking for straightforward answers, to those who yearn to belong, and to those who have an external locus of control, who feel that their lives are controlled by factors over which they have little influence. They are sometimes looking for values and a direction in life that they cannot find inside themselves; hence they are attracted to a charismatic leader and to a group that demands allegiance, sacrifice, and loyalty from its followers for the sake of an ideal.

Fundamentalists have built their lives on a narrow religious structure and system of beliefs. Sometimes this structure is simply one that they have grown up with and internalized from birth, so that they are heavily conditioned to believe its teachings. When development has led to a fragile sense of self or to deficits in the structure of the self, the structures of the tradition substitute for the internal self-structures needed to prevent fragmentation anxiety. Rigid adherence to traditional structures of belief and practice can be used to buttress the cohesion of the self. In the absence of personal goals and values, the fundamentalist falls back on an external set of clear rules and regulations such as those provided by a sacred text and the theological superstructure that tradition has erected upon it. Furthermore, to belong to a group of people who fervently share one's beliefs and mirror one's values helps to sustain one's sense of self. A tight-knit community meets any unmet alter ego or twinship needs in Kohut's (1984) sense, the need to feel like other people. The individual feels contained and safer within the protective shell provided by other members of his group, although this shell too often becomes a straightjacket. The adoption of strongly held ideals and values may compensate for internal fragility and buttress fragile intrapsychic structures needed to ward off dysphoric affects. Stein (2006) highlights the important difference between the religious sense of the sacred as the confrontation with the numinosum and fundamentalism as submission to the projected image of the internalized father, described as "the self-rejecting submission to an ideal authority that finally turns out to be submission to an alienated (projected), horrifying aspect of oneself" (p. 208).

One can integrate one's need for external structure with a pre-existing system of meaning such a religious or political (or psychotherapeutic!) system. The choice of the system's content is not important for this process to succeed psychologically. The intense, fanatical belief found among political and religious ideologues may also be used for defensive self-stimulation, and it is like an addiction used to ward off deadness in the absence of a firm sense of self. A charitable view of fundamentalist truth claims, and for some people of religious dogmas in general, is to see these beliefs as transitional phenomena that serve important psychological functions in Winnicott's (1971) sense.[1] This approach does not absolve such beliefs of criticism and says nothing about their claims to absolute historical truth.

Fundamentalists are often very tribal, and they split humanity into "us" and "them," "our goodness vs. their evil," or "we are the only saved or chosen ones." This kind of splitting defense shields the individual against the uncertainties of modern culture but has the effect of radically separating fundamentalists from others, sometimes leading to the formation of separate schools and communities for the sake of safety from a godless world. A high level of anxiety, projected and experienced as a fear of the modern world, may account for the fundamentalist's typical preoccupation with apocalyptic imagery and his sense that we are approaching the End Times or the Eschaton, the notion that world events will come to a climactic war of good and evil. The archetypal idea of a final Day of Judgment is found in all three Abrahamic faiths.

Fundamentalism brings a sense of certainty that simplifies some aspects of life because the tradition gives pre-formed answers to life's questions. However, the price for this illusion of certainty is a loss of individual decision making, a loss of the ability to express one's spirituality in unique ways, a narrow view of life, and a restricted imagination. Fundamentalist beliefs also tend to oversimplify the individual's approach to human nature and the complexity of human relationships.

Importantly, fundamentalists do not trust spontaneously occurring numinous imagery or religious experience that does not conform to orthodoxy. Authentic numinous experience may be considered to be demonic if it is non-traditional.

The attempt to maintain cognitive simplicity by adherence to a strict moral code defends against, or helps the individual cope with, powerful drives such as sexuality and painful affect states such as rage. In the process, normal feelings may become sources of guilt or shame, which may occur if the individual feels he is not living up to the moral standards of his tradition. Any tendency to have low self-esteem based on developmental failures of attunement may lead to tortuous feelings of being sinful. Fundamentalists often see human nature as fatally flawed and in need of redemption that can only be achieved through the rituals, prayers, and sacraments of their particular tradition. Some fundamentalists try desperately to control the behavior of other people as a way to vicariously control their own impulses. Typically, personal shadow material is split off and projected onto either the devil or non-believers. Because such splitting and projective defenses are protecting a vulnerable sense of self, they are particularly tenacious.

When the fundamentalist is able to rigidly adhere to a strict set of rules of behavior, he may achieve a sense of superiority compared to others. He has a variety of rituals, prayers, or other apotropaic mechanisms available to him that serve to bind anxiety. Nevertheless, religiously based anxiety, such as a fear of going to hell or a fear of the devil or of divine punishment, plague some fundamentalists. It is not clear whether anxious people are particularly drawn to fundamentalism or whether fundamentalist teachings induce anxiety in predisposed people. However, most empirical studies of fundamentalists do not show higher scores than other groups on measures of clinically important psychopathology (Hood et al., 1986), and some fundamentalists are more optimistic than liberal religionists because they see eschatological hope for the future (Sethi & Seligman, 1994). Nevertheless, the families of fundamentalists have been found to be less emotionally close, less flexible in dealing with change, less likely to encourage members to responsibly exercise their own judgment, and less likely to show caring without smothering (Denton & Denton, 1992).

Most fundamentalist traditions see men and women as unequal. They prevent women from having political power or religious authority, and they often control or prevent the education of women to the same level as men, both in secular matters and in the study of sacred texts. Women's sexuality is usually tightly controlled in fundamentalist societies. Such repression of women may occur because sexual desire threatens to reveal an area of weakness in men; sexual desire gives women power and threatens men's omnipotent defenses, leading to shame (Summers, 2006). Fundamentalists often use religious texts to justify prejudice such as homophobia. The biblical injunction that tells women to submit to their husbands (Eph. 5) can be used to rationalize misogyny and even sadomasochistic behavior.

Strozier (1994) points out that many fundamentalists have a history of trauma, which they learn to talk about using the rhetoric of Christian belief; their "born again" experiences are sometimes attempts at healing. Fundamentalists who were traumatized in childhood are drawn to mythologies that anticipate a violent, destructive final battle between good and evil, and they find consolation and hope in the mythic imagery of the expected End Times, the advent of a Messiah, and a Day of Judgment when all wrongs will be righted.

Barr (1981) believes that fundamentalism induces a strained, authoritarian, and suspicious outlook on the world in people who are raised in such societies. Religious fundamentalists tend to be politically conservative, authoritarian, and often anti-democratic. Lester and colleagues (2004) believe that suicide bombers show personality traits characteristic of the authoritarian personality, such as rigid adherence to conventional values, submission to an idealized authority, aggression, projection of their own difficulties onto an out-group, concern with strength, and devaluation of introspection. Lester believes that most Middle Eastern terrorists are raised in fundamentalist sects that foster these attitudes. Religious martyrdom is often a feature of fundamentalism, and martyrdom is sometimes a fundamentalist protest against modernism and liberal democracy. Yet it is not accurate to use the phrase "suicide bombers," because in their own mind those who blow themselves up for strictly religious reasons are not committing suicide.

Psychotherapy with religious fundamentalists

Psychotherapy with religious fundamentalists can be difficult for several reasons. Many of them have been raised to mistrust psychotherapy because it may threaten their belief system or lead them away from traditional practices. Fundamentalists are aware that classical Freudians saw religion as illusory forms of infantile dependency or as analogous to an obsessional state. Orthodox Jewish fundamentalists were told by earlier generations of psychoanalysts that circumcision is a sublimated form of castration. Religious mysticism has been reduced to an infantile wish to return to the womb. Christians have been told that their theology glorifies suffering, perpetuates the oppression of women, and that their image of God is that of a bloodthirsty child abuser. For these kinds of reason, fundamentalists in emotional distress will typically turn to their own clergy before seeking psychotherapy, and if they do turn to a therapist, they prefer that he or she belong to their own tradition. Psychotherapeutic work may be difficult if the individual sees his or her distress from a religious viewpoint; fundamentalists may see emotional difficulties such as depression as a divine punishment. When depressed, fundamentalists may assume this means that God has abandoned them, or that their depression is a sign of lack of faith or is a test of faith. These attitudes may complicate psychotherapy. Those Christian fundamentalists who have been raised by highly critical parents are particularly receptive to the insistence that human beings are basically sinful (Rom. 5: 12), leading to a punitive superego and the conviction that they are innately bad. It can be difficult to soften these attitudes in psychotherapy when they represent deeply ingrained identifications with parental or church attitudes. The therapist may also have to face very fixed ideas about gender roles or belief in creationism. Fundamentalist clergy may encourage harmful corporal punishment of children on biblical grounds, and adults who attended strict parochial schools may find it difficult to deal with chronic guilt and shame over minor peccadilloes or normal sexual behavior. The therapist's countertransference to such beliefs may lead him to over-pathologize fundamentalists without realizing how heavily acculturated they are.

It requires particular tact to work therapeutically with a fundamentalist without prematurely challenging his belief system, his sense of identity, or his loyalty to his family or tribal group; he may find such discussion intolerable. Especially when an ingrained belief system has been used to sustain the individual's sense of self and cope with anxiety, discussion of the individual's current or previous religious beliefs first requires the development of a trusting therapeutic relationship, in order to avoid shame or premature termination. Even when the individual has left his fundamentalist religion many years prior to entering psychotherapy, residual traces of his early conditioning may persist, especially with regard to sexuality and proneness to guilt and shame, which may remain problematic for a long time.

Recovery from fundamentalism is often difficult and prolonged, leading to a "shattered faith syndrome" that produces depression, isolation, estrangement from family and friends, loss of a sense of direction in life, and considerable self-doubt. Many ex-fundamentalists become very skeptical about all belief systems and any organized group that requires commitment. The therapist may be able to support the individual's search for alternative sources of meaning or a more liberal religious tradition. (Some of the problems raised in psychotherapy with fundamentalists are discussed in more detail in Corbett, 2011.)

Terrorism

Terrorism is typically understood to mean the use of violence against civilians to achieve political, ideological, or religious purposes and goals.[2] The phenomenon has been well known since antiquity. Terrorist operations are planned to shock, impress, and intimidate, so they make sure to produce enough violence to get the attention of the media, the government, and the public. The terrorist's goal is also to make the target population feel unsafe and create a sense of vulnerability. A terrorist act gives the responsible group a sense of power disproportionate to what would otherwise be its political or economic influence.

Terrorists typically claim that other approaches to political change have been ineffective, although it is noteworthy that they do not always exhaust non-violent approaches to their goals before becoming violent, and they may show little interest in peaceful approaches. With respect to the problem of evil, the important question for the psychologist is to understand how the terrorist is able to overcome normal human inhibitions about inflicting serious harm on innocent people, and how he is able to morally justify doing so. A further important issue is the way in which the obvious social, religious, and historical sources of terrorism interact with, or become integrated with, the terrorist's intrapsychic processes.

Groups are designated as terrorist by the target of the group, while people whose interests the terrorist represent might see the group as heroic. For instance, during India's struggle for independence from Britain, a fiery Sikh leader, Bhagat Singh, was called a terrorist by the British and a glorious martyr by the Indians. The same is true for groups like Hamas, which is viewed as evil by the Israelis but supported by many Palestinians. Yesterday's terrorist may become today's hero; Menachem Begin was a violent terrorist in his struggle against the British but was later revered by the Israelis. Yasser Arafat was a leader of the Palestinian Liberation Organization (PLO), which was considered by the Israelis to be a terrorist organization until 1991. He was regarded as a freedom fighter by many Palestinians, and he became a Nobel Peace Laureate in 1994.

The terrorist group's tactics and targets are shaped by the group's ideology and political aims. Left-wing or social revolutionary terrorists such as Germany's Red Army Faction and Italy's Red Brigades kidnapped and assassinated people whom they blamed for economic oppression or political repression. Their goal was to promote a Marxist revolution. Nationalist or ethnic groups such as the PLO, the Irish Repulican Army (IRA), and the Basque separatist Euskadi Ta Askatasuna (ETA; "Basque Homeland and Liberty") have been even more destructive than the left-wing groups. Religiously inspired terrorism is often seen as particularly deadly because it is motivated by apocalyptic fantasies and the wish to purify the world. Religious terrorists see non-believers as particularly evil, and they usually attack people who do not share their faith. They may also have political goals; radical Islamic terrorists are trying to expel Western influences from Muslim countries.

The psychological characteristics of this wide range of terrorist groups are obviously very different. It is difficult to understand the motivations of terrorists from a depth psychological point of view, not only because of their heterogeneity but also for the obvious reason that terrorists are not likely to be interviewed by analytically oriented researchers. Although terrorists often produce lengthy communiqués and ideological manifestos, these texts rarely describe the terrorists' emotional lives or their private thoughts and feelings apart from their ideology. A few terrorist memoirs have been published (Begin, 1977; Baumann, 1979; Iyad, 1981; Khaled, 1973), but this material largely consists of descriptions of their causes, the politics that drove them to terrorism, and the adversities they faced. Most of these memoirs give little information about the inner life of the terrorist.

Some people become involved in terrorist activity for conscious reasons, either religious or sociopolitical. They often feel that the state institutions have failed them, or that the state itself has persecuted them. They may see themselves as avenging the death of a loved one or as fighting for their community. Ethnic conflict is another potent source. In addition, psychodynamically oriented theorists assume that the terrorists' motives may be partly unconscious, so that, for example, the fact that Osama bin Laden objected to American soldiers in Saudi Arabia does not exclude the possibility that unconscious factors also played a part in his behavior.

Psychology and psychodynamics of terrorism

There are social, political, religious, and historical sources of terrorism, and there cannot be a straightforward or unifying psychological explanation for this phenomenon because it is so diverse. There are few empirical studies of the psychological sources of terrorism, although there is some information about their motivation derived from interviews of captured terrorists. There is also a great deal of theoretical speculation. Much of the literature suffers from the problem of applying a single theoretical perspective to a very complex phenomenon, leading to reductionism or overgeneralization. Nevertheless, if we apply multiple psychological perspectives, a certain amount can be said about the psychology of terrorism, both from the point of view of individual and group psychology. It is surely preferable to try to understand what motivates terrorists, rather than accusing them of being purely demonic, as if they are inhuman monsters committing terrible acts for their own sake, which is the impression given by some political speeches.

Post (2005) points out that for radical Islamic fundamentalist terrorists, "hatred has been bred in the bone," or instilled in them since childhood (p. 616). Post believes that explanations at the level of individual psychology are insufficient to explain why people become involved in terrorism, and that concepts of psychopathology are not useful in trying to understand the psychology of terrorism. He believes it is more useful to think in terms of group, organizational, and social psychology, especially the formation of a "collective identity." Based on interviews with incarcerated Islamic terrorists, Post found that they feel a moral obligation to their cause and a religiously sanctioned justification for their behavior. Post stresses the importance of the group leader, who "focuses the discontent of the group members on an external cause for their difficulties" (p. 618) and justifies their aggression. The leader helps the members of the group make sense of what they are doing in terms of what has happened to their lives, and he consolidates a group identity and group thinking. The individual's personal identity eventually fuses with the group identity, so that individuality is lost, as if there is a group self, and the goals of the individual and of the group become the same. There is enormous pressure to conform to the group beliefs and norms of behavior. Any member of the group who expresses doubts about the behavior of the group risks being expelled or severely punished.

Despite such insistence on the social causes of terrorism, and given that there will be no exclusive psychological explanation for it, I believe it is worth exploring the psychological processes that allow terrorists to mercilessly kill innocent civilians who have no responsibility for the terrorist's complaints. Some value, such as the need for justice or revenge, allows the terrorist to ignore ordinary moral constraints, so that they can murder innocent people in buses and markets, often killing themselves in the process. Bandura (1998, 1999) has described some of the psychological mechanisms that allow the usual self-sanctions against such inhuman behavior to be overridden, a process he refers to as moral disengagement.

I summarize his list of these processes here. Moral justification of killing others is accomplished by cognitively restructuring the moral value of killing, for example by seeing the victims as ruthless oppressors or by feeling that one is fighting an evil ideology. Killing others may be justified if non-violent options have proved to be ineffective and if the suffering inflicted by the enemy is seen to outweigh the suffering of the terrorist's victims. Euphemistic or sanitized language about the killing shapes the individual's thinking and becomes a device to make killing others respectable – hence the use of phrases such as "collateral damage" to describe killing civilians. Deplorable behavior can be favorably contrasted with the opponent's even worse behavior, so that one's own behavior seems less heinous in comparison. The mechanisms of moral justification and favorable comparison of atrocious behavior may actually become a source of self-approval and pride. Responsibility for damaging behavior may be displaced onto authorities that the individual sees as legitimate, so the individual does not feel responsible for the consequences. (This was the "just following orders" rationale displayed by many Nazi defendants at the Nuremberg trials, where it was decided that obedience to inhuman orders does not in fact relieve the individual of personal responsibility for his actions.) The division of labor among a terrorist group can diffuse responsibility for culpable behavior, so that each individual is carrying out one aspect of a larger program, and he only has to pay attention to his own work. Disregard for or distortion of the consequences of evil behavior allow the individual to minimize or ignore the results of his actions, especially if he does not see these results first hand, for example in the case of weapons that work remotely. If the perpetrator sees his victims in a dehumanized way, it is easier to mistreat them. The perpetrator who is able to blame his enemy can exonerate his own behavior, as if his antagonist forced him to behave badly.

Finally, self-deception is another possible way in which one might avoid self-censure. Bandura raises the difficult and much-debated philosophical issue of how one can be simultaneously a deceiver and the person deceived. If one lies to oneself, who is lying to whom? How can we believe something in the face of evidence to the contrary – can our emotionally laden desires and wishes override our rationality? This process requires some mechanism of intrapsychic splitting, so that part of the self is unconscious of what the rest of the self is doing, as if one could know and not know what one is doing at the same time. From a psychodynamic point of view, this seems plausible given the well-known defenses of compartmentalization, denial, disavowal, dissociation, and splitting, which may all contribute to self-deception. When the subject is anxious, or wishes to avoid guilt or shame or a threat to his self-esteem, he uses these defensive processes to transform his appraisal of the situation he is in or his evaluation of his behavior. Splitting allows part of the self to be unaware of or selectively able to ignore another part of the self. The subject can then avoid facing painful material such as greed, selfishness, feelings of incompetence, or envy. The subject's unconscious motivations and sense of responsibility for his behavior are thereby avoided. The self can lie to itself because it is unaware of the unconscious sources of its behavior, and it uses these defenses to avoid facing them; instead, the subject lives in his own version of reality. It may simply be too difficult to face the truth about oneself.

Self-deception is important to our study of evil and to our understanding of terrorism because self-deception can be a source of evil, as Peck (1983) pointed out. Self-deception contributes to the human ability to radically misunderstand and misjudge other people who are different. Self-deception therefore contributes to notions such as religious, national, or ethnic superiority and their attendant evils such as holy war, slavery, and racism.

From another perspective, the superego often has lacunae or internal contradictions within it, and it can be deceived, so that it may not be difficult to justify evil behavior. Psychopathic or narcissistic individuals often believe that the rules do not apply to them. From a Jungian point of view, self-deception may arise if we act out of a complex, which is a split-off fragment of the psyche that can become autonomous.

Are all terrorists pathological personalities?

There are few detailed psychological studies of individual terrorists. Some authors believe that most terrorists do not demonstrate serious psychopathology (Post, 1990; McCauley, 2004). This finding, if correct, may indicate that they are not very different in mental make-up from the rest of us, but special religious or social circumstances make them turn to extremism. Among Islamic extremists, these are circumstances such as the need for revenge, bitterness at the humiliations and frustrations imposed by an occupying power, the low standard of living of their society compared to the West, or the oppression by dictators whom they perceive as puppets of the USA. They prefer to feel strong in their hatred and resistance than to feel weak and powerless, and they are vulnerable to extremist preachers who can direct their rage by invoking jihadist ideology and a radical interpretation of the Qu'ran. Young people searching for an idealizable figure may be very attracted to such charismatic individuals and idealistic causes. The pain of their poverty, low status, and sense of oppression is soothed by action. Some of this behavior may be understandable, given their circumstances, and is not necessarily the result of significant psychopathology.

However, authors such as Volkan (1997), DeMause (2002), Lachkar (2013), and Piven (2004) insist that terrorists would not be able to carry out the mass murder of civilians unless they were suffering from a psychological disorder. In the view of these latter authors, at least some members of terrorist organizations are deeply traumatized people who suffered chronic physical abuse and humiliation in childhood. They grew up feeling unsafe, mistrusting others, hating feelings of passivity, and dreading any violation of their boundaries. Being passive makes them feel like a victim, and they feel they must ward off any such view of themselves. To do this they turn passive into active; instead of being a victim they victimize others. By devaluing others, they support their own self-esteem, leading to a form of malignant narcissism that may suppress moral feelings and justify sociopathic behavior and cruelty. They are often paranoid, seeing the world as a bad, dangerous place as a result of their childhood deprivation and privation. They rationalize their proclivity to violence with political explanations. Such individuals are often drawn to terrorist groups by economic deprivation, loss of territory, loss of civil liberties or state oppression; these factors mobilize narcissistic rage and may lead to the individual joining a terror group. Any personal sense of weakness can be split off and projected onto an outside group.

From a self-psychological point of view, the terrorist group provides a number of important psychological functions for its members, each of which would have a sustaining effect on narcissistically vulnerable members. Being with a group of like-minded individuals promotes the experience of a twinship or alter-ego transference to other members of the group (Kohut, 2011); it is helpful to be with people who are like oneself. In some ways, the group becomes an extension of the self, or one is part of a group self. The presence of a charismatic leader allows an idealizing transference, and the mutual support and acceptance provided by group members has an important mirroring function. The group's ideology also has a sustaining function on the individual's sense of self. These selfobject experiences within the group contribute to the individual's sense of self-cohesion and emotional stability and gives him a sense that he belongs, while making the group members interdependent. The group provides the individual with missing intrapsychic structure, combating internal emptiness or isolation. If the individual has experienced narcissistic rage due to persecution or humiliation by an enemy, violent action allows the expression of revenge and hatred, and gives the individual a sense of importance. To this list of factors, we might also add rewarding features such as excitement and the opportunity to display courage, not to mention the sense of power provided by membership in a group.

For some terrorists, identification with the group, the sense of identity and personal significance arising from their activities, and the psychological needs that the group meets make it difficult to relinquish their way of life. It may then be the case that the survival of the group becomes even more important than the achievement of its political goals.

Piven (2004) has attempted a psychodynamic interpretation of Islamic terrorists. He is among those writers who do not accept purely political explanations for terrorism, which he does not think account for the level of rage that allows terrorists to murder civilians. In his view, politics and religion cannot account for the terrorists' loathing of sensuality, their contempt for women, and their need to enforce their theology onto others. Piven believes that the lack of empathy required in order to commit acts of cruelty and violence cannot be derived from political injustice alone; such empathic lack in his view must derive from infantile neglect and abuse. Piven argues that terrorists often suffer from an absence of the kind of healthy psychological structures that usually develop with good maternal care. This lack results in a sociopathic and misogynistic personality "consumed with hostility and repressed fear of the feminine" (p. 152). For him, such men brutalize and demean women to overcome their own pathological rage and anxiety:

"Those who despise women are terrified of women and need to wreak vengeance on them" (p. 160), displacing onto all women the rage they feel towards their mothers because of neglect. This kind of individual needs what he despises, but he sees his need for love and sexuality as a disgusting weakness that renders him vulnerable. Social indoctrination that devalues anything feminine contributes to this misogyny. The feminine is regarded as innately inferior, "weak, messy, contaminated, and castrated" (p. 162). Male weakness and emotional needs are equated with emasculated effeminacy, so that misogyny represents these men's dread of helplessness and neediness that is displaced onto women. Because of their early emotional malnourishment, such men cannot help but see women as demons.

Writers such as Piven believe that, in addition to their early maternal deprivation, during their childhoods these individuals were also traumatized by men who viciously brutalized them and indoctrinated them into violence, which became their only source of self-esteem. This results in a hostile, paranoid, and even masochistic personality that can only survive by participating in a brutal social structure. Piven thinks that their shared social fantasy, the group ideology, protects them from succumbing to overwhelming rage, helplessness, and even psychotic fragmentation. For him, terrorist acts are partly a displacement of rage against their own society and they are partly masochistic, since they "orchestrate their own downfall to purify themselves in fantasies of re-merger with God (parents)" (p. 152). Terrorists are attempting to kill off their own weak and needy selves, "fantasizing grandiose triumph over helplessness and death through debasing and terrifying murder of others" (ibid.).

Piven does not believe that religiously based terrorists are violent simply because their religion commands them to be violent. Because some religionists selectively ignore their own tradition's messages of love and peace, and instead pay particular attention to scriptural encouragement of death and violence, he thinks they use religion to justify themselves. In his view, religions are "fantasy systems" that validate and offer divine sanction for the individual's desired beliefs and actions. He believes that psychological dependence on the projected fantasy of a deity is immensely gratifying, since the individual feels protected and loved by the parental surrogate and feels adored for pleasing his God. He is thereby absolved of any feelings of badness or inferiority and feels justified in destroying competing ideologies. Not only does he channel his rage into religious justification for his actions, but he also has the fantasy of destroying death itself through the violent domination of others. His religious group carries out a maternal function, and he participates in a communal merger with the group, absolving him of guilt when the group acts violently. Enemies are dehumanized and scapegoated in a way that inflicts onto others "the symbolic equivalents of what has been inflicted onto him" (p. 164). Such an individual tries to punish and retaliate enemies for his own experience of being violated and victimized. He may believe that the voice of his internal punitive objects belongs to God and sanctifies murder.

DeMause (2002) is also among those writers who see the sources of terrorism largely within the psychology of the terrorist, minimizing the social and political sources of terrorism and relying heavily on psychoanalytic theory, sometimes in a reductive manner. DeMause agrees that the roots of terrorism are found in extreme childhood abuse. He believes that children who grow up to become Islamic terrorists are products of violent, misogynistic cultures in which women are regarded as polluted and inferior. He believes that wife beating, rape, and the denial of pleasure are endemic in fundamentalist Islamic cultures. This produces mutilated, battered women who inflict their own misery onto their children, who are routinely physically abused. In his view, Islamic terrorists have been taught to kill those parts of themselves that want pleasure and freedom, and they kill those parts in projection by killing others.

Lachkar (2013) also believes that terrorists suffer from a psychological disorder; in particular, they have a vulnerability resulting from early trauma that contributes to their collective myths and fantasies – essentially what Jungians would refer to as a cultural complex. Their societies are traumatically bonded through war, loss, and a lifetime of government human rights violations. She sees parallels between terrorists and borderline personalities; both share similar defenses such as "splitting, projection, projective identification, shame, blame, guilt, envy, jealousy, control/submission and domination" (p. 1), as well as abandonment and annihilation anxieties. She sees them as suffering from paranoid anxiety, magical thinking, omnipotent denial, and massive depression. To this list one might add the possibility that the Islamic terrorists who criticize Western "immorality" might be projectively struggling with their own impulses that are forbidden in their religion. Here we might also note the effects of envy of the West and resentment at the apparently unfair advantages of Western societies, not to mention the feeling among some Islamic terrorists that the West devalues their religion and holds them in low regard as individuals. However, it is clear that the vast majority of Muslims do not subscribe to radical views and are not violent, so these psychological factors can at best be contributory but not a full explanation.

The terrorist leader

The terrorist organization typically has a leader who is often a traumatized but charismatic individual who exerts a fascinating and inspiring effect on others. This fascination is in part due to the longing of his followers to find some kind of power or omnipotence in which they can participate, or it is a form of primitive idealization. It is particularly easy for those who were orphaned in childhood to identify with powerful leaders who offer the fantasy of being a strong father figure, even when the leader is in fact destructive, for example in the cases of Milosevic and Saddam Hussein, both of whom were malignant narcissists. In a study based on interviews of Northern Irish terrorist leaders, researchers found that these leaders had typically been victims of terror themselves, and all had experienced "violations of their personal boundaries that damaged or destroyed their faith in personal safety" (Volkan, 1997, p. 160). Many had experienced early childhood victimization in the form of parental abuse, abandonment, or sexual molestation. Volkan believes that terrorist leaders are trying to shore up their own sense of self by "seeking the power to hurt and by expressing their sense of entitlement to power" (p. 161). Passivity risks further trauma.

Charismatic leaders of terrorist groups are often exploitative, domineering, authoritative, and self-aggrandizing, often with little regard for the feelings of others. The leader seems to embody the answers to the concerns of the terrorist group. He reinforces the group's ideology and mythology, he plays on members' fears of the outside world, and he fosters paranoid projections onto the group's enemies. For example, bin Laden was a hero for his followers, but his attitude was both apocalyptic and paranoid; he believed that crusaders and Zionists had been conspiring to destroy Islam (Gunaratna, 2002). Recently, however, some terrorist organizations have become decentralized, and for them the traditional role of a charismatic leader has become less important. In the long run, some authors point out that the terrorist group often cannot afford to succeed in its stated agenda, because if the group were to succeed it would no longer be necessary. The group's suffering and experience of being victimized would then have to be experienced instead of being externalized by victimizing others. The leader therefore unconsciously aims for the impossible.

Leaders often have a strong desire to be a leader. The classical research on individuals who are obsessed with being a leader explains this drive as the result of the lack of a father perceived as a strong, protective figure. Typically, the individual's father was absent, alcoholic, or uncaring (Popper, 1999). Another factor is narcissism, or the difficulty of working through one's infantile grandiosity, leading to the need to be adored. Such individuals learn early that they can charm others to get attention, but behind this need is profound insecurity. Such people were often abandoned or neglected in childhood, leading the child to feel that in order to be secure and gain approval he has to become special and develop an extraordinary gift to guarantee attention and admiration; this becomes a vehicle for obtaining emotional nourishment. Such people are primed by narcissistic parents for success; they feel that only success will allow parental acceptance, but they do not feel loved for themselves, and they feel internally empty. Kohut (2011) thought that charisma might result when a devoted and idealizing mother who has created a child with high self-esteem suddenly and unpredictably withdraws her empathy and support. The child compensates by idealizing himself; he is then identified with the grandiose self of childhood. He learns to charm others to deny his aloneness; he becomes empathic only with himself and his own needs. He uses others to regulate his self-esteem and assert his own perfection, needing control over others without regard for their rights or their humanity.

The followers of charismatic leaders are usually people who are struggling to achieve a cohesive sense of identity and selfhood. The followers try to draw strength from the leader, who offers a new family with himself as a kind of father figure. The leader uses oratory and bold actions to appeal to the members' infantile hunger for love and acceptance. He stresses the group's achievements. He reminds the group of their grievances and the injustices they have suffered, directing their aggression towards the group's target, thereby enhancing group cohesion. He diminishes the members' shame or guilt about their violence, and he allows them to project any felt inferiority onto an enemy, thus promoting prejudice and violence towards outsiders. The leader encourages group psychology and group thinking, thereby fostering a kind of group regression. Individual members lose their personal sense of morality and surrender their personal values for the sake of the approval of the group. They externalize their sense of being a victim by projecting victimhood onto others, with no concern for them. However, the externalization of victimhood prevents their underlying pain from being metabolized.

There is an important, well-known association between the experience of shame and humiliation and subsequent violent behavior, especially in men (Gilligan, 1996). Shame and humiliation are also important motivators of religiously inspired violence. It is often suggested that Muslim people who feel humiliated may be more likely to turn to fundamentalist Islam (Abi-Hashem, 2004), and humiliation is said to be one of the motivators of suicide bombers (Victoroff, 2005). Many of the recruits to militant Palestinian groups come from areas that have suffered greatly from humiliation by Israel (Post et al., 2003), and Chechens under Russian occupation or Iraqis under American occupation also feel humiliated and have turned to violence. Religions are particularly prone to either exacerbate or induce feelings of shame and humiliation in their adherents when they fail to live up to a high standard of behavior. Extreme religious movements that encourage prejudice against non-believers are readily able to incite violence against other people by channeling the violence the religion has induced by shaming its adherents (Jones, 2006).

Terrorism, fundamentalism, and purification

Fundamentalist religion can be a major motivator of terrorism, as we see in the case of ISIS. Many fundamentalist traditions see secular activities and secular governments as degenerate. As a result, fundamentalists often see themselves as at war with the larger society (Juergensmeyer, 2000), or at least under assault by it, as demonstrated today with complaints about attacks on Christianity in the USA. Jones (2006) points out that the split between pure and impure or between sacred and profane is a defining characteristic of the religious consciousness, particularly the more fanatical variety. Some fundamentalists prefer to withdraw from the world into islands of purity, whereas religious terrorists want to actively change and purify the world around them. Either way, the notion that the group must prevent defilement and maintain purity fosters a paranoid stance towards the world.

Jones points out the connection between traditional notions of sacrifice, often involving the shedding of blood, and purification by violent means, exemplified by the people who violently attack abortion clinics, killing doctors and other employees. These killers often insist they are acting for religious reasons. Stein (2006) notes that the notion of purification helps to explain how religious belief can deteriorate to the point that it develops the conviction that killing is good and righteous. One's own bad or impure parts can be projectively destroyed in this way.

As discussed on p. 146, many extreme religious movements subscribe to a doctrine of the End Times, which will be heralded by an apocalyptic battle between good and evil. In this mythologem, a final battle will purify the world, and such purification is seen as necessarily violent and bloody, as we see in the Book of Revelation. Apocalyptic fantasies always include a new world emerging from the ashes of the old. This kind of fantasy seems to originate in tremendous rage that is projected into the notion of world destruction and the need for renewal. Fantasies of purification through fire may be unconsciously motivated by a sense of personal badness that can only be ameliorated through extreme punishment. These fantasies are often accompanied by the notion that the religious martyr will be reunited with the divine father in heaven, who it is believed will lovingly accept the martyr's sacrifice, a notion that seems to be driven by the need to pacify and gain the acceptance of harsh internal imagoes.

The desire for union with the divine often becomes linked with violence in the mind of the religiously motivated terrorist. The terrorist is sacrificing himself as well as his victims, and he sees this as a form of sanctification, a deeply religious act carried out for the sake of God. The Palestinian Hamas movement believes that martyrdom is the epitome of *jihad* (which means effort for the sake of Allah), which has an important position in Islam. Belief in *jihad* is part of a moral code that Hamas believes justifies attacks against Israel. Islamic radicals who blow themselves up are often referred to in the Western press as suicide bombers, but Islam expressly forbids suicide, so these individuals would repudiate that designation because they believe they are in the service of Allah. The phrase "suicide bomber" is also inaccurate from a clinical point of view, because the motives and mental state of the suicidal person and the religious martyr are entirely different, and so is their attitude toward death. Religious martyrs are not necessarily depressed. A preferable term is "human bombers."

Individuals who martyr themselves are regarded as sacred by their community, where they are elevated to a lofty level of holiness. The martyr is thought to be instantly transported to heaven; his sins are forgiven, he faces no reckoning on the Day of Judgment, and he can intercede for others. (However, many commentators have noted that few of the jihadi fighters have much background in Islamic texts or theology.) The theme of martyrdom as a guarantee to entrance into heaven is found in several religious traditions. In this context, of interest to depth psychologists is the Islamic tradition that the martyr may be given prior knowledge of his death in a dream or a waking vision. This tradition continues among modern Islamic martyrs, and their friends often dream of dead martyrs who reassure the dreamer that they are happy in paradise, which is important for Jihadist ideology.

Jones (2006) notes that the association of the shedding of blood and redemption is connected to a particular image of God as vengeful and punitive. Such a believer often feels profoundly unworthy and guilty, and he believes that the divine must be placated with a bloody sacrifice. Such a God-image is often associated with immature object relations, an external locus of control, anxiety and depression, and abusive early caregivers. In contrast, a benevolent God-image is often associated with more mature psychological structures and object relations, and benign early attachment figures. As Jones points out, it makes sense that a person who envisions God as wrathful or punitive would tend to use defenses such as rigid splitting and have a reduced capacity for empathy, which are traits that seem to characterize many religiously motivated terrorists. Indeed, fundamentalists typically have a judgmental image of God, a drive for purification, prejudice towards outsiders, and concern with authority and submission, all of which reinforce their motivation for martyrdom (Altemeyer & Hunsberger, 1992). They tend to be politically conservative and often anti-democratic. Patriarchal religions that focus on obedience, guilt, submission to God, and the need to earn divine favor are particularly prone to violence.

All terrorists live for what they believe will be a glorious future. For religious groups this will be at a divinely chosen time, but the group may feel chosen to hasten it. Secular terrorists feel that their cause is so righteous it will be successful because they are the wave of the future. They imagine a utopia that may require the destruction of the society in which they live. However, in practice most terrorist groups do not last long, with the exception of ethno-nationalist groups such as the PLO, the IRA, and the Basque ETA. These are resilient apparently because they are supported by their constituency, such as their ethno-national brethren. They have a clear goal such as a homeland. In contrast, the left- and right-wing political terrorist groups have to proselytize among uncommitted people. Left-wing groups have historically not been successful partly because they cannot articulate what will replace the capitalist state.

The victims of terrorism

The victim of a terrorist attack suffers in several ways apart from physical injury. As well as the risk of post-traumatic stress disorder, many victims no longer feel that the world is safe or predictable, and they suddenly feel excessively vulnerable. Questions about the meaning of their lives may come to the fore. They can no longer believe in a just and orderly world, and they often become preoccupied with thoughts of death. They realize how close they came to death, and they may be haunted by memories of the dead bodies they saw during the attack. They often suffer a combination of rage and grief, sometimes accompanied by fantasies of revenge. Whatever personal difficulties the individual has been struggling with, such as addiction, may become magnified by exposure to a terrorist attack. If the victim has experienced previous trauma, his previous symptoms may re-surface. Some victims develop a phobic avoidance of anything or any place that reminds them of the scene of the trauma. These fear cues may produce somatic distress, and psychophysiological problems such as poor sleep and appetite or gastrointestinal symptoms may occur. Many victims of terrorist attacks benefit from long-term psychotherapy. (Miller [2004] has a valuable discussion of the necessary approaches.)

The terrorist and his victims

Casoni and Brunet (2002) (using an object relations approach) suggest that there is a parallel between the intrapsychic phenomena experienced by witnesses of terrorism and the psychodynamics of the perpetrators of terrorism. Terrorists seem to "unconsciously wish to draw witnesses into a psychic realm similar to their own" (p. 5). Among witnesses to terrorism, despair and distress occur, not only because of the insecurity produced by witnessing literal destruction, but also because such destruction seems to threaten the existence of good internal objects with which the witness identifies. These authors believe that being a witness to such destruction may lead to either an empathic identification with the victims or with the terrorist. Although it seems easier to identify with the victims, the witness may also have violent components within his personality due to an identification with internal violent objects, so the witness might experience anxiety or distress simultaneously from these two different processes of identification. Association of the attack with good internal objects produces distress because these seem to be under attack, leading to fear, helplessness, and sadness. The witness is reminded of the vulnerability of these good objects, and he feels helpless. At the same time, the witness may simultaneously identify with the terrorist as well as with the victims. The part of the self that identifies with the terrorist and bad internal objects feels hatred and rage or destructive fantasies stirred up by terrorist attacks. These two aspects of the personality then conflict with each other, possibly leading to despair.

After a terrorist attack, many people are tempted by revenge fantasies, maintaining the illusion that killing external persecutors will free one of one's own destructive impulses and internal bad objects. The result is a wish for the destruction not only of the terrorists but also of any group of people who are identified with persecutory internal objects. Hence, the authors point out, the reaction of some governments to terrorist attacks, using the restriction of civil liberties or the promotion of totalitarian laws. All evil is projected onto the enemy. The authors note that the wish for revenge contributes to a sense of self-protection, suppresses feelings of helplessness, and can be used to avoid grief. Fantasies of vengeance alleviate sadness and depression, but this process requires continual splitting and defensive projection. However, this is only a temporary solution that prevents psychological freedom and condemns us to perpetual cycles of rage and fear of retaliation. In contrast, to restore the link to good internal objects permits hope and allows us to sustain the predominance of love over hostility. A more realistic vision of oneself and others is then possible, but to achieve this inner peace requires that we deal with the pain and sorrow produced by identification with both the victims and the terrorists.

Casoni and Brunet (2002) believe that these two sets of identifications also occur within the terrorist. He may rationalize his destructive acts, but he also identifies with his victims, creating internal fantasies of damaging internal objects with whom he identifies. Profound identification with his victims and his own victimhood leads to a resort to vengeance as a way to deal with his own anxiety and despair. His hatred calms the dread of an internal or external world devoid of good objects. When he identifies with the aggressor, and with his murderous act, the terrorist must then project his internal good objects outward, onto his leader or onto God, to protect them from destruction. Massive identification with the aggressor requires a way to counterbalance despair at one's actions by seeing oneself as a heroic figure.

The splitting of reality into all good and all bad is an important dynamic. Fairbairn (1954) described the way in which an abused child needs to maintain the experience of his parents as good, because the child is dependent. The child therefore takes on the sense of badness himself, while maintaining an idealized view of his parents. He does so at the cost of his own self-esteem, taking on the burden of his parents' badness. Religions that teach that people are innately bad or sinful take advantage of this dynamic by making their devotees feel unworthy in the face of an idealized image of divinity. Or, one might project one's own sense of badness onto another religion and identify with an idealized vision of one's own religion. The target of this projection may then be demonized and attacked, and this may lead to religiously motivated terrorism. Not surprisingly, the most fanatical religious groups are the most racist and homophobic (Altemeyer & Hunsberger, 1992).

Stein (2006, 2002) believes that the intense wish for union with the masculine, paternal God of traditional monotheism found in coercive fundamentalism represents a violent, homoerotic father-son relationship. She uses the notion of father-son love to understand the ecstatic willingness of the terrorist to carry out what he perceives as the will of God. Terrorists want to change the image of the internalized, feared father from a persecutor into an idealized love object; what was a persecutory inner object then becomes an exalted one, so that hatred is transformed into idealizing love. She bases this notion in part on the letter written by Mohammed Atta, one of the 9/11 perpetrators. This letter frequently mentions love of God and the requirements for entry into paradise. Stein sees in this letter the intimacy of the father-son connection and the seeking of a marriage to God. She notes that Atta seemed to have been in an ecstatic state of mind as a result of the conviction that he was doing God's will and because of the prospect of merger with God. This state of mind allows a "smooth passage" from life to death. She believes that such an individual is experiencing a transcendent mystical experience that allows the transformation of self-hatred and envy into love of God. This love obliterates parts of the self that are antagonistic to the perpetrator's sense of purity. Stein points out that to kill others with no sense that one is committing a crime and no sense of evil requires that we see other human beings as worthy of extermination, as if they were insects or diseases. Then the act of killing is spiritualized, because God wills it. The terrorist kills any bad parts of himself that have been projected outwards, which allows peace of mind.

Another possible contribution to the problem of terrorist attacks comes from evolutionary psychology, which suggests that we have evolved with a predisposition to resentment at other groups who seem to have more resources than we do. Or, there may have been survival advantages to parents who gave limited resources to a single child, leaving others to fend for themselves. Those who survived would be those who were the most sensitive to the potential for sibling competition. That is, terrorism may arise from the resentment that arises from sensitivity to inequality and unfairness. At the same time, we have also evolved to be altruistic toward others in distress.

Jungians might see the phenomenon of terrorism linked to fundamentalism as the result of possession by an archetypal image such as the archetype of the apocalypse (Edinger, 2002). Identification with the archetype leads to enormous inflation. This is clearly seen in the case of ISIS, which subscribes to a medieval form of Islam that believes in a Day of Judgment. Members of ISIS read their sacred texts literally, reviving ancient traditions such as slavery and crucifixion that they feel the Qu'ran justifies. Now that ISIS has declared a caliphate, the organization feels obliged to expand into other countries ruled by non-Muslims. ISIS's commitment is to bring about the apocalypse (Wood, 2015). This is a very typical example of the way in which fundamentalists adhere concretely and rigidly to a mythic image with no modification by the ego. The symbol becomes frozen and loses its metaphoric sense; essentially, symbol is turned into history. ISIS attaches great importance to the Syrian city of Dabiq, near Aleppo, which is the place they believe the Prophet said that the armies of Rome (infidel armies) will be defeated. They believe in the coming of an anti-Messiah named Dajjal; according to the myth, he will be killed by Jesus in a great battle that will lead the Muslims to victory. Another example of the literalizing of a mythic image occurred during the U.S. invasion of Iraq, where many people believed that this war signaled the beginning of the End Times, and they anticipated the arrival of the Mahdi, a messianic figure destined to lead Muslims to victory. In this context, I'm reminded of a comment of Jung's that the more clearly the archetype is constellated, the more fascinating it is, and the more it is formulated as something divine (CW 11). When a mythic image is overvalued it tends to lead to magical thinking.

Mythic imagery is symbolic, not literal history, and a true symbolic capacity is crucial for the development of mature religion. A religious symbol is a bridge between the human and the divine. But symbols are not objective facts with one meaning; they are metaphors, and they have many meanings, some of which are paradoxical. Jung believes that archetypal phenomena are inherently paradoxical because they are expressing something transcendental that cannot be expressed in an either-or fashion. He points out that paradox is spiritually important, and a religion becomes impoverished when it loses its paradoxes, because only paradox allows us to comprehend the fullness of life. Non-ambiguity is invariably one-sided, and so cannot express the incomprehensible (CW12). The image of God portrayed in the sacred texts of our major monotheistic traditions is often paradoxically loving and punitive, creative and destructive at the same time. The text itself may contain problematic elements. Primitive personalities are unable to contain such paradoxes, and they tend to split and project one side of these opposites in order to hold onto an uncomplicated God-image or to insist on the superior value of their own sacred text. Competing traditions can then be devalued instead of being seen as valuable in their own right.

Jung's typology is relevant in this context. Adherents of fundamentalist religions who are feeling types and who are gripped by archetypal imagery such as that of the apocalypse cannot easily moderate this material with more evolved religious thinking or with a more differentiated thinking function. Adherents who are thinking types are often lacking in empathy for their victims and able to rationalize sadism with doctrine.

On reconciliation

If reconciliation between hostile groups is attempted, such as the handshake between Rabin and Arafat in 1995 at the White House, one could see this as a move from the paranoid to the depressive position. In the paranoid position the subject feels: "I have all the goodness," and badness is externalized; the world is black and white. The subject feels like a victim and the other is the oppressor. Feelings of mistrust and rage predominate. In the depressive position, it is acknowledged that "I am not all good" and the other is not all bad; empathy appears with the possibility of gratitude for what has been received, along with guilt or sadness at having hurt others and the need to repair damage done to the other. Reality testing improves and the possibility of a reciprocal relationship develops, along with letting go of grudges, making compromises, and settling for a less-than-ideal solution.

Revenge has the value of allowing the subject to feel active rather than like a passive victim, but the possibility of reconciliation is impaired by the repetition of the attack-revenge cycle, which is repeated over and over again until its futility is finally seen. The destructive energy may then fade and non-hostile exchanges are tried. Both parties realize that their revenge has done damage and neither is innocent. Both have been hurt and caused hurt, which may lead to a degree of empathy and forgiveness. Acknowledgment by the perpetrators that they have hurt the victims helps the victim to recover from trauma, but denial that anything bad has been done does further damage. Reconciliation is more likely if the perpetrator shows signs of repentance, apologizes, and offers some kind of reparation, either material or emotional. This helps the victim's self-esteem and allows further mourning, which may eventually allow the grief to diminish. The victim can then reconsider, elaborate, and revise what he remembers. Forgiveness, and letting go of some anguish, may then become possible.

Youth in terrorist groups

Young men are commonly found in terrorist groups. They are often idealistic, looking for meaning, and they have existential questions and questions of identity. Youth in these groups want to believe and belong; they often enter the group feeling alienated and suffering from low self-esteem. They are often individuals who have been hurt by ethnic conflict or who have lost family members in protests. Adolescents enjoy being part of a group, and when the young person is exposed to a charismatic leader and a group that offers an apparent antidote to their unhappiness, they are very susceptible to the group's influence and to ideological indoctrination. Group members have a sense of purpose and feel fulfilled. They are part of a community or a quasi-family of like-minded individuals, which is preferable to feeling like a nobody. The group gives them a reason to live, and they feel they are contributing to the well-being of others. They often want to face danger in a heroic way and be admired for doing so. A young group member might be unconsciously exerting independence and autonomy, trying to individuate by rebelling against authority or his parents' values. He can feel powerful as a member of the group, which also allows him to express anger. He can escape parental dominance, using the group to emancipate from his parents. He may benefit emotionally from peer acceptance and community. He may like the structure, protocols, rules, and rituals of the group, which may help him contain internal turmoil, acting as a therapeutic community. He may enjoy being in a community of true believers who feel morally superior to others. Committed group members may feel notorious or special and privileged. Young members of the group have often been brought up to hate and demonize a particular enemy. However, even zealous individuals with dedicated energy to a cause often burn out over time, and eventually re-direct their energy to family and careers or political action. Many people who were radical in their youth became pillars of their communities in later life and take up an ordinary existence in society.

Notes

1 Transitional phenomena are important in play, the imagination, religious feelings, artistic and scientific creativity, and other cultural phenomena.
2 I should note that there is no agreed-upon definition of *terrorism*. Different agencies define it in their own terms, either as a political act, a criminal act, or an act of war.

Chapter 9

Is evil part of human nature?

Are there evil characters or only evil actions?

This chapter considers the question of whether evil can be an essential quality of a person's nature, or whether evil is only a description of what a person does. It is possible that a deeply flawed character disorder, such as a malignant narcissist, may behave in an evil way but not be evil at the deepest level of his being. Alternatively, he may have developed his character disorder *because* he is essentially evil, so that his character expresses his real nature. Such an individual could have an evil character but not be in a situation that allows him to carry out evil acts, in which case actions or the lack of them are not essential criteria for deciding if someone is evil. As Haybron (1999) points out, Hitler would have had an evil character even if he had not been able to do what he did politically. As previous discussions have shown, it is clearly possible that one could do evil without being an essentially evil person.

Various authors have suggested criteria for determining whether a character is truly evil. We might recognize a malevolent character because he has what Haybron calls a "deep seated enmity towards goodness" (p. 136). But the situation is complicated. McGinn (1997) believes that to have an evil character is to feel pleasure in the face of other people's pain and feel pain at others' pleasure. McGinn describes this malice for its own sake as pure evil, although to the clinician it sounds like a description of envy, which could be confined to one sector of a personality that is not necessarily entirely pervaded by evil. Furthermore, an evil person may not take pleasure at the suffering of others; some people cause intentional harm but feel nothing – for the psychopath, the other person is just a nuisance. Some people are involved in the administration of evil without much feeling of any kind. McGinn thinks the capacity for this kind of evil may be a psychologically primitive, hard-wired disposition analogous to altruism, which makes it sound deeply embedded in human nature. In that case, it is radically immanent rather than something transcendent that can be laid at the feet of a supernatural being such as the devil. Evil is then not something beyond our understanding and essentially mysterious; it can be approached rationally.

If evil is a potential within human nature, perhaps because of our evolutionary endowment or because it is an aspect of the dark side of the transpersonal Self, it may be found within all of us. Otherwise evil is confined only to some people. Authors who believe that evil is an inevitable feature of being human point to the primitive, barbaric aspects of human beings. If this is a universal attribute of our nature, we must take total responsibility for evil. Dews (2012) believes that ultimately "we are what is wrong with the world" (p. 232), and this is a popular view. Svendsen (2010) insists that evil is a problem of human relationships; he believes it is attributable to human free will: "To be free, moral agents necessarily implies that we are both good and evil" (p. 234). Haybron (1999) also points out that the extent to which one is evil does not only depend on the degree to which one has evil psychological traits; it also depends on how much one is responsible for having these traits.

Perrett (2002) sees five possible positions about the relationship between evil and human nature: (1) optimism says human nature is primarily good; (2) pessimism sees it as primarily evil; (3) dualism sees it as both; (4) neutralism sees it as neither good nor evil; and (5) individualism says there is no such thing as human nature – only individuals are good or evil. Perrett points out that the last two are implausible since we all share some innate dispositions.

Optimism says that humans are naturally predisposed to do good, but internal or external conditions may prevent this innate propensity from being realized. Ignorance and weakness, which have psychological and social causes, account for our evil, not a deep aspect of human nature. The counter to the optimistic position is the observation that many evil acts are perpetrated by people who are fully aware that their actions violate moral principles, and they may have no subsequent remorse.

Pessimism says we have a primary potential for evil, and we act in an evil manner when we do not control our impulses; we tend to pursue our own desires at the expense of others. When we do behave well towards each other, pessimists believe this is the result of the influence of civilization on our instincts. For pessimists, it is natural for us to be selfish and pursue our own desires at the expense of others; in this view, only moral teaching and social penalties will curb evil. The problem with pessimism is that it has to explain the existence of goodness, which it tries to see as somehow always egoistic, or in the individual's self-interest, but this seems too forced an explanation for all acts of altruism and does not explain conscious self-sacrifice.

Dualism suggests that human nature is a mixture of potentials that predispose us in opposite directions; we do evil because the good part of our nature does not override the bad. Kekes (1993) believes that this is the only plausible explanation for the coexistence of both altruism and evil. However, dualism has to explain why, in the face of good behavior, the individual's natural propensity to evil did not assert itself and why, in the face of evil, the propensity to do good did not triumph. To explain this difference, the depth psychologist would invoke factors such as the individual's capacity to contain intense affect such as rage without acting out, pressure from complexes or from the shadow, the level of development of the superego, and other personality factors.

What is an evil person?

Wilson (2003) writes that an evil person may be described as "one who intentionally inflicts serious physical harm on another person or persons in pursuit of a personal, ideological or religious goal, and who experiences intense psychological pleasure in doing so" (p. 3). The value of this approach is that it stresses motivation and intentionality, although as we have seen motivation alone is not sufficient to call something evil because harm could be due to negligence or recklessness. It is not unusual for people to claim that an evil act is a wrong act that is pleasurable (e.g., Steiner, 2002). However, as noted above, the criterion of experiencing pleasure seems to be unnecessary, since evil may occur in its absence; one could do evil without enjoying doing so. Calder (2013) points out that the criterion that an evildoer must experience pleasure for an evil act to be evil would mean that a trivial wrong that the person enjoys doing could be considered evil.

Haybron believes that to be an evil person is to be consistently vicious, in the sense that one is "not aligned with the good to a morally significant extent" (2002, p. 270). In this view, evil people have no good side; they show no real compassion or conscience even if they never perform evil acts or do any harm at all, although that is unlikely. Evil people may do their duty as long as this is not grounded in respect or concern for others. An evil person might be actively opposed to the good, but such misalignment from the good is vicious; it requires complete or near-complete lack of concern for the welfare of others. Haybron believes that evil people are motivated in ways that are radically different from ordinary wrongdoers. He suggests that the concept of an evil person is one pole of a moral continuum at the opposite pole of which is the moral saint.

The objection to thinking of the individual himself as evil, rather than only seeing his actions as evil, is that this would require a very complex assessment of the person, and we rarely have that much information. To condemn a person as evil we would have to take into account conscious intention, unconscious motivation, genetics, developmental history, the details of the immediate situation, and the individual's overall psychology. Yet some writers believe it is possible to simplify this question; Darley (1992) suggests that a person is evil if he has committed many evil actions. Darley believes that our culture intuitively believes that the evil person contains an element or kernel of evil, almost like a physical characteristic. He calls this a quantum of evil and suggests that it may be masked by an ordinary persona. This makes the evildoer almost demonic rather than a pathetic figure in the grip of an impulse. Darley suggests that the idea of a world containing evildoers preserves our belief in an otherwise just and ordered world, a belief we are reluctant to give up because it allows us to go into the world and send our children into the world. Darley contrasts his view of a quantum of evil with the views of social scientists who claim that ordinary people can behave in evil ways given the right situation. These latter "situationist" writers suggest that many evil actions are not the result of the evil will of individual evildoers, but they are products of social forces and organizations that make the individual do terrible things. In this process the individual is changed, becoming evil himself. An organization such as a dictatorship is necessary to train, reinforce, and sustain this kind of socially evil activity. (However, a purely situationist view of evil does not take into account the fact that evil social conditions begin with the psychology of those who create and foster such conditions.)

Darley points out that the essence of the process that socializes people to do evil is that they are placed under pressure "to take small steps along a continuum that ends with evildoing" (1992, p. 208). Although each step is small, the process is continuous and each lapse in the individual's morality is rationalized by invoking a higher good or a regrettable necessity. Darley believes that if the process goes far enough for the person to initiate evil actions, he has become evil himself, and this potential lies in all of us and can be activated by a socialization process.

Kekes (1993) suggests that there are various types of evil character: those who cause evil autonomously such as Hitler or Stalin, whom he calls moral monsters; evil characters who cause evil non-autonomously such as Eichmann; and well-meaning but heartless people who don't realize what they are doing, to whom he refers as moral idiots. Moral idiots are not evil themselves, but they cause evil. Calder (2003, p. 373) adds: "Moral monsters are the more basic type of evil character: they simply have a consistent propensity to desire other people's significant, real harm for an unworthy goal such as their own pleasure or entertainment value." He suggests that moral idiots also have this propensity, but they believe that they have a goal that justifies the harm they cause, so they too may be evil characters unless their belief in this goal is defensible for scientific or sociological reasons.

In contrast to the view that there are evil characters, Read (2014) is among those writers who believe that the root of evil lies in only action, not in humanity itself. She supports the view that the notion of a purely evil person is as artificial a construct as the notion of a purely good one. In this view, perpetrators of evil are extraordinary because of what they do, not because of who they are, and we should not extend the title of evil from actions to their agents. The issue that arises here is the difference between Kekes's (1993, p. 5–7) "soft reaction to evil," meaning that we are reluctant to allow evil actions alone to be evidence for the perpetrator being evil, and the "hard reaction" that says that evil is inexplicable without the existence of evil characters. The soft reaction prefers to explain evil in terms of the corruption of the human disposition to goodness, while the hard reaction believes that the disposition to do evil is an integral part of human nature. This is a parallel discussion to the debate in psychoanalytic circles between those who believe that aggression and destructiveness are innate and those who believe that these reactions only occur in response to frustrations and developmental trauma. Similarly, Waller (2007) believes that a purely evil person is "just as much an artificial construct as a person who is purely good. Perpetrators of extraordinary evil are extraordinary only by what they have done, not by who they are" (p. 19). They are not beyond understanding. Therefore, the root of evil is action, not the person who commits it. However, writers such as Benn (1985) point out that it is not enough to talk about evil behavior, since a person could be evil but unable to act, and Calder (2003) points out that an evil character could be too cowardly or incompetent to succeed in committing an evil act. He claims that, at least conceptually, ordinary people without an evil character may cause evil. In fact, Haybron (1999) believes that "most evil actions are not the product of evil people . . . the connection between evil-doing and evil character is much lower than most writers suppose" (p. 279). Morton (2004, p. 54) points out that "far more evils are performed by perfectly normal people out of confusion or desperation or obsession than by violent individuals or sociopaths." Human beings are often thoughtless, sometimes stupid, and easily influenced, factors that may lead to evil as it were by default. We are not good at resisting situational pressures. Horne (2008) also believes that the term *evil* should be restricted to evil acts rather than evil characters; for him, *evil* is an adjective rather than a noun, and "it should be employed to qualify acts of persons rather than their character" (p. 669), and these acts must be examined only in their specific contexts.

Is moral behavior innate?

The notion that human beings are naturally possessed of morality is an ancient one, at least going back to Aristotle. Bloom (2013) believes that babies have an innate, rudimentary moral sense that is subsequently modified by life experiences and cultural values. Based on his study of infants, Bloom argues that there is in human beings an inborn knowledge of good and bad; infants seem to be more attracted to helping behavior than to uncooperative behavior. Even a very young child seems to be able to sense whether the experimenter needs help with a task. For example, the child appears to realize the difference between a pencil that is dropped deliberately and one that is dropped accidentally, and the child behaves accordingly. However, these experiments are not entirely convincing because they do not rule out the possibility that the child is picking up subliminal cues from the experimenter. But there are other lines of evidence for the innateness of moral behavior, found for example in studies showing that empathy, which is important for the moral treatment of others, has some genetic basis. Another view is that moral behavior is largely based on learned cooperation and interaction with others in childhood, leading to reciprocally helpful behavior. We feel positively toward those who have helped us in the past, and in families this help fosters the development of pro-social behavior that is positively reinforced over time (Tomasello & Vaish, 2013).

Moral emotions are very important in our evaluation of an action as good or evil. Moral emotions are those such as horror and revulsion that arise spontaneously when we witness certain events, but they also include feelings such as pride, shame, empathy, and guilt. Pride occurs when we feel that our behavior is in accord with our personal moral values, or with those of our society. Shame and guilt occur when our behavior falls short of these values. The individual's ethical behavior may also be based on values, on empathy, on the feeling function, on principles, or on relationships. A morally mature individual has a personal set of values, and her intentions and reasons for behavior may be a more important basis for her behavior than the achievement of a particular outcome. The morally mature individual is able to perceive another person's distress, and can see a situation from another's point of view. He is motivated to help the distress of others. He has personal principles – conscious or not – that enable him to evaluate and choose behavior. He values ethics for its own sake, and he evaluates behavior on the basis of several criteria, including the individual's intention and the situation he is in. The morally mature person recognizes her interconnectedness with others, and acts in accordance with her responsibility to others. Overall, our moral reasoning largely depends on a combination of our cultural context and also on our relationships with early caregivers. However, it is important to note that different moral choices may occur among people who are at equivalent levels of moral development and among people who reason with similar levels of moral maturity. The individual's degree of moral maturity is therefore more about the process of choosing an action than the actual choice that is made.

Miller (2004) makes the case that psychotherapy is an implicitly moral endeavor, and moral judgments and moral emotions are implicit in clinical judgments. Therapists often make judgments about patients' intentions or motivations based on the therapist's moral approval or disapproval. Such judgment is not purely cognitive; it is based on spontaneous emotional reactions in the therapist, such as approval or disgust. Whenever the therapist tries to help someone reduce shame or guilt, or tries to mitigate a patient's exaggerated self-blame, the therapist is making an intrinsically moral assessment of the patient's situation.

Morality can be seen as an evolutionary development, because among our hominid ancestors mutual support would have been beneficial to group and individual survival. Corresponding to the evolutionary account of the development of morality, it has been claimed that moral standards are a function of human neurobiology. However, it is important that we do not succumb to the temptation to reduce morality to brain mechanisms. We see this tendency in suggestions that we could investigate an ethical issue by scanning the brain of a person thinking about it. However, at the moment the correlations between observable brain mechanisms and moral decision making are much too crude, and even if a clear correlation could be made, knowing the brain mechanism involved would tell us nothing about the validity of the ethical decision that was reached, and nothing about the personal and social values involved. Brain mechanisms cannot account for the difference in ethical systems found in different societies. Brain mechanisms do not tell us the nature of moral truths or decide on what is good or evil – these decisions belong to the community and to the individual. Ethical behavior is about treating other people as we would like to be treated, about conscience, and about decency, respect, and empathy for others.

References

Abe, M. (1989). *Zen and Western thought*. Honolulu: University of Hawai'i Press.

Abi-Hashem, N. (2004). Peace and war in the Middle East. In F. Moghaddam & A. Marsella (Eds.), *Understanding terrorism* (pp. 64–90). Washington, DC: American Psychological Association.

Adams, M. M. (1999). *Horrendous evils and the goodness of God*. Ithaca, NY: Cornell University Press.

Alford, C. F. (1997). *What evil means to us*. Ithaca, NY: Cornell University Press.

Alford, C. F. (1999). A psychoanalytic study of evil. *American Imago, 56*(1), 27–52.

Alford, C. F. (2001). Reply to Michael Levine's "See no evil." *Psychoanalytic Studies, 3*(1).

Altemeyer, B., & Hunsberger, B. (1992). Authoritarianism, religious fundamentalism, quest, and prejudice. *International Journal of Psychology Religion, 2*, 113–134.

Amen, D. G., Stubblefield, M., Carmichael, B., & Thisted, R. (1996). Brain SPECT findings and aggressiveness. *Annals of Clinical Psychiatry, 8*(3), 129–137.

Apostolou, M. (2013). The evolution of rape: The fitness benefits and costs of a forced-sex mating strategy in an evolutionary context. *Aggression and Violent Behavior, 18*(4), 494–490.

Aragno, A. (2013). The devil within: A psychoanalytic perspective on evil. *Issues in Psychoanalytic Psychology, 35*(1), 101–123.

Arendt, H. (1965). *Eichmann in Jerusalem*. New York: Penguin Books.

Arendt, H. (1973). *The origins of totalitarianism*. New York: Harcourt, Brace, Jovanovich.

Arendt, H. (1994). *Essays in understanding, 1930–1954*. New York: Schocken Books.

Arendt, H. (2007). *The Jewish writings*. New York: Schocken Books.

Arendt, H., & Jaspers, K. (1992). *Hannah Arendt/Karl Jaspers correspondence 1926–1969*. New York: Harcourt Brace Jovanovich.

Armstrong, K. (2001). *The battle for God*. New York: Ballantine Books.

Athens, L. (1997). *Violent criminal acts and Actors revisited*. Chicago, IL: University of Illinois Press.

Bandura, A. (1998). Mechanisms of moral disengagement. In W. Reich (Ed.), *Origins of terrorism: Psychologies, ideologies, theologies, states of mind*. Washington, DC: Woodrow Wilson Center Press.

Bandura, A. (1999). Moral disengagement in the perpetration of inhumanities. *Personality and Social Psychology Review, 3*, 193–209.

Baron-Cohen, S. (2012). *The science of evil: On empathy and the origins of cruelty*. Philadelphia, PA: Basic Books.

Barr, J. (1981). *Fundamentalism*. Philadelphia, PA: Westminster Press.

Barth, K. (1994). *Church dogmatics*. Ed. H. Gollwitzer. Louisville, KY: Westminster John Knox Press.

Basoglu, M., Jaranson, J. M., Mollica, R., & Kastrup, M. (2001). Torture and mental health: A research overview. In E. Gerrity, T. M. Keane, & F. Tuma (Eds.), *The mental health consequences of torture* (pp. 35–62). New York: Springer Science+Business Media.

Bauer, Y. (1982). *A history of the Holocaust*. New York: Watts.

Baumann, M. (1979). *Terror or love? Bommi Baumann's own story of his life as a West German urban guerrilla*. New York: Grove Press.

Baumeister, R. F. (1997). *Evil: Inside human violence and cruelty*. New York: Henry Holt.

Baumeister, R. F. (2012). Human evil: The myth of pure evil and the true causes of violence. In M. Mikulincer & P. R. Shaver (Eds.), *The social psychology of morality: Exploring the causes of good and evil* (pp. 367–380). Washington, DC: American Psychological Association.

Baumeister, R. F., & Campbell, W. K. (1999). The intrinsic appeal of evil: Sadism, sensational thrills, and threatened egotism. *Personality & Social Psychology Review, 3*, 210–221.

Becker, E. (1974). *The denial of death*. New York: Free Press.

Becker, E. (1975). *Escape from evil*. New York: Free Press Division of Simon Schuster.

Begin, M. (1977). *The revolt: Story of the Irgun*. Jerusalem, Israel: Steimatsky Agency.

Benn, S. (1985). Wickedness. *Ethics, 95*(4), 795–810.

Berger, P. L. (1999). *The desecularization of the world: Resurgent religion and world politics*. Washington, DC, Grand Rapids, MI: Wm. B. Eerdmans Publishing Co.

Berkowitz, L. (1968). The devil within. *Psychoanalytic Review, 55*(1), 28–36.

Berkowitz, L. (1999). Evil is more than banal: Situationism and the concept of evil. *Personality & Social Psychology Review, 3*(3), 246–253.

Bernstein, R. J. (2002). *Radical evil: A philosophical investigation*. Cambridge: Malden, MA: Wiley-Blackwell.

Bernstein, R. J. (2008). Are Arendt's reflections on evil still relevant? *The Review of Politics, 70*, 64–76.

Blair, R. J. (2003). Neurobiological basis of psychopathy. *British Journal of Psychiatry, 182*(1), 5–7.

Blass, T. (1991). Understanding behavior in the Milgram obedience experiment: The role of personality, situations, and their interactions. *Journal of Personality and Social Psychology, 60*, 398–413.

Blass, T. (1993). Psychological perspectives on the perpetrators of the Holocaust: The role of situational pressures, personal dispositions, and their interactions. *Holocaust and Genocide Studies, 7*, 30–50.

Bloom, P. (2013). *Just babies: The origins of good and evil*. New York: Random House.

Bollas, C. (1995). *Cracking up: The work of unconscious experience*. New York: Routledge.

Brennan, T. (1997). Social evil. *Social Research, 64*(2), 211–234.

Breytenbach, C., & Day, P. L. (1995). Satan. In K. van der Toorn, B. Becking & P. van Horst (Eds.), *Dictionary of deities and demons in the Bible* (pp. 1369–1380). New York: E.J. Brill.

Browning, C. (1998). *Ordinary men: Reserve Police Battalion 101 and the final solution in Poland*. New York: HarperCollins.

Burton, J. (1997). *Violence explained: The sources of conflict, violence and crime and their prevention*. Manchester, UK: Manchester University Press.

Bushman, B. J. (2002). Does venting anger feed or extinguish the flame? Catharsis, rumination, distraction, anger, and aggressive responding. *Personality and Social Psychology Bulletin, 28*, 724–731.

Calder, T. (2003). The apparent banality of evil: The relationship between evil acts and evil character. *Journal of Social Philosophy, 34*(3), 364–376.

Calder, T. (2013). Is evil just very wrong? *Philosophical Studies, 163*(1), 177–196.

Camus, A. (1991). *The plague.* New York: Vintage Books.

Card, C. (2002). *The atrocity paradigm: A theory of evil.* New York: Oxford University Press.

Casoni, D., & Brunet, L. (2002). The psychodynamics of terrorism. *Canadian Journal of Psychoanalysis, 10*(1), 5–24.

Cenkner, W. (1997). Hindu understandings of evil: From tradition to modern thought. In W. Cenkner (Ed.), *Evil and the response of world religion* (pp. 13–141). St. Paul, MN: Paragon House.

Christie, R. (1970). Why Machiavelli? In R. Christie & F. Geis (Eds.), *Studies in Machiavellianism.* New York: Academic Press.

Coen, S. J. (1986). The sense of defect. *Journal of the American Psychoanalytic Association, 34*, 57–67.

Cohen, A. (1988). *Tremendum: A theological interpretation of the Holocaust.* New York: Crossroad Publishing.

Cole, P. (2006). *The myth of evil.* Edinburgh, Scotland: Edinburgh University Press.

Comas-Diaz, L., & Amado, M. (1990). Countertransference in working with victims of political repression. *American Journal of Orthopsychiatry, 60*(1), 125–134.

Cooper-White, P. (2003). The concept of the vertical split in self psychology in relation to Christian concepts of good and evil. *Journal of Pastoral Theology, 13*(1), 63–84.

Corbett, L. (2011). *The sacred cauldron: Psychotherapy as a spiritual practice.* Wilmette, IL: Chiron publications.

Corbett, L. (2012). *Psyche and the sacred.* New Orleans, LA: Spring Journals and Books.

Corbett, L., & Whitney, L. (2016). Jung and non-duality: Some clinical and theoretical implications of the self as the totality of the psyche. *International Journal of Jungian Studies, 8*(1), 15–27.

Covington, C. (2012). Hannah Arendt, evil, and the eradication of thought. *International Journal of Psychoanalysis, 93*(5), 1215–1236.

Covington, C. (2016). Witnessing evil. In R. C. Naso & J. Mills (Eds.), *Humanizing evil: Psychoanalytic, philosophical and clinical perspectives* (pp. 188–203). New York: Routledge/Taylor & Francis Group.

Cramer, M. (1980). Psychopathology and shamanism in rural Mexico: A case study of spirit possession. *British Journal of Medical Psychology, 53*(1), 67–73.

Darley, J. M. (1992). Social organization for the production of evil. *Psychology Inquiry, 3*, 199–218.

Davies, A. T. (1993). Evil and existence: Karl Barth, Paul Tillich, and Reinhold Niebuhr revisited in light of the Shoah. In S. L. Jacobs (Ed.), *Contemporary Christian responses to the Shoah.* New York: University Press of America.

Davion, V. (2009). Feminist perspectives on global warming, genocide, and Card's theory of evil. *Hypatia, 24*(1), 160–177.

Delbanico, A. (1996). *The death of Satan: How Americans have lost the sense of evil.* New York: Farrar, Straus, and Giroux.

DeMause, L. (2002). The childhood origins of terrorism. *The Journal of Psychohistory*, *29*(4), 340–348.

Denton, R. T., & Denton, M. J. (1992). Therapists' ratings of fundamentalists and non-fundamentalist families in therapy: An empirical comparison. *Family Process*, *31*(2), 175–185.

Dews, P. (2012). *The idea of evil*. Hoboken, NJ: John Wiley.

Diamond, S. A. (1996). *Anger, madness, and the daimonic*. Albany, NY: SUNY Press.

Dicks, H. V. (1972). *Licensed mass murder: A socio-psychological study of some SS killers*. New York: Basic Books.

Dodge, I. A., Bates, J. E., & Pettit, G. S. (1990). Mechanisms in the cycle of violence. *Science*, *250*, 1678–1683.

Duntley, J. D., & Shackelford, T. K. (2008). Darwinian foundations of crime and law. *Aggression and Violent Behavior*, *13*(5), 373–382.

Edinger, E. (1973). *Ego and archetype*. Baltimore, MD. Penguin Books.

Edinger, E. (2002). *Archetype of the Apocalypse: Divine vengeance, terrorism, and the end of the world*. Peru, IL: Open Court Publishing.

Eibl-Eibesfeldt, I. (1979). *The biology of war and peace*. New York: Viking Press.

Eigen, M. (1984). On demonized aspects of the self. In. M. Nelson & M. Eigen (Eds.), *Evil: Self & culture*. New York: Human Sciences Press.

Ellenberger, H. F. (1981). *The discovery of the unconscious*. New York: Basic Books.

Ellenbogen, S. (2013). Against the diagnosis of evil: A response to M. Scott Peck. *Philosophical Practice*, *8*(1), 1142–1148.

Erikson, E. (1950). *Childhood and society*. New York: Norton.

Fairbairn, R. (1954). *An object relations theory of the personality*. New York: Basic Books.

Fingarette, H. (1969). *Self-deception*. New York: Routledge & Kegan Paul.

Formosa, P. A. (2008). A conception of evil. *The Journal of Value Inquiry*, *42*(2), 217–239.

Formosa, P. A. (2013). Evils, wrongs, and dignity: How to test a theory of evil. *The Journal of Value Inquiry*, *47*, 235–253.

Freidman, S. H., Cavney, J., & Resnick, P. (2012). Child murder by parents and evolutionary psychology. *Psychiatric Clinics of North America*, *35*(4), 781–795.

Freud, S. (1915/1981). Thoughts for the times on war and death. *The Standard Edition of the Complete Psychological Works of Sigmund Freud*. 24 vols. Trans. and ed. James Strachey. London: Hogarth Press, *14*, 275–300.

Freud, S. (1916). Some character-types met with in psychoanalytic work. *The Standard Edition of the Complete Psychological Works of Sigmund Freud*. 24 vols. Trans. and ed. James Strachey. London: Hogarth Press, *14*, 309–333.

Freud, S. (1923/1981). A seventeenth century demonological neurosis. *SE*, *19*, 72–105.

Freud, S. (1930/2002). *Civilization and its discontents*. London: Penguin Books.

Frey-Rohn, L. (1967). Evil from the psychological point of view. In The Curatorium of the C.G. Jung Institute of Zurich (Ed.), *Evil* (pp. 151–200). Evanston, IL: Northwestern University Press.

Frick, P. J., & Marsee, M. A. (2005). Psychopathy and developmental pathways to antisocial behavior in youth. In C. J. Patrick (Ed.), *Handbook of psychopathy* (pp. 353–374). New York: Guilford Press.

Friesen, J. G. (1992). Ego-dystonic or ego-alien: Alternate personality or evil spirit? *Journal of Psychology & Theology*, *20*(3), 197–200.

Fromm, E. (1964). *The heart of man: Its genius for good and evil*. New York: Harper and Row.

Fromm, E. (1973). *The anatomy of human destructiveness*. New York: Holt, Rhinehart and Winston.

Funkhauser, G. R. (1991). Cross-cultural similarities and differences in stereotypes of good and evil: A pilot study. *Journal of Social Psychology, 131*(6), 859–874.

Garrard, E. (1998). The nature of evil. *Philosophical Explorations, 1*(1), 43–60.

Garrard, E. (2002). Evil as an explanatory concept. *The Monist, 85*(2), 320–336.

Garrison, J. (1983). *The darkness of God: Theology after Hiroshima*. Grand Rapids, MI: Eerdmans Publishing.

Gilligan, J. (1996). *Violence: Our deadly epidemic and its causes*. New York: Grosset-Putnam Books.

Goldberg, C. (1995). The daimonic development of the malevolent personality. *Journal of Humanistic Psychology, 35*(3), 7–37.

Goldberg, C. (1996). The privileged position of religion in the clinical dialog. *Journal of Clinical Social Work, 24*(2), 125–136.

Goldberg, C. (2000). *The evil we do: The psychoanalysis of destructive people*. Amherst, NY: Prometheus Books.

Goldhagen, D. J. (1992). The evil of banality. *The New Republic*, July 13–20.

Goldhagen, D. J. (1997). *Hitler's willing executioners: Ordinary Germans and the Holocaust*. New York: Vintage Books.

Goldman, H. E. (1988). Paradise destroyed: The crime of being born – A psychoanalytic study of the experience of evil. *Contemporary Psychoanalysis, 24*, 240–251.

Gozlan, O. (2016). Trauma and evil: Questions of ethics and aesthetics for a profession in crisis. In R. C. Naso & J. Mills (Eds.), *Humanizing evil: Psychoanalytic, philosophical and clinical perspectives* (pp. 171–187). New York: Routledge/Taylor & Francis Group.

Graham, J., & Haidt, J. (2012). Sacred values and evil adversaries: A moral foundations approach. In M. Mikulincer & P. R. Shaver (Eds.), *The social psychology of morality: Exploring the causes of good and evil* (pp. 11–31). Washington, DC: American Psychological Association.

Grand, S. (2000). *The reproduction of evil: A clinical and cultural perspective*. Hillsdale, NJ: Analytic Press.

Grand, S. (2015). Responding to the problem of evil and suffering. In D. F. Walker, C. A. Courtois, & J. D. Aten (Eds.), *Spiritually oriented psychotherapy for trauma* (pp. 253–271). Washington, DC: American Psychological Association.

Gross, J. T. (2001). *Neighbors: The destruction of the Jewish community in Jedwabne, Poland*. Princeton, NJ: Princeton University Press.

Grossi, G., Kelly, S., Nash, A., & Parameswaran, G. (2014). Challenging dangerous ideas: A multidisciplinary critique of evolutionary psychology. *Dialectical Anthropology, 38*(3), 281–285.

Grossman, D. (1996). *On killing*. Boston, MA: Little, Brown.

Groth, A. A. (1979). Sexual trauma in the life histories of sex offenders. *Victimology, 4*, 6–10.

Gunaratna, R. (2002). *Inside Al Qaeda: Global network of terror*. New York: Berkley Books.

Hall, K. (2012). "Not much to praise in such seeking and finding": Evolutionary psychology, the biological turn in the humanities, and the epistemology of ignorance. *Hypatia, 27*(1), 28–49.

Hallie, P. P. (1981). From cruelty to goodness. *Hastings Center Report, 11*(3), 23–28.

Hamilton, R. (2008). The Darwinian cage: Evolutionary psychology as moral science. *Theory, Culture, and Society, 25*(2), 105–125.

Haybron, D. M. (1999). Evil characters. *American Philosophical Quarterly, 36*(2), 131–148.

Haybron, D. M. (2002). Moral monsters and saints. *The Monist, 85*(2), 260–284.

Hayden, P. (2010). The relevance of Hannah Arendt's reflections on evil: Globalization and rightlessness. *Human Rights Review, 11*, 451–467.

Heckel, R. V., & Shumaker, D. M. (2001). *Children who murder: A psychological perspective.* Westport, CT: Praeger.

Henson, H. K. (2006). Evolutionary psychology, memes, and the origins of war. *Mankind Quarterly, 46*(4), 443–459.

Hering, C. (1996). Beyond understanding? Some thoughts on the meaning and function of the notion of evil. *British Journal of Psychotherapy, 14*(2), 209–220.

Herman, J. (1992). *Trauma and recovery.* New York: Basic Books.

Hick, J. (1997). *Evil and the God of love.* New York: Palgrave Macmillan.

Hohne, H. (1989). *The order of the death's head.* New York: Ballantine.

Hollander, P. (2014). Grappling with evil in our time. *Hedgehog Review, 16*(1), 48–56.

Hood, R. W., Morris, R. J., & Watson, P. J. (1986). Maintenance of religious fundamentalism. *Psychological Reports, 59*, 547–559.

Horne, M. (2008). Evil acts not evil people. *Journal of Analytical Psychology, 53*(5), 669–691.

Horney, K. (1933). *The neurotic personality of our time.* New York: W.W. Norton.

Ivey, G. (1993). The psychology of satanic worship. *South African Journal of Psychology, 23*, 180–185.

Ivey, G. (2002). Diabolical discourses: Demonic possession and evil in modern psychopathology. *South African Journal of Psychology, 32*(4), 54–59.

Iyad, A. (1981). *My home, my land: A narrative of the Palestinian struggle.* New York: New York Times Books.

Jakobsen, M. D. (1999). *Negative spiritual experiences: Encounters with evil.* Lampeter, Wales. Retrieved from http://repository.uwtsd.ac.uk/id/eprint/473

James, W. (1958). *The varieties of religious experience.* New York: Mentor Books.

Jonason, P., Webster, G., Schmitt, D., Li, N., & Crysel, L. (2012). The antihero in popular culture: Life history theory and the dark triad personality traits. *Review of General Psychology, 16*(2), 192–199.

Jones, J. (2006). Why does religion turn violent? A psychoanalytic exploration of religious terrorism. *Psychoanalytic Review, 93*(2), 167–190.

Juergensmeyer, M. (2000). *Terror in the mind of God.* Berkeley: University of California Press.

Jung, C. G. (1965). *Memories, dreams, reflections.* New York: Vintage Books.

Jung, C. G. (1970). Good and evil in analytical psychology. In R. F. C. Hull (Trans.), *Civilization in transition* (2nd ed., pp. 456–468). Princeton, NJ: Princeton University Press (Original work published in 1964).

Jung, C. G. (1975). *Letters*, vol. 2. Eds. G. Adler and A. Jaffe. Trans. R. F. C. Hull. Princeton, NJ: Princeton University Press.

Jung, C. G. (2006). *The undiscovered self.* New York: Penguin Books.

Kant, E. (1998/1793). *Religion within the boundaries of mere reason.* New York: Cambridge University Press.

Kantemir, E. (1994). Studying torture survivors: An emerging field in mental health. *Journal of the American Medical Association, 272*(5), 400–401.

Kast, V. (1992). How fairy tales deal with evil. In M. Jacoby, V. Kast, & I. Riedel (Eds.), *Witches, ogres, and the devil's daughter* (pp. 16–39). Boston, MA: Shambhala.

Katz, F. (1993). *Ordinary people and extraordinary evil: A report on the beguilings of evil.* Ithaca, NY: Suny Press.

Keener, C. S. (2010). Spirit possession as a cross-cultural experience. *Bulletin For Biblical Research, 20*(2), 215–235.

Kekes, J. (1993). *Facing evil.* Princeton, NJ: Princeton University Press.

Kekes, J. (1998). The reflexivity of evil. *Social Philosophy and Policy, 15*(1), 216–232.

Kekes, J. (2005). *The roots of evil.* Ithaca, NY: Cornell University Press.

Kelman, H. C., & Hamilton, V. L. (1989). *Crimes of obedience: Toward a social psychology of authority and responsibility.* New Haven, CT: Yale University Press.

Kerenyi, C. (1967). The problem of evil in mythology. In The Curatorium of the C. G. Jung Institute of Zurich (Ed.), *Evil.* Evanston, IL: Northwestern University Press.

Kernberg, O. (1984). *Severe personality disorders: Psychotherapeutic strategies.* New Haven, CT: Yale University Press.

Kernberg, O. (1992). *Aggression in personality disorders and perversions.* New Haven, CT: Yale University Press.

Kernberg, O. (1997). The almost untreatable narcissistic patient. *Journal of the American Psychoanalytic Association, 39*, 45–73.

Kerr, G. A. (2011). A Thomistic response to the problem of evil. *Yearbook of the Irish Philosophical Society*, 38–50.

Kershaw, I. (1991). *Hitler.* London: Longman.

Khaled, L. (1973). *My people shall live: The autobiography of a revolutionary.* London: Hodder and Stoughton.

Kiehl, K., Smith, A., Liddle, P., et al. (2001). Limbic abnormalities in affective processing by criminal psychopaths as revealed by functional magnetic resonance imaging. *Biological Psychiatry, 50*(9), 677–684.

Kim, B. (1998). Ontology without axiology? A review of Masao Abe's account of the problem of good and evil from a western philosophical perspective. *The Eastern Buddhist, 31*(1), 85–108.

Kirschenbaum, H., & Henderson, V. L. (1989). *Carl rogers: Dialogues.* London: Constable.

Klein, M. (1927). Criminal tendencies in normal children. *British Journal of Medical Psychology, 7*, 177–192.

Klein, M. (1934). On criminality. *British Journal of Medical Psychology, 14*(4), 312–315.

Klein, M. (1946). Notes on some schizoid mechanisms. *International Journal of Psycho-Analysis, 27*, 99–110.

Klose, D. A. (1995). M. Scott Peck's analysis of human evil: A critical review. *Journal of Humanistic Psychology, 35*(3), 37–66.

Knight, Z. G. (2007). Sexually motivated serial killers and the psychology of aggression and "evil" within a contemporary psychoanalytical perspective. *Journal of Sexual Aggression, 13*(1), 21–35.

Knoll, J. (2008). The recurrence of an illusion: The concept of "evil" in forensic psychiatry. *Journal of the American Academy of Psychiatry and the Law, 36*(1), 105–116.

Koestler, A. (1968). *The ghost in the machine.* London: Palgrave Macmillan.

Koestler, A. (1978). *Janus: A summing up.* New York: Random House.

Kohut, H. (1972). Thoughts on narcissism and narcissistic rage. *Psychoanalytic Studies of the Child, 27*, 369–399.

Kohut, H. (1977). *The restoration of the self*. New York: International Universities Press.

Kohut, H. (1979). The two analyses of Mr. Z. *International Journal of Psychoanalysis*, *60*, 3–27.

Kohut, H. (1984). *How does analysis cure?* Chicago, IL: University of Chicago Press.

Kohut, H. (2011). *The search for the self*. London: Karnac Books.

Krueger, D. (2013). Christianity and violence. *Religion Compass*, *7*, 243–251.

Kubarych, T. (2005). Self-deception and Peck's analysis of evil. *Philosophy, Psychiatry, & Psychology*, *12*(3), 247–255.

Kulka, O. D. (2013). *Landscapes of the metropolis of death: Reflections on memory and imagination*. New York: Penguin Books.

Kushner, H. S. (2004). *When bad things happen to good people*. New York: Bantam Doubleday Publishing.

Lachkar, J. (2013). The psychopathology and profiles of terrorism: A cultural V-spot. *Journal of Psychohistory*, *41*(2), 81–99.

Lester, D., Yang, B., & Lindsay, M. (2004). Suicide bombers: Are psychological profiles possible? *Studies in Conflict and Terrorism*, *27*(4), 283–295.

Levi, P. (1989). *The drowned and the saved*. New York: Vintage Books.

Levine, M. (2000). See no evil, hear no evil, speak no evil: Psychiatry, psychoanalysis and evil. *Psychoanalytic Studies*, *2*(3), 265.

Lewis, D. O., Mallouh, C., & Webb, V. (1989). Child abuse, delinquency, and violent criminality. In D. Ciccetti & V. Carlson (Eds.), *Child maltreatment: Theory and research on the causes and consequences of child abuse and neglect*. New York: Cambridge University Press.

Lifton, R. J. (1986). *The Nazi doctors: Medical killing and the psychology of genocide*. New York: Basic Books.

Lifton, R. J., & Markusen, E. (1992). *The genocidal mentality: Nazi Holocaust and nuclear threat*. New York: Basic Books.

Lipstadt, D. (2011). *The Eichmann trial*. New York: Nextbook/Schocken.

Lisak, D., & Roth, S. (1990). Motives and psychodynamics of self-reported, unincarcerated rapists. *American Journal of Orthopsychiatry*, *60*(2), 268–280.

Littman, R., & Paluck, E. L. (2015). The cycle of violence: Understanding individual participation in collective violence. *Advances in Political Psychology*, *36*(1), 79–99.

Lu, C. (2004). Agents, structures and evil in world politics. *International Relations*, *18*, 498–509.

Lu, K. (2013). Can individual psychology explain social phenomena? An appraisal of the theory of cultural complexes. *Psychoanalysis, Culture, and Society*, *18*(4), 386–404.

Mackie, J. L. (1971). Evil and omnipotence. In B. Mitchell (Ed.), *Philosophy of religion*. New York: Oxford University Press.

Magid, B. (1988). The evil self. *Dynamic Psychotherapy*, *6*(2), 99–113.

Mandel, D. R. (2002). Evil and the instigation of collective violence. *Analyses of Social Issues and Public Policy*, *2*(1), 101–108.

Mariano, S. A. M. (2009). The banality of radical evil. *International Journal of the Humanities*, *7*(1), 123–138.

Maslow, A. H. (1943). A theory of human motivation. *Psychological Review*, *50*(4), 370396.

Masters, B. (1997). *The evil that men do: From saints to serial killers*. London: Black Swan.

May, R. (1969). *Love and will*. New York: Norton.

May, R. (1977). *The meaning of anxiety*. New York: W.W. Norton.

May, R. (1982). An open letter to Carl Rogers. *Journal of Humanistic Psychology*, *22*(3), 10–21.

Mayr, E. (1997). *This is biology: The science of the living world*. Cambridge, MA: Harvard University Press.

McCauley, C. (2004). Psychological issues in understanding terrorism and the response to terrorism. In C. E. Stout (Ed.), *Psychology of terrorism: Coping with the continued threat*. Westport, CT: Praeger.

McGinn, B. (1994). *Antichrist: Two thousand years of the human fascination with evil*. San Francisco: Harper.

McGinn, C. (1997). *Ethics, evil, and fiction*. New York: Oxford University Press.

McHoskey, J. W., Worzel, W., & Szyarto, C. (1998). Machiavellianism and psychopathy. *Journal of Personality and Social Psychology*, *74*(1), 192–210.

Mearns, D., & Thorne, B. (2000). *Person-centred therapy today: New frontiers in theory and practice*. London, England: Sage.

Meloy, J. R. (2000). *Violence risk and threat assessment: A practical guide for mental health and criminal justice professionals*. San Diego, CA: Specialized Training Services.

Midgley, M. (2001). *Wickedness: A philosophical essay*. Boston, MA: Routledge & Kegan Paul.

Milgram, G. (1974). *Obedience to authority: An experimental view*. New York: Harper and Row.

Miller, A. (1991). *Banished knowledge*. New York: Anchor Books.

Miller, A. (1996). *Prisoners of childhood: The drama of the gifted child and the search for the true self*. New York: Basic Books.

Miller, A. G. (1986). *The obedience experiments: A case study of controversy in social science*. New York: Praeger.

Miller, A. G., Gordon, A., & Buddie, A. (1999). Accounting for evil and cruelty: Is to explain to condone? *Personality and Social Psychology Review*, *3*(3), 254–268.

Miller, L. (2004). Psychotherapeutic interventions for survivors of terrorism. *American Journal of Psychotherapy*, *58*(1), 1–16.

Miller, P. A., & Eisenberg, N. (1988). The relation of empathy to aggressive and externalizing antisocial behavior. *Psychological Bulletin*, *103*, 324–344.

Miller, R. B. (2004). *Facing human suffering: Psychology and psychotherapy as moral engagement*. Washington, DC: American Psychological Association.

Mills, J. (2016). The essence of evil. In R. C. Naso & J. Mills (Eds.), *Humanizing evil*. New York: Routledge.

Milo, R. (1984). *Immorality*. Princeton, NJ: Princeton University Press.

Mitchell, S. A. (1993). *Hope and dread in psychoanalysis*. New York: Basic Books.

Montagu, A. (1957). *Anthropology and human nature*. Boston, MA: Porter-Sargeant.

Morrison, D., & Gilbert, P. (2001). Social rank, shame and anger in primary and secondary psychopaths. *Journal of Forensic Psychiatry*, *12*, 330–356.

Morton, A. (2004). *On evil*. New York: Routledge.

Morton, A. (2005). Atrocity, banality, self-deception. *Philosophy, Psychiatry, & Psychology*, *12*(3), 257–259.

Muslin, H. (1992). Adolf Hitler: The evil self. *Psychohistory Review*, *20*, 251–270.

Neiman, S. (2015). *Evil in modern thought: An alternative history of philosophy*. Princeton, NJ: Princeton University Press.

Neumann, E. (1990). *Depth psychology and a new ethic.* Boston, MA: Shambhala Publications.

Niebuhr, R. (1996). *The nature and destiny of man: A Christian interpretation.* Louisville, KY: Westminster John Knox Press.

Noakes, J., & Pridham, G. (1988). *Nazism: A history in documents and eyewitness accounts.* New York: Schoken.

Noddings, N. (1989). *Women and evil.* Berkely, CA: University of California Press.

Ogden, T. H. (1989). On the concept of an autistic-contiguous position. *International Journal of Psycho-Analysis, 70,* 127–141.

Pagels, E. (1996). *The origins of Satan.* New York: Vintage books.

Panksepp, J., & Panksepp, J. B. (2000). The seven sins of evolutionary psychology. *Evolution and Cognition, 6*(2), 108–131.

Peck, M. S. (1978). *The road less traveled.* New York: Simon and Schuster.

Peck, M. S. (1983). *People of the lie.* New York: Simon and Schuster.

Perrett, R. (2002). Evil and human nature. *The Monist, 85*(2), 304–319.

Phillips, G. L. (1949). *England's climbing-boys: A history of the long struggle to abolish child labor in chimney sweeping.* Cambridge, MA: Harvard University Press.

Philp, H. L. (1958). *Jung and the problem of evil.* London: Salisbury Square.

Pierrakos, J. (1990). Anatomy of evil. In C. Zweig & J. Abrams (Eds.), *Meeting the shadow: The hidden power of the dark side of human nature* (pp. 88–90). New York: Putnams.

Piven, J. S. (2004). The psychosis (religion) of Islamic terrorists and the ecstasy of violence. *Journal of Psychohistory, 32*(2), 151–201.

Platinga, A. (1979). *The nature of necessity.* New York: Oxford University Press.

Pogge, T. (2002). *World poverty and human rights.* New York: Cambridge: Polity Press.

Pogge, T. (2005). World poverty and human rights. *Ethics and International Affairs, 19,* 1–7.

Popper, M. (1999). The sources of motivation of personalized and socialized charismatic leaders. *Psychoanalysis and Contemporary Thought, 22*(2), 231–246.

Post, J. M. (1990). Terrorist psycho-logic: Terrorist behavior as a product of psychological forces. In W. Reich (Ed.), *Origins of terrorism: Psychologies, ideologies, theologies, states of mind* (pp. 25–42). New York: Cambridge University Press.

Post, J. M. (2005). When hatred is bred in the bone: Psycho-cultural foundations of contemporary terrorism. *Political Psychology, 26*(4), 615–638.

Post, J. M., Sprinzak, E., & Denny, L. (2003). The terrorists in their own words: Interviews with 35 incarcerated Middle Eastern terrorists. *Terrorism Political Violence, 15*(1), 171–184.

Prince, R. (2016). Predatory identity. In R. C. Naso & J. Mills (Eds.), *Humanizing evil.* New York: Routledge.

Prins, H. (1992). Besieged by devils: Thoughts on possession and possession states. *Medicine, Science, and the Law, 32*(3), 237–246.

Raine, A., Lencz, T., Taylor, K., Helige, J. et al. (2003). Corpus callosum abnormalities in psychopathic antisocial individuals. *Archives of General Psychiatry, 60*(11), 1134–1142.

Raine, A., & Yang, Y. (2006). The neuroanatomical bases of psychopathy: A review of brain imaging findings. In C. J. Patrick (Ed.), *Handbook of psychopathy* (pp. 278–295). New York: Guilford Press.

Raine, K. (1982). *The human face of God: William Blake and the book of Job.* New York: Thames and Hudson.

Read, M. (2014). Elements of evil: On the role of violence and emotion in our observances of evil. *Dialogue, 57*(1), 51–56.

Reimann, M., & Zimbardo, P. G. (2011). The dark side of social encounters: Prospects for a neuroscience of human evil. *Journal of Neuroscience, Psychology, and Economics, 4*(3), 174–180.

Richardson, R. C. (2007). *Evolutionary psychology as maladapted psychology.* Cambridge, MA: MIT Press.

Ricoeur, P. (1967). *The symbolism of evil.* Erie, PA: Beacon Books.

Ricoeur, P. (1985). *Evil: A challenge to philosophy and theology.* Cambridge, MA: MIT Press.

Ricoeur, P. (2000). *Fallible man.* Trans. A. Kelbey. New York: Fordham University Press.

Rogers, C. R. (1961). The process equation of psychotherapy. *American Journal of Psychotherapy, 15*, 27–45.

Rogers, C. R. (1963). The actualizing tendency in relation to "motives" and to consciousness. In M. R. Jones (Ed.), *Nebraska Symposium on Motivation* (Vol. 11., pp. 1–24). Lincoln, NE: University of Nebraska Press.

Roper, T. (1987). *The last days of Hitler.* Chicago, IL: University of Chicago Press.

Rosenbaum, R. (1998). *Explaining Hitler.* New York: Random House.

Ross, D. (1988). *The right and the good.* Indianapolis, IN: Hackett Publishing.

Rubenstein, R. L. (1992). *After Auschwitz.* Baltimore, MD: Johns Hopkins University Press.

Russell, J. B. (1992). *The prince of darkness: Radical evil and the power of good in history.* Ithaca, NY: Cornell University Press.

Russell, L. (2007). Is evil action qualitatively distinct from ordinary wrongdoing? *Australasian Journal of Philosophy, 85*(4), 659–677.

Sanford, J. A. (1982). *Evil: The shadow side of reality.* New York: Crossroad Publishing.

Scarre, G. (2012). Evil collectives. *Midwest Studies in Philosophy, 36*(1), 74–92.

Schlesinger, L. B. (2000). *Serial offenders.* Boca Raton, FL: CRC Press.

Schmid, P. (2013). Whence the evil? A personalistic and dialogic perspective. In A. C. Bohart, B. S. Held, E. Mendelowitz, & K. J. Schneider (Eds.), *Humanity's dark side: Evil, destructive experience, and psychotherapy* (pp. 35–55). Washington, DC: American Psychological Association.

Schopenhauer, A. (1958). *The world as will and representation,* vol. 2. Indian Hills, CO: Falcon's Wing press.

Schwartz-Salant, N. (1986). *Narcissism and character transformation: The psychology of narcissistic character disorders.* Toronto: Inner City Books.

Scott, M. S. M. (2015). *Pathways in theodicy: An introduction to the problem of evil.* Minneapolis, MN: Fortress Press.

Sethi, S., & Seligman, M. E. P. (1994). The hope of fundamentalists. *Psychological Science, 5*(1), 58.

Shafranske, E. P. (1990a). The psychology of evil. *Journal of Pastoral Counseling, 25*, 1–113.

Shafranske, E. P. (1990b). Evil: A discourse on the boundaries of humanity, an introduction. *The Journal of Pastoral Counseling, 25*, 1–7.

Shay, J. (1995). *Achilles in Vietnam: Combat trauma and the undoing of character.* New York: Simon and Schuster.

Singer, M. G. (2004). The concept of evil. *Philosophy, 79*(2), 185–213.

Singer, T., & Kimbles, S. (2004). *The cultural complex.* New York: Brunner-Routledge.

Smith, M., & Prader, L. (1980). *Michelle remembers*. New York: St. Martin's Press.

Spinelli, E. (2000). Therapy and the challenge of evil. *British Journal Of Guidance & Counselling, 28*(4), 561–567.

Staub, E. (1989). *The roots of evil*. New York: Cambridge University Press.

Staub, E. (2003). *The psychology of good and evil*. New York: Cambridge University Press.

Stein, D. J. (2000). The neurobiology of evil: Psychiatric perspectives on perpetrators. *Ethnicity & Health, 5*(3/4), 303–315.

Stein, D. J. (2005). The philosophy of evil. *Philosophy, Psychiatry, & Psychology, 12*(3), 261–263.

Stein, R. (2002). Evil as love and as liberation. *Psychoanalytic Dialogues, 12*(3), 393–421.

Stein, R. (2006). Ideologies of war: Fundamentalism, father and son, and vertical desire. *The Psychoanalytic Review, 96*(2), 201–229.

Steiner, H. I. (2002). Calibrating evil. *The Monist, 85*, 183–193.

Stone, W. F., & Lederer, G. (1993). *Strength and weakness: The authoritarian personality today*. New York: Springer-Verlag.

Stout, M. (2005). *The sociopath next door: The ruthless versus the rest of us*. New York: Broadway Books.

Strozier, C. B. (1994). *Apocalypse: On the psychology of fundamentalism in America*. Boston, MA: Beacon Press.

Summers, F. (2006). Fundamentalism, psychoanalysis, and psychoanalytic theories. *Psychoanalytic Review, 93*(2), 329–352.

Svendsen, L. F. H. (2010). *A philosophy of evil*. London: Dalkey Archive Press.

Tajfel, H. (1981). *Human groups and social categories*. Cambridge, UK: Cambridge University Press.

Taylor, R. (2000). *Good and evil: A new direction*. Amherst, NY: Prometheus Books.

Thomas, L. M. (1993). *Vessels of evil: American slavery and the Holocaust*. Philadelphia, PA: Temple University Press.

Tillich, P. (1936). *The interpretation of history*. New York: Scribner's Publishing.

Tomasello, M., & Vaish, A. (2013). Origins of human cooperation and morality. *Annual Review of Psychology, 64*, 231–255.

Tooby, J., & Cosmides, L. (2005). Conceptual foundations of evolutionary psychology. In D. M. Buss (Ed.), *The handbook of evolutionary psychology* (pp. 5–67). Hoboken, NJ: Wiley.

Van Bernschoten, S. C. (1990). Multiple personality disorder and satanic ritual abuse: The issue of credibility. *Dissociation: Progress in the Dissociative Disorders, 3*, 22–30.

Verene, D. P. (2010). The sociopath and the Ring of Gyges: A problem in rhetorical and moral philosophy. *Philosophy and Rhetoric, 43*(3), 201–221.

Verhoef, A. (2014). The relation between evil and transcendence: New possibilities? *South African Journal of Philosophy, 33*(3), 259–269.

Vetlesen, A. J. (2005). *Evil and human agency: Understanding collective evildoing*. New York: Cambridge University Press.

Victoroff, J. (2005). The mind of the terrorist: A review and critique of psychological approaches. *Journal of Conflict Resolution, 49*(1), 3–42.

Viding, E. (2005). Evidence for substantial genetic risk for psychopathy in 7-year-olds. *Journal of Child Psychology and Psychiatry, 46*(6), 592–597.

Virtanen, H. (2013). The King of Norway: negative individuation, the hero myth and psychopathic narcissism in extreme violence and the life of Anders Behring Breivik. *Journal of Analytical Psychology, 58*(5), 657–676.

Volkan, V. D. (1997). *Blood lines: From ethnic pride to ethnic terrorism*. New York: Farrar, Strauss, Girard.

Von Franz, M. L. (1967). The problem of evil in fairy tales. In The Curatorium of the C. G. Jung Institute of Zurich (Ed.), *Evil*. Evanston, IL: Northwestern University Press.

Von Franz, M. L. (1972). *Problems of the feminine in fairy tales*. Washington, DC: Spring Publications.

Von Franz, M. L. (1995). *Shadow and evil in fairy tales*. Boston, MA: Shambhala.

Waller, J. E. (2007). *Becoming evil: How ordinary people commit genocide and mass killing*. New York: Oxford University Press.

Ward, D. (2002). Explaining evil behavior: Using Kant and M. Scott Peck to solve the puzzle of understanding the moral psychology of evil people. *Philosophy, Psychiatry, and Psychology, 9*(1), 1–12.

Weisstub, E. (1993). Questions to Jung on "Answer to Job." *Journal of Analytical Psychology, 38*(4), 397–418.

White, V. (1955). Jung on Job. *Blackfriars, 36,* 52–60.

White, V. (1959). Psychology and religion: Book review. *Journal of Analytical Psychology, 4*(1).

Widom, L. S. (1989). The cycle of violence. *Science, 244,* 160–166.

Wilson, E. O. (1979). *On human nature*. New York: Bantam Books.

Wilson, P. (2003). The concept of evil and the forensic psychologist. *International Journal of Forensic Psychology, 1,* 1–9.

Winnicott, D. W. (1945/1975). *Through pediatrics to psychoanalysis*. New York: Basic Books.

Winnicott, D. W. (1957). Aggression. In J. Hardenberg (Ed.), *The child and the outside world*. London: Tavistock publications.

Winnicott, D. W. (1960). The theory of the parent-infant relationship. *International Journal of Psycho-Analysis, 41,* 585–595.

Winnicott, D. W. (1965). *Maturational processes and the facilitating environment*. London: Hogarth Press.

Winnicott, D. W. (1971). *Playing and reality*. New York: Basic Books.

Winnicott, D. W. (1989). *Psychoanalytic explorations*. London: Karnac Books.

Wolfe, A. (2011). *Political evil: What it is and how to combat it*. New York: Knopf.

Wood, G. (2015). What ISIS really wants. *The Atlantic*, March 2015.

Yoon, J. E., & Lawrence, E. (2013). Psychological victimization as a risk factor for the developmental course of marriage. *Journal of Family Psychology, 27*(1), 53–64.

Youngblade, L. M., & Belsky, J. (1990). Social and emotional consequences of child maltreatment. In R. T. Ammerman & M. Hersen (Eds.), *Children at risk: An evaluation of factors contributing to child abuse and neglect*. New York: Plenum Press.

Zillmer, E. A., Harrower, M., Ritzler, B. A., & Archer, R. P. (1995). *The quest for the Nazi personality: A psychological investigation of Nazi war criminals*. Hillsdale, NJ: Erlbaum.

Zimbardo, P. G. (2007). *The Lucifer effect: Understanding why good people turn evil*. New York: Random House.

Zuckerman, M. (2014). *Sensation seeking: Beyond the optimal level of arousal*. New York: Psychology Press.

Zukier, H. (1994). The twisted road to genocide: On the psychological development of evil during the Holocaust. *Social Research, 61*(2), 423–455.

Index